*In the Shadow
of the Buddha*

In the Shadow of the Buddha

*One Man's Journey of Spiritual Discovery
and Political Danger in Tibet*

Matteo Pistono

HAY HOUSE

Australia • Canada • Hong Kong • India
South Africa • United Kingdom • United States

First published by Dutton, a member of Penguin Group (USA) Inc., 375 Hudson Street, New York, New York 10014, USA

First published and distributed in the United Kingdom by:
Hay House UK Ltd, 292B Kensal Rd, London W10 5BE. Tel.: (44) 20 8962 1230; Fax: (44) 20 8962 1239. www.hayhouse.co.uk

Published and distributed in Australia by:
Hay House Australia Ltd, 18/36 Ralph St, Alexandria NSW 2015. Tel.: (61) 2 9669 4299; Fax: (61) 2 9669 4144. www.hayhouse.com.au

Published and distributed in the Republic of South Africa by:
Hay House SA (Pty), Ltd, PO Box 990, Witkoppen 2068. Tel./Fax: (27) 11 467 8904. www.hayhouse.co.za

Published and distributed in India by:
Hay House Publishers India, Muskaan Complex, Plot No.3, B-2, Vasant Kunj, New Delhi – 110 070. Tel.: (91) 11 4176 1620; Fax: (91) 11 4176 1630. www.hayhouse.co.in

Distributed in Canada by:
Raincoast, 9050 Shaughnessy St, Vancouver, BC V6P 6E5. Tel.: (1) 604 323 7100; Fax: (1) 604 323 2600

MIX
Paper from
responsible sources
FSC® C013056

*The book is dedicated to the fulfillment of the visions
and aspirations of Tertön Sogyal Lerab Lingpa (1856–1926)*

for Namkhai Lhamo

Contents

Part III 113

ᏈᏈ

Chapter 8

Chapter 9

Chapter 10

Part IV 179

ᏈᏈ

Chapter 11

Chapter 12

Foreword

For more than a decade, Matteo Pistono has lived in Nepal and Tibet, and worked in the fields of human rights and religious freedom. He knows the territory well, and it shows in both the grit and scope of his narrative. In the many years and many places that I've known him, from India to Washington, Matteo has remained an informed, reliable, skillful, and joyously energized individual. He is a true student of Buddhism, and has had the great fortune of having received significant teachings from some of the world's greatest teachers, including His Holiness the Dalai Lama, Sogyal Rinpoche, and the late Khenpo Jikmé Phuntsok inside Tibet—a rarity indeed.

The book you hold in your hands is the story of how great spiritual practitioners from Tibet, like the mystic Tertön Sogyal, and the thirteenth and fourteenth Dalai Lamas, are able to bring the full force of the bodhisattva commitment—the burning desire to free all beings from suffering—into whatever situation they face, including the world of politics. The experiences Matteo writes about in this context are often esoteric, but never less than deeply human. He speaks to us of the vital importance of a complete commitment to nonviolence and of an insistence, as Gandhi used to say, on the truth—the profound truth of interdependence and selflessness—as the only doors that can lead us and others to genuine happiness. For Matteo, the world of politics only has meaning when motivated by a selfless compassion, at which point politics and social action can themselves become a powerful spiritual practice.

In the Shadow of the Buddha is a fascinating journey to the Tibet of the present and of the past, which at times is both heartbreaking and inspiring, as the people Matteo writes about demonstrate what courage and commitment to truth are really about when you are motivated by a vast sense of responsibility to all beings—be they friend or enemy. So if you want to venture beyond the Himalayas to glimpse a sacred world that is almost lost, or whether your interests lead you to the halls of political power, or to finding your path in the Western Dharma world, I trust this book will give you a deeper appreciation of the ancient wisdom tradition of Tibet and how vitally relevant it is to us today—in your heart, your community, or in the world at large.

Richard Gere

Buddhas work for the benefit of others,
Ordinary people work for the benefit of themselves,
And just look at the difference between them.

Shantideva, seventh century

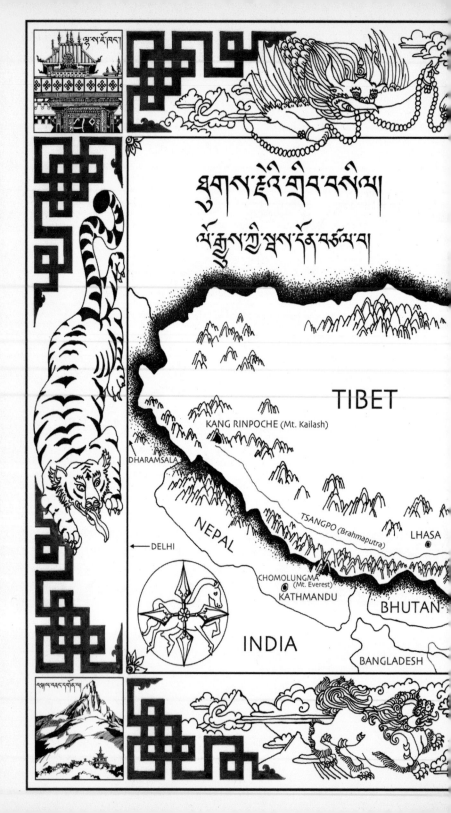

Part I

A pilgrimage through wild, open lands provides visions that help shape the proper attitude and inner awareness for religious practice.

THE XIV DALAI LAMA OF TIBET

Chapter 1

The Mission Begins

When I first journeyed to Tibet in 1999, I was on a pilgrimage in the footsteps of a nineteenth-century Tibetan mystic named Tertön Sogyal. A horseriding bandit turned meditation master, Tertön Sogyal eventually became the teacher of the XIII Dalai Lama, the predecessor to the current Dalai Lama. Such was the prevailing belief that Tertön Sogyal's mantras and prayers could protect Tibet from foreign armies that the Dalai Lama summoned him to Lhasa to serve the nation. Not unlike the Dalai Lama today, Tertön Sogyal was a master at integrating his political duties with spiritual practice, while never losing the pure motivation that holds others' well-being as the priority.

I first learned of Tertön Sogyal in 1996 when I met his reincarnation, Sogyal Rinpoche. I was in graduate school in London studying Indian philosophy. I was drawn to Tertön Sogyal's life story because I know politics matter. My parents had instilled in me an awareness that social action is not so much a choice as a responsibility—to ourselves and to our community.

There was something in Tertön Sogyal—the way that he pursued the path of spiritual enlightenment even while in the unsavory theater of politics—that I wanted to understand more deeply.

The two years before coming to London I had lived in extreme contrasts—on the one hand meditating in Nepal and on the other involving myself in partisan environmental politics in America. In Nepal, I had spent months meditating under the guidance of a Tibetan lama in the foothills outside Kathmandu. I was introduced to ancient methods of meditation and yoga that are meant to uncover the indwelling potential of spiritual awakening that each and every one of us possesses. After six months of meditation retreats, I returned to the Western American state of Wyoming and began working in environmental politics, battling oil and gas lobbyists in legislative hearings. I continued to practice meditation in Wyoming, but it did not take long before the serenity that I had experienced in Nepal was but a memory. In the face of my political adversaries, a vindictive mind would arise with ferocity. The divide between my social activism and spiritual practice was vast because I didn't know how to take the insights and peace I experienced on the meditation cushion into the world.

Tertön Sogyal Lerab Lingpa (1856–1926) was one of Tibet's great mystics of the late nineteenth and early twentieth centuries, teacher of the XIII Dalai Lama, and protector of the Tibetan nation. This is the only known photo of him taken in 1913 near Rebkong in northeast Tibet.

When I arrived in London for graduate school and began studying meditation with Sogyal Rinpoche, as well as the history and the works of the mystic Tertön Sogyal, I realized that here was an example of what I aspired toward. Tertön Sogyal possessed an endless reservoir of wisdom and strength to draw from while working in the volatile political realm of late nineteenth-century Tibet. This reservoir was something that I needed to tap into. So after I graduated, I decided to see where Tertön Sogyal's saintly life had played out—and deepen my own meditation practice—in hallowed caves and hermitages high on the roof of the world and among Tibet's sacred temples and shrines. I set up a base in Kathmandu as a freelance journalist to fund my travels and began making frequent trips to Tibet.

The road map for my pilgrimage was Tertön Sogyal's own far-ranging travels across the Tibetan plateau; his life was not bound to isolated mountain retreats. Soon I was meditating among hermits in remote sanctuaries and cliffside grottoes. I slept in the caves where Tertön Sogyal had experienced spiritual visions and revelations. On foot, horseback, and dilapidated buses, I crossed the same glacier-covered passes that he used to travel from eastern Tibet to Lhasa. And I sought out the masters and yogis still alive who uphold Tertön Sogyal's spiritual lineage and could tell me the oral history of his life and teachings.

But the pilgrimage took an unexpected turn.

The more time I spent in Tibet delving into the nineteenth-century spiritual teachings of Tertön Sogyal, the more often I met Tibetans who wanted to tell me their story of frustration and pain, and about their never-ending hope that one day the exiled Dalai Lama would return to Tibet. Traveling as a Buddhist pilgrim, I gained Tibetans' trust. Political prisoners who had experienced abuse and torture in Chinese prisons showed me scars. Monks and nuns who had been kicked out of their monastery gave me their expulsion notices from the local security bureau. I was taken to meet a Buddhist leader who had been scalded with boiling water and then jailed for five years for publicly praying to the Dalai Lama.

Tibetans not only told me their stories, but early into my pilgrimage they asked me to spirit such firsthand accounts of human rights abuses out of Tibet and into the hands of Western governments and advocacy groups. While I still wanted to search out Tertön Sogyal's meditation techniques, I became a courier of often graphic accounts of torture and abuse. This required evading China's vast security network of plainclothed security agents, undercover cops in monks' robes, and the sophisticated cyberpolice. And I began photographing Chinese secret prisons where Tibetan monks and nuns are incarcerated for their Buddhist beliefs. The journey in Tertön Sogyal's footsteps became a different kind of pilgrimage.

AUTUMN 2002, YEAR OF THE WATER HORSE

Larung Buddhist Encampment, Eastern Tibet

Screeching brakes brought the rusty Dong Feng cargo truck to a halt. A rolling cloud of dust followed, adding yet another layer atop my driver's cargo. I heard Dawa speaking to the Chinese police officer about the contents in the back. The pulse in my neck pounded as I attempted to lie motionless while hidden in the bed of the truck. I did not want to meet the security officer again. Four body-size bolts of maroon felt, twenty wicker baskets filled with cabbage and bruised apples, and two wind-burnt nuns were between that officer and me.

Dawa offered a smoke to the policeman—the same cop who had spat cigarette-stained insults at me two days earlier. A roaming security unit had discovered me evading its monitoring posts, trying to enter the sprawling monastic complex of the Larung Buddhist Encampment. I knew my way around this place, having first come here three years earlier in 1999.

At over thirteen thousand feet, I was too exhausted to argue in the cold rain with one Tibetan and two Chinese policemen who'd stopped me on foot. They'd taken me to the Larung Encampment's security post at the base of the valley to meet their senior officer.

"Absolutely, you are banned from entering Larung Monastery!"

The quickest way out of the police station was to admit my crime against the Chinese Motherland, absorb the officer's verbal abuse, sign a document to that effect, and walk away, tail between my legs.

"Yeah, I'm wrong," I said, looking into the sergeant's bloodshot eyes, trying to assure him. "I know this is a closed area for foreigners. I should not be here." I would tell him anything he wanted to hear. I just needed to get out of his security outpost so I could find a different route back into the encampment.

"Fine. I'll take tomorrow's early bus back to Chengdu from Serthar town," I lied. I had no intention of leaving the area until I had completed my mission of delivering a message from Tibet's exiled spiritual leader, the Dalai Lama, to the monk-abbot of Larung, Khenpo Jikmé Phuntsok. Khenpo was the only meditation master living in Tibet who was a teacher of the Dalai Lama. Khenpo was also my Buddhist teacher.

The police put me in the backseat of their van and we slid through muddy Sichuan roads to the town of Serthar. It was not the first time I had been kicked out of a closed area on the Tibetan Plateau by Chinese security—nor would it be the first time that I returned to the same area within forty-eight hours of being expelled.

I exhaled as Dawa's cargo truck started rolling after being cleared by the police. Twenty minutes later, as we were lumbering up the winding road, one of the nuns pulled at my parka. Emerging from my hideout, I peered over the truck's side rails. I saw thousands of wooden and adobe huts packed tightly together across the mountain like a massive honeycomb, each a home to two or three meditating monks or nuns who study under Khenpo. Four pagoda-roofed temples were set in the middle of the vast encampment, around which thousands of monks and nuns shuffled between scriptural study classes and philosophical debate sessions.

When Dawa stopped the truck, I gripped the rusty chains hanging on the side and climbed down. One of the nuns flung my backpack off the other side into the sagebrush. Pointing with his lips, Dawa silently indicated which cabin I should enter. He had already arranged a hideout for me—I had not involved any monks from Larung, as that could have endangered them.

Less than a year earlier in June 2001, Communist Party officials from Beijing, accompanied by hundreds of Party cadres, descended upon Khenpo and the congregation of eight thousand monks and nuns at Larung. The Larung Buddhist Encampment had grown beyond the Chinese government's comfort level. The officials evicted thousands. Monks and nuns watched work crews hack down nearly three thousand of their homes. This was the largest-scale physical destruction of a religious institution in Tibet or China since the Cultural Revolution. I had gone there to bring out photographic evidence of the devastation to the West.

Though heartbroken at the destruction, I was at least encouraged that the rest of the world had learned of the tragedy at Larung. It became known that the demolition orders had come directly from Chinese president Jiang Zemin. Other dramatic images and firsthand reports appeared in *Newsweek* and the *New York Times*. I learned later that U.S. State Department officials had called on Chinese diplomats in Washington, D.C., to explain the destruction at Larung, using the photos that I had smuggled. Their red-faced silence spoke volumes to the American officials who called the Chinese on their duplicity.

This time, in the fall of 2002, I returned to the Larung Encampment not only because I wanted to see my aging teacher Khenpo, but also because I was carrying a message for him—an urgent one from the Dalai Lama.

I first came to know about human rights when I was sixteen at a music concert in Italy in 1988. I was attending high school as an exchange student in Ravenna, the same year Amnesty International's *Human Rights Now!* concert toured the world with Bruce Springsteen, Sting, and Peter Gabriel headlining. With our peace and anarchy pins secured to army satchels, my friends and I attended the show in Turin along with sixty thousand screaming fans. I signed a few petitions on the way into the soccer stadium, not knowing anything about the causes to which I was putting my name. We listened to Tracy Chapman and Sting speak about the fortieth anniversary of the Universal Declaration of Human Rights, but we were really just waiting for the music.

After six hours, Peter Gabriel took the stage. He began telling of an oppressive country where racism was enshrined in its constitution, and of a man, Stephen Biko, who dared to stand against such injustice. Biko was an antiapartheid leader in South Africa who was jailed, brutally tortured, and murdered in police custody in 1977. For me, Biko seemed the very epitome of courage and strength, and a man who spoke truth to unjust power, paying the ultimate price. The feeling that I experienced when Peter Gabriel sang "Biko" branded my heart with a call to work against social and political injustice, and I took the words of the song, *"and the eyes of the world are watching now, watching now,"* as a personal call to expose crimes of any government.

I began writing letters and postcards to presidents and prime ministers around the globe, demanding that they release prisoners of conscience.

I always concluded my notes with the handwritten line *"The eyes of the world are watching now, watching now."* Later, in college, I ran the campus Amnesty International group organizing anti–death penalty demonstrations in front of maximum-security prisons in Wyoming and Colorado. My study of anthropology and political science in university led to a deeper understanding of how past and current policies of governments lead to an abuse of power. In particular, I studied the United States' wanton destruction of the native peoples of North America. Having grown up on the edge of the Shoshone and Arapaho's Wind River Indian Reservation, it was readily apparent what happens to an indigenous culture when its life force is fading.

I attended my first political rally in a Little League baseball uniform, watching my father, chairman of Wyoming's largest labor union, hoist homemade signs calling to raise the minimum wage for janitors, teachers, and other state employees. Many evenings in my teens were spent with my mother placing stamps on mailings, campaigning against proposed nuclear waste storage in our county. And I saw the determination of my Italian, Polish, and Irish grandparents who had worked in Wyoming's coal mines, built railroads, and farmed in Montana. In my own home, after my brother and I chopped and stacked firewood, weeded the garden, or shoveled snow off the sidewalks, politics was often the topic of conversation over a dinner of elk or deer meat we had hunted in the autumn.

My parents' example was the seed of political activism that led me to coordinate field operations for a gubernatorial race in Wyoming in the early 1990s soon after I graduated from college. Though we were predicted to win the governorship, the neoconservative tidal wave overwhelmed us in the Rocky Mountains, and I did what most Democrats wanted to do the morning after Election Day—I escaped. I lost confidence in people whom I'd trusted to vote into office the candidate who I believed cared more about increasing the minimum wage for workers than corporate subsidies, and who would fight to protect the environment rather than work backroom deals for the oil and gas companies' profits. I felt my efforts in the political process had been futile. The Himalayas seemed as far away from American politics as I could get.

I contacted a principal of a Nepalese school before arriving in Kathmandu and told him I wanted to help. The school's principal was the son of a refugee who had left Tibet when the Dalai Lama fled in 1959, after Communist China invaded Lhasa. Of the hundred thousand refugees who followed the Dalai Lama, escaping over the Himalayas into exile, thousands remained in the Kingdom of Nepal, including the principal's father. The principal welcomed my offer and housed me with a dozen extended family members and his white-haired uncle, Apu.

The first morning in Kathmandu I was awakened by barking street dogs to find Uncle Apu waving a small urn of smoking sandalwood and juniper incense around my backpack and me. He was chasing away the malevolent spirits I might have brought from America. He left the room murmuring a mantra.

I began exploring the curry-scented streets of Kathmandu, with its legless beggars and mendicant ascetics, decrepit shanty houses, hundreds of Hindu and Newar shrines, and rickshaw drivers weaving between sacred cows gnawing on plastic bags. After a few weeks, my notion of normality had been stretched and twisted. So when the school principal's offer came to attend a Buddhist ceremony that sounded similar to an exorcism, it did not seem out of the ordinary.

I awoke the next day just after dawn and looked down to the courtyard at a dozen freshly tonsured monks scurrying to finish preparations for the ceremony. Brightly colored brocaded scroll-paintings of Buddhist deities were hung. Laid out before the sacred images were silver bowls filled with saffron-dyed water, platters of fruit, and garlands of marigolds. Carpets and prayer tables were set up with ceremonial instruments close by, including standing drums, ritual bells, and long trumpetlike horns. Uncle Apu's wife brought me a cup of sweet Nepali tea, and gestured for me to get dressed and join them downstairs.

My parents raised my older brother and me in the Roman Catholic faith. At weekly services, the sweetness of frankincense, chiming of bells, and my mother's singing usually stirred us from our Sunday drowsiness. I studied catechism in my youth, and donned the woolly brown Franciscan habit as an altar boy at Holy Rosary Church twice a month. I later trained as a Eucharistic minister in my first year of college, administering the sanctified body and blood of Christ at the campus Mass. By my sophomore year, however, I felt increasing skepticism toward the theology I studied. I saw a contradiction in the church's guidance that insisted I rely upon something outside of myself to confirm the truthfulness of my experience. This was not an aversion to authority; rather I wanted the responsibility of my spiritual maturation placed where it belonged—on my own shoulders. I soon left the Catholic Church, not disgruntled or angry, but knowing that it was not my path. Still, ritual and ceremony spoke to a deep place inside me.

The school principal sat next to me on the carpet-covered courtyard when the ceremony began, with Uncle Apu presiding on an elevated seat with the monks seated in front of him. Uncle Apu had spent many years in meditation retreat in snow-lined hermitages in the Himalayas and now spent most of his day in dusty Kathmandu meditating and drinking tea, leaving the house only to conduct Buddhist ceremonies in others' homes when requested. My senses were saturated after an hour of hypnotic chants, alarmingly high-pitched horns, the rattling of hand drums, and the eating of sacred herbal pills. Then, as the chanting and rhythm faded into a meditative stillness, two monks approached Uncle Apu with a triangular metal container the size of a shoe box. Inside the metal container was an effigy of a man made of barley dough. The figure was presented to Uncle Apu, whose gaze was at once vast and piercingly direct. He did not blink for what seemed the entire ceremony.

Using elegant hand gestures and reciting mantras, Uncle Apu summoned a malicious spirit to enter and possess the effigy. This particularly rowdy spirit was not only causing a disturbance in the sleep of most members of the family of the house, but also had threatened to sap the vitality of Uncle Apu. Staring intently at the effigy that was now occupied by the spirit, Uncle Apu slowly reached across his prayer table and retrieved a *phurba*—a three-edged ritual dagger—from among the implements in front of him. He raised the phurba and rolled it back and forth between his hands. He then plunged it decisively into the center of the effigy's chest. Ice shot through my spine. Medicinal herbs and sacramental liquids were dripped on top of the effigy before it was taken away to be buried.

"I hope I'll finally be able to sleep tonight," the principal admitted, confident the exorcism was successful. As the concluding prayers were chanted, he slid closer to me. "You must know, you can only perform these rituals if you have truly conquered negativity within your own heart and mind."

"But your uncle was . . ." I paused to collect my thoughts. "He was stabbing away as if he was some kind of warrior. I thought Buddhism was about compassion," I said, having only a cursory acquaintance with Buddhism through books.

"Indeed, he *is* a warrior. And one who is steeped in compassion. He's called a *bodhisattva,* which means a compassionate warrior. A bodhisattva is someone who has aroused the wish to attain enlightenment for the benefit of all beings, and does everything possible to bring others to that state of enlightenment, free of suffering. Oh, and if you are wondering about the spirit—it's not destroyed, it's liberated, through compassion, to proceed toward a state of ultimate happiness."

"But the phurba? Enlightenment with what looks like a weapon?"

"The phurba dagger is used to vanquish the ego, which is the source of our greed and anger. This is about getting rid of the ego so that we will be liberated from the endless cycle of birth, sickness, old age, and death. People cannot perform these kinds of practices if they have not conquered the demons within their own hearts. That is what Uncle Apu was doing for the nearly twenty years he spent in meditation retreat."

During Uncle Apu's years as a hermit-yogi in the caves of Yolmo north of Kathmandu, he mastered the very phurba practice I had just witnessed. The phurba practice is one of many found in the vajrayana, the form of Buddhism practiced in Tibet. Vajrayana utilizes the tantric teachings of the Buddha, I came to learn, which begin with the view that the goal of the spiritual path is within us already, here and now, but only veiled by ignorance. The powerful methods of the vajrayana, which include visualization, mantra, and meditation, transform our perception to reveal directly our enlightened nature. Once this enlightened potential fully manifests, we can truly benefit others.

A few weeks later I went with the principal to ask Uncle Apu to teach me the phurba practice. I thought it might be useful in the political sphere in America—maybe I could remove a few politicians from their ill-earned pedestals. The principal translated my request into Tibetan. Uncle Apu chuckled, not because I wanted to wield the phurba in America, but because I had the gumption to think that I had the ability to perform the ceremony. Uncle Apu suggested I stay at different monasteries and hermitages in Nepal for much of the next year to practice meditation. Uncle Apu sent me away, saying, "Enlightenment abides within you—it is not to be found somewhere outside yourself."

During the next weeks and months, I was taught meditation and yogic breathing techniques by a lama, or teacher, at a Buddhist monastery. In the mornings on the mountainsides above Kathmandu, I sat cross-legged and applied the teachings. Relaxed but aware, I allowed rising thoughts and emotions to move through my mind without thinking about them, simply observing the movement but leaving no trace—like the falcon's flight path in the sky. And as I entered the sleep state, I tried to recognize that which is aware of dreams rather than following the drama in the dream itself. My efforts were directed toward glimpsing, if only for a moment, the light of enlightenment that Uncle Apu had said is within my being.

Nearing the end of my stay in Nepal, I received a message that Uncle Apu wanted to speak with me. I squeezed into a motor rickshaw with three Nepali carpet weavers who worked below the hermitage and we bounced into Kathmandu. Uncle Apu suggested I travel to India to see the Dalai Lama and take the vows of a bodhisattva in order to commit myself to realize fully my enlightened potential, not only for myself, but for all beings. "Coupled with meditation, your bodhisattva vow will set the foundation for your future phurba practice."

When I first went to Nepal, I had no plans to set foot upon the Buddhist path, and certainly not to commit to any precepts or spiritual vows. Yet, after more than six months of meditation and contemplations on the logic of how all things are woven in a web of interdependence, and the truth of the impermanence of all phenomena, the fundamental tenets of the Buddha's teachings became an evident truth. For me this was an investigation into reality, not religious dogma or academic philosophy. But the most compelling experience that had arisen while at the hermitages was my fleeting encounters in meditation with my own undistracted awareness of the ever-changing present moment. The experiences went beyond the books I read or teachings I received. Brief moments arose in meditation when my awareness was aware of itself. This was convincing evidence of the power of the mind to transcend the endless chain of thoughts that click by, one after another, as if someone were channel-surfing in my mind. Transcending the thinking-mind in meditation, it was as though I glimpsed that indwelling potential for enlightenment.

It took me a week of solo travel by road through Nepal and by rail across northern India to arrive in Dharamsala. I was on a well-trodden path by Westerners, with the likes of Gary Snyder and Allen Ginsberg traveling here in the early 1960s, followed by philosophers and Christian mystics such as Thomas Merton, and today by neuroscientists, molecular geneticists, and movie stars. For more than forty years, beatnik poets, renowned scientists, world leaders, and global celebrities have journeyed to Dharamsala with the same motivation—to see the XIV Dalai Lama.

When the Dalai Lama escaped a pursuing Chinese army and fled Tibet in 1959, India accepted him as a guest of their country, providing him a home and a daily rupee stipend that they still honor today. Over 120,000 Tibetans journeyed on foot over the Himalayas to follow into exile their spiritual and political leader. While many refugees were scattered in colonies throughout the Indian subcontinent, the Tibetan government-in-exile eventually set up operations near Dharamsala in the north Indian foothills, where the Dalai Lama currently resides.

Teachings began a few days after I arrived. Together with thousands of Tibetans and hundreds of Westerners, we entered the football-field-size cement courtyard between the Dalai Lama's bungalow residence and Namgyal Monastery. Chanting crackled over the loudspeaker as nouveau hippies and monks jockeyed for seats with the best view of the Dalai Lama. Monkeys clambered on the tin roof of the surrounding buildings. I sat in a section cordoned off for Westerners, where a local radio signal transmitted the voice of the Dalai Lama's translator. A kind lady from Italy shared one of the earphones from her handheld radio, as I had not picked up a similar fifty-rupee radio from a vendor up the street.

A breeze of silence blew over the crowd as the Dalai Lama left his residence and walked into the courtyard. Security guards with automatic rifles and monks carrying incense walked shoulder to shoulder clearing a path through the crowd. I was sitting at the edge of the Tibetan leader's walkway.

Thousands of Tibetans' eyes spontaneously filled with tears, hands devotedly folded at their chests. This was the first time I had set my eyes on the man whom Tibetans regard as a manifestation of the Buddha's compassion. As the Dalai Lama passed by, I heard two sounds that would later come to symbolize for me how he works in both the political and spiritual worlds—a soft, deep-knowing chuckle, and the flapping of his ubiquitous rubber flip-flops.

After a week of teaching, on the morning the Dalai Lama was to give the bodhisattva vow, he told us that undertaking the vow did not apply only to this life, but we were pledging ourselves to benefit others in all of our future lives, until we attained enlightenment. According to the Buddhist view, this might be a couple hundred thousand years of working for others, depending on how many lifetimes the vow took to accomplish—for the completion of the bodhisattva's task means that everyone, every single being, is free from suffering. "Whether we attain enlightenment today or ten lifetimes from now," he said, "our job is still the same—to work for others' happiness."

The crowd repeated the vow to attain enlightenment not just for ourselves, but for the benefit of all beings—and then committed to the path of diligently cultivating within ourselves qualities such as patience, generosity, and meditation. With a snap of the Dalai Lama's fingers the ceremony was complete.

Commotion began. Chanting broke over the loudspeaker. Teams of monks streamed into the monastery courtyard to serve tea to the masses. Tibetan grandmothers returned to thumbing their prayer beads. Kids from the Tibetan Children's Village were rounded up by their teachers to go back to their classrooms up the mountain. Monkeys began howling at the action below. I watched the Dalai Lama on his throne, quietly smiling. I concentrated on him as both the source and the benevolent witness to the vow I had just taken. In gratitude to him for inspiration and wisdom, I recited a verse he had used in the ceremony:

For as long as space exists
And sentient beings endure,
May I, too, remain,
To dispel the misery of the world.

Little did I know at the time that this vow would mature seven years later as a clandestine mission to deliver a message inside Tibet from the Dalai Lama.

Chapter 2

Following in the Footsteps of the Master

Soon after taking the bodhisattva vow in India, I returned to America, where I found a letter of acceptance into graduate school from the University of London's School of Oriental and African Studies. Even though I had lived on a shoestring budget, my bank account was dry from travel around the Indian subcontinent. Deferring entry into graduate school for a year to save cash, I worked for the Wyoming Outdoor Council and Sierra Club contesting the oil and gas industry efforts to drill in Wyoming's desert and mountain wilderness. Our political battlefields were the hallways and conference rooms of the Wyoming State Legislature.

It was not long before the taste of meditative serenity that I experienced in the Himalayas faded into the political rancor. And my bodhisattva vow to work for the benefit of everyone, not just my family and friends, was straining under the weight of animosity. As I meditated at my house in Cheyenne, anger erupted within my mind. It was directed at my adversaries—the Exxon and Chevron lawyers with whom I quarreled at legislative meetings, public hearings, and in the press. Meditation sessions were soon reduced to briefly sitting on a cushion by my bed and trying to hold back waves of aggressive thoughts toward those who were destroying Wyoming's environment and fleeing the state with the profits. The gap between my spiritual practice and my involvement in politics was vast. I wanted to be that compassionate warrior who could fiercely and skillfully benefit others, a bodhisattva like the Dalai Lama and Uncle Apu.

After saving enough money for tuition while working for the environmental groups, in the late summer of 1996 I left Wyoming for graduate school in England to study Indian philosophy. The transition brought a drastic change in both my physical and mental landscape. I found the challenge of academia and the study of the Upanishads, the Bhagavad-Gita, and early Indian Buddhism, as well as the Tibetan language, invigorating. I also reconnected in London with Tibetans and their exiled culture through the refugee community, including relatives of Uncle Apu. Though I had lived among Tibetan refugees in Nepal and at monasteries, I was, like many Westerners in Kathmandu, trying to work out my own spiritual path and did not delve into the issues of social injustice that were plainly before me. But in London I began to be more involved in the nonviolent struggle of the Dalai Lama and Tibetan people for self-determination in their homeland. Feeling appreciation for the techniques of meditation that I had learned from Uncle Apu and other Tibetan Buddhist teachers, I wanted to give something back.

One afternoon at university, over tea, Dominique, a fellow graduate student, invited me to attend an evening talk by her teacher, Sogyal Rinpoche, whom I only knew from reading his book *The Tibetan Book of Living and Dying*.

Sogyal Rinpoche was born in the late 1940s, in the region of eastern Tibet known as Kham. Neighbors reported seeing rainbows arc over the family home in which he was born, and as a small child he spontaneously started reciting mantras while being carried to a monastery. Sogyal Rinpoche

Sogyal Rinpoche is one of the most prominent Tibetan Buddhist teachers in the world and is the author of *The Tibetan Book of Living and Dying.* He is one of two simultaneous reincarnations of Tertön Sogyal.

was soon recognized as the reincarnation of Tertön Sogyal, a great mystic who had passed away twenty years before. Had the Chinese not taken over Tibet, Sogyal Rinpoche would have likely grown to assume the traditional role of a reincarnate lama, following in the footsteps of the past saints from Kham. However, for him this traditional world of a Tibetan lama from eastern Tibet did not come to pass.

After China's invasion of Tibet in 1949–1950, and its subsequent forced conversion of the Buddhist society to Marxist collectivism, when monasteries were either destroyed or used by the state as granaries and barnyards, Sogyal Rinpoche and his family fled into exile in 1955 with his teacher Jamyang Khyentsé Chökyi Lodrö. They settled in the Himalayan kingdom of Sikkim, where he continued his training as an incarnate lama. After Jamyang Khyentsé passed away in 1959, Sogyal Rinpoche pursued his studies under a number of highly revered teachers. He also began to receive a Western education at a school run by Catholic fathers, which led to a scholarship to study comparative religion at Cambridge University. Starting in England in the 1970s, Sogyal Rinpoche began translating for the Tibetan masters who were beginning to travel to Europe and America. Because of his fluency in English and his acquaintance with Westerners' psychological disposition, Sogyal Rinpoche's own teachers encouraged him to begin instructing students in Tibet's wisdom tradition. A worldwide organization gradually grew around him, which focused on presenting Buddhist teachings and meditation practices, and also, I discovered, on giving spiritual care for the dying. Called Rigpa, its members also assisted in the Dalai Lama's early visits to the West, and helped the Tibetan community in the years before the Tibet issue became widely known. After the publication of *The Tibetan Book of Living and Dying,* and its widespread popularity, Sogyal Rinpoche's prominence, and Rigpa's meditation centers all over the world, grew significantly and soon thousands of people of all faiths came to him seeking spiritual guidance.

Sogyal Rinpoche's meditation center in London was down the street from my student apartment at the chaotic intersection of King's Cross, where the clatter of dope dealers, junkies, and buskers welcomed me each time I stepped onto the street.

During the evening talk, Sogyal Rinpoche spoke about how, at the most subtle level, there is no difference between the mind of a Buddha and our own mind. Sogyal Rinpoche's phrase "Your buddha nature is as good as any buddha's buddha nature" stuck in my mind. We all have the same potential for enlightenment—we are all buddhas-to-be. It does not matter whether we are Buddhists or Muslims, Christians, Jews, or atheists, each one of us possesses the same capacity to transcend the limitations set upon us by our own destructive emotions such as anger and aggression. At the fundamental level of being, Sogyal Rinpoche said, we are no different from the Buddha. Yet we fail to recognize this inherent potential for enlightenment, which, like our face, is so close but we cannot see it. And as long as we do not recognize our enlightened potential, we dwell in confusion and distraction, forever dissatisfied with our lives.

The similarity of the message that Sogyal Rinpoche was articulating and what Uncle Apu had told me in Kathmandu was apparent—if I wanted to be truly content, here and now, I owed it to myself to realize this potential. Sogyal Rinpoche's presence and his words struck directly at my core. It was as if he were providing what I most deeply needed.

Halfway through the talk, Sogyal Rinpoche taught us how to turn inward to see the essence of our minds, our enlightened nature—to arrive at a natural recognition, in the way a child recognizes his or her mother in a crowd. As I watched him move his own hands slowly downward to rest on his knees, and as I turned my mind inward according to his instruction, it was as if dark drapes were pulled away from the gateway of my awareness, and clarity dawned from within. There was no flash of lights, no visions. There were no booming voices, rapture, or levitation. It was exceedingly uncomplicated, while, at the same time, extraordinarily profound. I merely remained in the vivid and visceral awareness of the ever-changing present moment, as if all my senses and the world itself had been stripped naked. It was unlike anything I had ever experienced, and seemed, if only for a moment, a glimpse of freedom from distraction.

When the evening concluded and the crowd left the meditation hall to walk the foggy London streets, I remained seated on a round cushion in the shrine room. Above the statues and the pictures on the shrine hung a black-and-white photograph of Sogyal Rinpoche's previous incarnation, Tertön Sogyal. In the picture he sat wrapped in a cloak, holding prayer beads in his left hand, dreadlocks wound around his head as if a crown. Tertön Sogyal was as stable and majestic as a Himalayan mountain peak, his piercing eyes commanding, if not unsettling.

Over the course of the next year and a half in London, I attended various retreats and talks by Sogyal Rinpoche. I also researched the nineteenth-century life of Tertön Sogyal. Though a highway robber in his youth, Tertön Sogyal later became renowned as Tibet's great champion and protector, using practices such as phurba rituals to combat not only military aggression from Great Britain and China, but also warring factions within Tibet. He was also a meditation teacher and political confidant to the previous Dalai Lama, the thirteenth.

After a few years of study with Sogyal Rinpoche, I wanted to meditate in the same caves in Tibet that his predecessor had used for retreat and visit the shrines he had consecrated. I wanted to cross the same mountain passes and camp in the same valleys where Tertön Sogyal had journeyed. If I were really intent on following in the footsteps of Tertön Sogyal, Sogyal Rinpoche suggested I travel to the Larung Buddhist Encampment in Tibet to meet Khenpo Jikmé Phuntsok, another reincarnation of Tertön Sogyal.

Reincarnation, the migration of a single consciousness into another body, is analogous to how a flame from a single candle can light another, where the second flame is both the same yet different from its source. Before Tertön Sogyal died in 1926, the Year of the Fire Tiger, he told his disciples that he would reincarnate in not only one, but in two individuals simultaneously. In Tibet it is rare but not unheard of that a meditation master reincarnates in more than one body at the same time. But as one of the purposes of reincarnating is to complete tasks that were started in previous lives, more than one incarnation is a very practical solution. As a bodhisattva who vowed to work for all beings until they attain enlightenment, Tertön Sogyal chose to continue his work in both the East and the West. A prophecy regarding Tertön Sogyal's reincarnation states that one of the reincarnations would "have a voice that resounds throughout the world like a lion's roar," and the other would be like "a turquoise dragon holding up a jewel for all to see." It is believed that the lion's roar refers to Sogyal Rinpoche, and that the powerful dragon refers to Khenpo Jikmé Phuntsok.

Just before my first visit to eastern Tibet, I visited Sogyal Rinpoche at his retreat center, Lerab Ling, in southern France. One afternoon he took me to his private shrine room. Juniper incense rose from a small urn and the smoke hung in a powerful silence. Sogyal Rinpoche approached the altar and took from a porcelain plate a small gold-painted relic of his own master, Jamyang Khyentsé. He told me to wear the relic as protection while traveling, even while reminding me that the ultimate pilgrimage place is simply to dwell in the profound state of meditation, and that "is not an external journey."

WINTER 1999, YEAR OF THE EARTH HARE

Larung Buddhist Encampment, Eastern Tibet

I sat in the back row in the middle seat of a cigarette-smoke-filled bus with two-dozen Chinese migrant workers from Yunnan. I could see the gravel road through a hole in the floorboard. We were traveling eighteen hours a day northwest from Chengdu onto the Tibetan Plateau, halting late at night to sleep in grungy truck-stop dormitories and then departing before daybreak. The second day the driver nearly rolled the bus down a steep ravine but instead careened across the road, raking the bus alongside a granite wall, shattering glass into the lap of the man next to me. Everyone was so cold in the bus, nobody yelled during the crash, nor seemed to remark about the incident.

On the third day, two Tibetan monks smelling of campfire boarded and squeezed into the seats next to me. I welcomed the warm bodies. They, too, were en route to the Larung Buddhist Encampment to continue studying under Khenpo Jikmé Phuntsok. On the fourth day of travel, after a flat tire at dawn and then climbing two sixteen-thousand-foot icy passes, we drove toward the golden plains of the region of Serthar, which stretched north-south with mountain ranges on either side. Near the southern end of a valley leading to the encampment, the monks and I descended from the groaning bus. A southerly wind blew from the frozen plains as we walked silently with our belongings on our backs.

After a half-hour trek, we entered the valley and with each step the massive encampment began to unfold to my view. Thousands of mud-walled huts were set upon the valley's parched hillsides, built by the monks and nuns who studied at Larung. As we walked higher toward the ridgeline, with each breath in the thin air, my lungs squeezed. We moved off the trail to rest as a group of nomads with long, raven-black braids, looking like Sioux warriors, rode past us on horseback returning to their yak herds. The sky above was as wide as it was high. In this frigid, remote corner of the Tibetan Plateau, I felt I was coming home.

Khenpo Jikmé Phuntsok founded the Larung Encampment in this desolate valley in 1980 in accordance with a prophecy given to him by a local spirit. Over the next twenty years, the encampment grew to accommodate more than eight thousand ordained monks and nuns from as far away as Mount Kailash and Mongolia, as well as Tibetan monks who came from exile in India. Over a thousand Chinese disciples also arrived, including many affluent doctors, engineers, and artists from Shanghai and Beijing. Many of the Chinese disciples told me of different ways in which they had seen through the smoke screen of consumerism's unfulfilled promise of happiness, and were now more than willing to endure the rugged and inhospitable landscape in eastern Tibet. By late 2000 the enormous encampment with its ten thousand students, bigger than most towns in eastern Tibet, was the largest concentration of monastics anywhere in Tibet, China, and indeed the world.

During the dark years of Mao's Cultural Revolution, Khenpo evaded the Red Guards and their attempts to scrub the Tibetan Plateau of religion and its indigenous culture. He wandered with a few companions and a small herd of goats in the remote wilderness, sustained by wild vegetables and spring water. On the occasions when Khenpo encountered Chinese officials or the Red Guards, he used skillful ruses to escape, and sometimes even gave the impression that he had contracted a contagious disease, thereby being banished to the highlands. There, in the silence of the mountain meadows of Serthar and Golok, Khenpo had visionary encounters with saints and deities who instructed him with prophecies about how to strengthen Buddhism in Tibet in the future. He also spent months on end meditating in solitude, recalling by memory all the meditation instructions his teachers had given him as a young monk.

At the end of the Cultural Revolution in the late 1970s, when Deng Xiaoping relaxed the suppression of religion in Tibet and China, Khenpo began teaching the meditation techniques he had perfected in the mountains. Though he could have remained secluded in a quiet hermitage, Khenpo's bodhisattva vow propelled him to offer spiritual medicine to his fellow Tibetans who had experienced decades of death and the destruction of their culture. Over time, Khenpo's reputation spread as the most learned of Buddhist scholars and an accomplished meditator. Thousands of students arrived at the Larung Encampment in the late 1980s. Nearly every major Tibetan Buddhist teacher had fled into exile or perished after 1959. Khenpo was one of the last alive in Tibet.

The younger monk with whom I had traveled in the bus to the encampment had space on his kitchen floor for me to sleep. We wound our way through the muddy alleyways of the encampment to his shack. Monks and nuns chanted scriptures behind the doors we passed. Smoke rose from simple tin chimneys in the homes of those who had money to buy yak dung for fuel. A few refugee dogs were curled against the doors of some of the huts, trying to stay warm. My head pounded from the lack of oxygen at this altitude. When we arrived at my host's small home, he started a fire as I fell into a corner, exhausted from the journey. The monk put a kettle of water on to boil and then ran out the door halfway down the valley to Khenpo's residence to deliver my request to meet the teacher, and pass along a letter Sogyal Rinpoche had written for me requesting assistance on my pilgrimage.

For the next week, while waiting for a response to the request to speak privately with Khenpo, I attended his teachings in the huge, three-tiered, open-air assembly hall of Larung, huddled together with thousands of monks. Nuns sat on the opposite side of the hall, which was separated by thousands of plastic flowers. During the afternoons, after adjusting to the altitude, I wandered the surrounding ridgelines as the shadows of the mountains lengthened across the valley and plains below.

One day after an early-morning prayer session, while exiting with the other seven thousand monks and nuns, I was pulled from the flood of maroon robes that flowed out of the assembly hall.

"Yishin Norbu—Wish-Fulfilling Jewel—will see you now, but only briefly," the monk whispered, tearing my jacket as he dragged me against the human tide.

Through a snow-covered courtyard of the pagoda-style temple, up three flights of rickety wooden stairs, I tiptoed past two sleeping mastiffs. Then, as I rounded a corner of the temple, I found myself before Khenpo. He was seated as if a huge mountain, not unlike the stoic photograph of his predecessor, Tertön Sogyal. I saw next to his wooden bowl of steaming tea the letter of introduction from Sogyal Rinpoche, his spiritual brother. A piece of ripped cardboard was set out for me to sit on.

I presented a series of scroll paintings that Sogyal Rinpoche had sent with me for Khenpo. Khenpo inquired about his brother-by-incarnation and told me the immense kindness he had felt when he visited Sogyal Rinpoche in France in 1993 on his only visit to the West. Khenpo asked me to convey to Sogyal Rinpoche an invitation to come to Larung to teach Khenpo's disciples.

We spoke for half an hour, then Khenpo become suddenly still, arresting all sound and movement around us. His eyes widened, unblinking and unmoving. And then, just as when a cloud dissolves effortlessly in the sky, there was an expansive spaciousness, free of tension, free of thinking. Looking into his eyes, I felt Khenpo's thought-free awareness being poured into me. Only crystal-clear awareness remained. I was looking into the face of awareness itself, where the looker, the looking, and that which is being looked at dissolve of their own accord. Time did not stand still—there was no time; there was nothing before or after, only freedom.

With a slow blink, Khenpo reclined.

"You will need protection on your journey," he said softly.

Khenpo Jikmé Phuntsok (1933–2004) was the most prominent teacher who emerged from the Cultural Revolution to begin teaching and reviving Buddhism in Tibet. He is one of two simultaneous reincarnations of Tertön Sogyal and, here, holds the tertön's phurba dagger.

He reached to his belt and pulled out an eight-inch, three-sided, single-pointed phurba, not unlike the first phurba I had seen Uncle Apu using years before in Kathmandu. Khenpo's attendant handed him a smaller phurba, shorter than my index finger. Khenpo wrapped his coral prayer beads around the two, as if to bind the transfer of blessing from the mother-phurba to the smaller child-phurba. His eyes turned upward with only the whites visible.

Rolling the two phurbas and crimson beads between his hands, he chanted the mantra of the enlightened deity Vajrakilaya, *"Om Benza Kili Kilaya Hung Phet, Om Benza Kili Kilaya Hung Phet . . ."*

"Wear this phurba for protection. By reciting the mantra, *Om Benza Kili Kilaya Hung Phet,* and continually visualizing Vajrakilaya, you will remove obstacles to your spiritual path." He dropped the small phurba into a silk pouch, tying it closed with a red cord, and placed it around my neck.

"Now, go to Kalzang Monastery in Nyarong, the Cave That Delights the Senses near Palpung Monastery, the Jokhang Cathedral in Lhasa, and then, go to Nyagar in Golok. You will find what you need to know about Tertön Sogyal, and how to wield the phurba for your own and others' benefit."

Khenpo had told me to visit four places that figured prominently in Tertön Sogyal's life; Kalzang Monastery, where Tertön Sogyal met his first teacher; the Jokhang Cathedral in Lhasa, where Tertön Sogyal entered the Dalai Lama's court; the Cave That Delights the Senses near Palpung Monastery, where he revealed a powerful phurba practice; and Nyagar in Golok, where Tertön Sogyal passed away.

I ventured to Kalzang Monastery in late 2000. The secluded temple, set among forests of fir and spruce, had been established by the great meditator Pema Duddul, in the region of Nyarong in eastern Tibet. Its library houses the hand-carved woodblocks for Tertön Sogyal and his teacher's collected writings, as well as the only known biography of Tertön Sogyal, *The Marvelous Garland of White Lotus,* written by one of his monk students named Tsullo.

Tsullo's biography is based on Tertön Sogyal's journals of his mystical visions and wide-ranging travels. The journals were destroyed during the Cultural Revolution, it is said, so the biography is as close as we can get to a document that traces Tertön Sogyal's movements. Yet, even for Tibetan scholars of the highest caliber, much of this spiritual biography is incomprehensible. The meaning of passages is often concealed in arcane language; historians find it perplexing. Given that Tertön Sogyal's life was exceptional even by the standards of the Tibetan religious and scholarly elite, as an American pilgrim, my only hope of accessing the biography's deeper meaning meant radically expanding my perception of the possible. In it, a Western sense of chronology hardly exists. As in most Tibetan hagiographies, Tertön Sogyal's past, present, and future lives are playfully interchanged. We read of Tertön Sogyal simultaneously inhabiting heavenly realms, pure lands, and the caves of eastern Tibet and valleys around Lhasa. Coded language, referencing Tertön Sogyal and other key people like the Dalai Lama by various secret names, makes cross-checking with other biographies a complex task. And Tertön Sogyal's interactions with long-dead saints and ethereal protector spirits are mixed with actual historical events.

The woodblocks for Tertön Sogyal's biography and other Buddhist texts had been taken away individually and hidden by villagers underground and in the earthen walls of their homes during the dark years of the Cultural Revolution, when frenetic mobs burned libraries and temples across Tibet. In the mid-1980s, when there was a relative relaxation on religious suppression, former monks, still wearing green fatigues and Mao caps instead of burgundy robes, collected the woodblocks from the villagers and returned them to the libraries. When an elderly one-eyed monk named Wangde was let out of prison after eighteen years of incarceration for defending his Buddhist beliefs, he took it upon himself to reconstitute the library at Kalzang, picking up the remains of a thirteen-hundred-year-old spiritual tradition, woodblock by woodblock.

When I came to Kalzang Monastery, One-Eye Wangde held the keys to the iron padlocks on the door to the dusty library on the top floor of the temple. As we walked to the temple library, I held his bony elbow as his curved knuckles gripped a cane. Ascending a leaning stairwell, we lit two candles to illuminate the room. The library consists of the hundreds of woodblocks stored in shelves that reach the ceiling with enough space for pilgrims to walk underneath. The aging One-Eye Wangde told me that I was the first "long-nose," or Westerner, ever to visit this inner sanctum of the temple at Kalzang—permission was granted likely because of the letter from Sogyal Rinpoche I continued to carry.

One-Eye Wangde arranged for a copy of Tertön Sogyal's hagiography from the woodblocks, directing three younger novices to print the book manually on handmade paper. One novice traveled by horse for four hours to collect the paper from Chagdud Monastery. Another monk ground ink powder by hand and then mixed it with the nearby holy spring water, adding a dash of gold out of respect for the story the ink would tell. It took an additional two days for the monks to print the manuscript and a half day to dry the text in the mountain sunlight before binding the elongated sheets of paper between thin wood slats, secured with a leather strap.

While I waited for the book, every morning I went to One-Eye Wangde's one-room, wood-cabin hermitage. A plastic sheet had been nailed around the window for insulation, casting a mellow bluish light against the walls, thick with soot from the dung-fire stove. He sat on what served both as his bed and his meditation cubicle. There was a small bookshelf with volumes read hundreds of times over and a dented tea thermos. Only prayer broke his days of silence. One-Eye Wangde had a toughness about him that seemed to welcome discomfort.

One-Eye Wangde had his own copy of the hagiography, oil- and dirt-stained at the top edges from use. He chanted the entire text, offering me the traditional oral transmission where the disciple hears the text directly from his teacher, just as his teacher had given it to him, so the continuity of blessing is secured.

Upon my return to Nepal with the text, I turned to two British scholar-friends in France and Kathmandu to help extrapolate Tertön Sogyal's travels across the Tibetan Plateau from the mystical verses, prophetic statements, and cryptic dreams. Although the text purportedly narrates Tertön Sogyal's life, locating him in a specific time and place in a chronological sense was a difficult task. Over the course of the next years, my English friends and I spoke to elderly lamas in Tibet, Nepal, and India. We tried to unlock the meaning of various passages, and researched different biographies of the XIII Dalai Lama and other spiritual luminaries who spent time with Tertön Sogyal. In my room in Kathmandu, I had a map on my wall of present-day Tibet. I highlighted Tertön Sogyal's apparent travels on foot and on horseback, and in dreams, across Tibet, and into China. I made tentative itineraries and plans to travel along the same caravan routes, and circled with a red marker the locations where his most significant revelations and visions occurred. Most places had no road to them. I eventually came away with a cartographer's sketch of the Tibetan Plateau crisscrossed by Tertön Sogyal's life of nonstop movement. I now had a map to guide me—but the map is not the territory.

After receiving the oral transmission for Tertön Sogyal's biography from One-Eye Wangde in the fall of 2000, I asked to remain in retreat at a cave above Kalzang Monastery. One-Eye Wangde suggested that I stay in a small log cabin instead of the cave, as he knew I would last only a day or two in the frigid grotto.

"Use the caves for inspiration, but for now, you can stay in a retreat hut with a woodstove," he suggested.

This was my first solitary meditation retreat in Tibet, at one of the most sacred mountains associated with Tertön Sogyal, Shangdrak Peak. It was here that his teacher, Pema Duddul, stayed many years and later gave Tertön Sogyal his first meditation instructions. My retreat cabin had once belonged to Tertön Sogyal's wife; she had died there in the late 1940s. Her thick, tattered meditation cloak remains in the cabin. One-Eye Wangde encouraged me to drape the cloak over my shoulders when I meditated, as he did not think my North Face down jacket was warm enough. I felt the blessings of the shack and its dusty garments the moment I entered. I wanted to start the retreat straightaway the next day.

"Enthusiasm is as strong as a horse, but as short as a sheep's tail!" the old monk chuckled, reading my character. "Take a few days to settle down, and then you can begin your retreat."

That first evening, after I swept my room with a pine branch fashioned as a broom, I placed three photographs on the shelf: Tertön Sogyal, Khenpo, and Sogyal Rinpoche. My pack hung on a bent nail so the resident mice would not chew through it during the next weeks. I rolled out a sleeping bag in an elongated wooden box, shorter than I was tall, which was both my bed and meditation seat. The wind blowing through the walls reminded me of camping in Wyoming's Wind River Mountains, where the yaps of coyotes punctuate the night sky.

While I was tending a fire to boil some potatoes for dinner, One-Eye Wangde returned to talk about my retreat schedule. He suggested the traditional four daily meditation sessions, each lasting two hours, during which time I was to sit unmoving in a cross-legged posture. Additionally, I needed to schedule an hour in the morning to place water bowl offerings on the shrine, offer a few hundred prostrations, and make a smoke offering of juniper branches as rent payment to the local mountain spirits. No need to read any books or write, he told me, but rather, "continually recall your teacher's blessed words and advice on recognizing the nature of mind, and then simply rest in the awareness of that recognition.

"Reading philosophy and theories in books is just a distraction from recognizing one's buddha nature," he said grinning, as I thought about how much money I had paid to study philosophy at university in London. "And writing about it makes it more so." I slid my journal under my sleeping bag.

Before One-Eye Wangde departed for the evening, he offered advice on the deeper purpose of retreat. He told me to think about the next weeks in terms of establishing boundaries: external, internal, and secret. The external boundary is literally the perimeter that I decided not to walk beyond nor allow anyone else to enter into during the retreat. A few cedar trees that surrounded my cabin marked that boundary. The internal boundary binds the retreatant to a schedule of meditation sessions and yogic practices, free from mundane activity.

"This is where freedom begins, where we progress along the spiritual path," the old monk said, speaking from experience. "And the secret boundary is to make the solemn promise to yourself that you will strive to abide in awareness of your buddha nature."

I was a bit skeptical. Meditating at such a subtle state of awareness for a moment or two during each session seemed remotely possible. But to do so continually day after day seemed unlikely. My doubt was confirmed during my retreat.

"Your promise is to strive and persevere, for your own and others' benefit," he instructed, answering the silent question in my mind. "The meditator's life—to continually abide in a state of pristine awareness—is not an easy one, but that is why we call it *the path*."

"A pot of tea will be delivered at four thirty A.M. and eleven A.M. each day at that cedar tree," he said, pointing to the boundary for solitude. "You can start tomorrow on the new moon. I will see you after twenty-one days."

When I returned to eastern Tibet over the next two years, I continued short meditation retreats at various hermitages and caves, sometimes for just a few days. I traveled mostly in the regions where Tertön Sogyal had wandered and meditated in the early part of his life, the Nyarong valleys and highlands of Tromthar. The expansive plains of Golok spread to the north, where Tertön Sogyal spent much of his later years. In between Nyarong and Golok is the wild-west town of Kandze, which is at the center of eastern Tibet's firm opposition against forces that have tried to conquer the region in the past and today. Monks, nuns, farmers, and nomads speak openly of their passionate opposition to what they see as China's occupation of their homeland.

The more time I spent around Kandze with elderly monks, local shamans, and old-timers who shared with me the oral history of eastern Tibet and Tertön Sogyal's life, the more trust I seemed to garner. It did not take long before their stories changed from Tertön Sogyal's spiritual life to current-day political injustices and suppression of religion. In a country where China suppresses Tibetan Buddhism, talk of the spiritual path evokes strong feelings of political injustice and Tibetan nationhood.

"This is my brother's arrest record for chanting 'Long Live the Dalai Lama,'" one woman said tearfully, showing me a Chinese court document. "He was beaten with an iron pipe by the police."

"Please take this to your country," I was asked by another man while being handed documents marked FOR INTERNAL DISTRIBUTION ONLY from the Sichuan Provincial Government. "It outlines how Tibetan language will no longer be taught in school. Only Mandarin."

I heard of imprisoned monks in the villages around Kandze; the forced settlement of nomads to the south in Litang; I was given photographs of demolished monks' homes to the west in the Yachen Encampment; and was told of a recent execution with a single bullet to the back of a Tibetan's head in Dartsedo.

Carrying this type of firsthand information and photographs in Tibet or China not only heightened my awareness of my surroundings, but often resulted in sleepless nights. Nightmares of Tibetans being beaten and tortured scared me from sleep. I knew that the real danger was to them. Increasingly I found myself in the middle of the night praying to Tertön Sogyal to protect the Tibetans, repeating the mantra that Khenpo had given me, *"Om Benza Kili Kilaya Hung Phet, Om Benza Kili Kilaya Hung Phet . . ."*

Tibetans were asking me to plug their stifled voices from the Tibetan Plateau into an amplifier in the West for the world to hear and act upon. Rather than meditating, I spent more time worrying about being caught by the Chinese police carrying handwritten descriptive notes and digital memory sticks full of human rights abuse information.

"Go to Tibet," I once heard the Dalai Lama respond to a Westerner who asked how to help Tibet. "Then tell the world what you have seen. Bear witness."

Bearing witness is one thing. Actually doing what the Chinese government considers "endangering state security" is another. If caught carrying such politically sensitive information, the worst-case scenario for me would be an expensive air ticket home, "deported" stamped in my passport, and a prohibition against my ever being allowed in China or Tibet again—I could deal with that. But the real risk was for the Tibetans who find ways to skirt their stories out of China. Arrest, torture, long prison sentences, and the death penalty are the consequences for those caught trying to send information to journalists and human rights groups.

The black tassels plaited into a long ponytail, threaded through a four-inch-thick ivory ring and wound around the head, were a sure sign the men I spotted in the Kandze street market hailed from Nyarong in Kham. They both had high, chiseled cheekbones like Apache warriors and arm-length knives run through a bloodred sash. Such swords are a symbol of Khampa brotherhood and, at the same time, a warning to those same brothers not to overstep unstated boundaries. Today, blades also signify resistance. In 2002, I saw posted announcements from local public security bureaus declaring an official ban on carrying knives in marketplaces or on public transport. In practice, few blades were left at home.

I asked the two swashbuckling twenty-year-olds on the muddy street about cheap transport to Nyarong, the region where Tertön Sogyal was born. Yes, they would take me, but there was a catch. Lifting their chins, they pointed to the newest of the many Sichuanese migrants' *jyoza* shops. A couple of bowls of steaming pork-filled mini-raviolis was cheaper than renting a jeep, so I happily agreed to the exchange.

After wiping drips of chili sauce from their chins with their coat sleeves and whistling at a passing group of local girls, Phuntsok and Orgyen jumped with me into the back of a rickety pickup truck. The vehicle was driven by their uncle, wearing a pinstripe suit over a Chicago Bulls T-shirt, trousers tucked into his Dingo boots, and a requisite stiletto attached to his belt. His life's savings were his two gold front teeth. Heading due east out of Kandze to the Kawalungri Mountain Range, Uncle Buccaneer, as I called him, took a sharp southerly turn to enter Nyarong.

Bumping over icy dirt roads, Phuntsok and Orgyen protected themselves from the skin-splitting wind by sinking down in the back of the truck and leaning on my rucksack. Anxiousness kept me from the usual travel banter. In my mind's eye was the frightened look of a Tibetan from the previous night who had asked me to carry secret prison sentencing documents from the Sichuan provincial court. I concealed the papers by sewing them into the shoulder straps of my backpack, upon which Phuntsok and Orgyen were reclining. The papers itemized the offenses of a recently jailed Buddhist scholar:

> In order to achieve his aim to split the country and sabotage the unity of the nationalities, the accused illegally organized a mass gathering with 2,000 participants at the Puse Township of Kandze County to pray for the long life for the Dalai, the exile who has engaged in activities to split the Motherland. At this prayer gathering, the accused raised a giant photograph of the Dalai, which he had brought himself. . . . During the religious teaching session, the accused not only chanted long-life prayers for the Dalai, but also openly urged monks and other people to believe in the Dalai.

The court-stamped documents attested that the scholar-monk was try-ing to split Tibet from the Motherland of China by praying to the Dalai Lama and displaying a large photograph of the Tibetan leader. The Chinese government equates religious faith in the Dalai Lama with the criminal of-fense of "separatism" or "splittism." He was sentenced to five years in prison. Before the monk was brought before a judge in Chengdu, he was beaten with rubber tubing and his left shoulder and back scalded with boiling water. When news got back to Kandze of the abuse, Tibetans hung even more por-traits of the scholar-monk next to the forbidden photographs of the Dalai Lama.

Possessing such official documents from Chinese courts is rare. They are extremely useful to human rights monitors and governments concerned about human rights because they bring into sharp focus how the Chinese legal system functions. Within two months, the dozen folded pages upon which my yak-herding companions reclined were hand-carried by different individuals from Chengdu, to Bangkok, to Amsterdam, and finally Wash-ington, D.C. The documents were passed to the U.S. State Department and European government officials, who soon called upon their Chinese coun-terparts to explain themselves.

AUTUMN 2002, YEAR OF THE WATER HORSE

Larung Buddhist Encampment, Eastern Tibet

During my first trip to Larung in 1999 there was no need to enter surrepti-tiously; the Chinese authorities did not restrict foreigners from the area. Not only did I meet Khenpo, but he had given me the phurba for protection. In the few years since my pilgrimage began, I had completed a few meditation retreats in Tibet, and also personally seen and heard the Tibetan people's pain. In late 2002, when I sneaked into the Larung Buddhist Encampment in the back of Dawa's truck to take the message to Khenpo from the Dalai Lama, I was fully aware of the dangers. Tibetans' tears were still flowing over the destruction just a year before when the Chinese government ordered work teams to hack down over three thousand meditation huts. The Chinese security forces still patrolled the encampment hourly and I knew if I was discovered, Dawa the driver, any monks who had seen me, and even Khenpo would face serious consequences. Nobody from Larung had asked me to return, but I needed to deliver the message.

I threw a few more pieces of yak dung chips on the fire and warmed my hands. I had been hiding in the cabin for a day, holding in my mind the message from the Dalai Lama for Khenpo.

The message had been given to me by the Dalai Lama's envoy, Lodi Gyari, a few weeks earlier in New Delhi. We discussed how even a message that only concerned the health care of a lama might be construed as political by the Chinese authorities.

"Khenpo needs medical care in Europe; then he can return to his encampment in Larung. But, he needs proper medical attention. The Dalai Lama is very concerned for Khenpo's deteriorating health. Sogyal Rinpoche can arrange the flights and care. This is not politics. This is about Khenpo living longer," Lodi Gyari said.

"We need Khenpo to remain in this world. He needs immediate medical treatment."

The logistics of getting Khenpo to Europe for medical care were simple. The political situation at the Larung Encampment was not. As I waited in that one-room shack I thought of Khenpo looking down the valley, watching the wind stirring the dusty skeletons of his students' demolished homes that had been razed by the Chinese government just a year before. Chinese work crews and security bosses still roamed the encampment. Khenpo's attendants told him under their breath that young nuns had committed suicide in the distant hills, that disheartened monks were spat upon as they begged on sidewalks in inhospitable Chengdu, and that hundreds of Khenpo's students were still arriving monthly in the United Nations refugee center in Nepal.

The only interruption to my solitude while hoping to see Khenpo and deliver the message had been thermoses of butter tea that arrived with a knock at the door, and a thump of boots on frozen ground. The tea warmed me. An oil lamp burned on the small shelf with a faded photograph of Khenpo and small copper statue of Buddha.

Suddenly the door of my hut burst open without warning, filling the room with icy air. A monk with a long goatee stood for a moment holding a burlap bag, and then walked to the fireplace without saying a word. Putting the bag down, he pulled a knife from a woodblock and cut open the bag's tie, revealing my dinner—a thigh-size, dry chunk of yak meat, a bag of roasted barley flour, and a leather pouch of butter. I did not dare tell him that I was a vegetarian.

"I make the tea for you now. Tomorrow and next day you stay here. Don't go out. There are Chinese policeman and army looking for a foreigner," he said in a strong local dialect. He left just as abruptly as he had entered.

Two days went by; I left the cabin only when nature called. Late in the afternoon on the third day, the goateed monk returned to my cabin. I had spent enough time in Tibet to know that Tibetans rarely knock when they want to come into a house, even if it is the house of a stranger. After taking his seat by the fire, he looked at me silently and stroked his beard.

Tension at Larung had remained high since the demolitions and expulsions a year earlier. Khenpo's attendants were suspicious of everyone—Tibetans, Chinese, Americans—and they questioned whether the international press that had berated China had actually benefited the encampment, or had simply caused the Chinese authorities to clamp down tighter. It was still an open question. Anyone outside the close-knit group of relatives and attendants of Khenpo was deemed untrustworthy. There could not have been a more difficult time to get a message from the outside to Khenpo, much less for a foreigner to see him.

Dawa had told me he planned to send a bearded monk to my house the second or third night if he was successful in telling Khenpo that I was carrying a message from the Dalai Lama's office in India.

"If the monk sits for more than fifteen minutes, then tell him the message you have for Khenpo." Dawa had instinctively done a risk assessment. "If he comes and leaves quickly, it means that I will come back for you the same night to drive you away. You may not be able to stay or give the message to Khenpo."

I poured the monk a cup of tea. He finally spoke.

"Tertön Sogyal predicted that if his two reincarnations, Khenpo and Sogyal Rinpoche, and especially their respective students, get along well, and if they help each other out, then each teacher's benefit for all beings will be as vast as space itself."

It was a signal to communicate to him the message from the Dalai Lama. It also meant that I would not see Khenpo on this visit.

After I had entrusted him with the Dalai Lama's message encouraging Khenpo to seek medical care in Europe, the monk pulled a silk scarf and blessed relic pills from beneath his robes. "These are from Khenpo. He sends them to you with his blessing and this instruction, *'If you want the blessings of Tertön Sogyal, and to learn how to wield the phurba, visit the four pilgrimage places that I told you.'*"

Part II

Beings are by nature buddhas,

But this is concealed by temporary stains.

When the stains are purified, their buddhahood is revealed.

BUDDHA

Chapter 4

From Bandit to Saint

Nyarong, Eastern Tibet

The tires sprayed gravel as we rounded a bend, heading toward the mountain pass that leads into the deep Nyarong Gorge. I looked out from the back of yet another pickup truck in which I'd hitched a ride with a group of herders. Young yaks jumped and kicked their back legs, scared by the passing vehicle. Motherly *dri* stared impassively, steam freezing into icy droplets around their noses. I was returning to Kalzang Monastery to see One-Eye Wangde.

We were driving through the canyon that lay in the shadow of Eternal Snow Mountain Range. This is the home of the protective deity, Eternal Snow, who is a minister in the celestial court of the powerful God over the Plains near Lhasa, the mountain deity who oversees the entire Himalayan Range and is charged with protecting the Buddha's teachings. As we crossed a mountain pass, rock cairns marked the northern boundary of the mountain abode of Eternal Snow. Strings of vaporous prayer flags stretching between trees painted the sky with mantras and sacred scripture. We passed a solo farmer on the roadside placing juniper on a small fire, sprinkling rice wine, sending billowing clouds of incense smoke to appease and honor Eternal Snow and the local spirits.

Tibetans view wilderness through a dual prism of their ancestral shamanistic animism and Buddhist cosmology, much of which they inherited from India. Glaciated peaks and high altitude lakes, vast plains, and even the pure sky above, are given meaning through their relationship with the deities of the land and clan spirits who reside there. Offering incense and alcohol to the local spirits is a matter of respecting latent forces; failure to do so can invite obstacles. I began to shift my outlook from seeing the terrain as wilderness to conceiving it as a sacred topography in which the mountains and rivers, streams and glaciers, the very pebbles upon which my boots fall, are woven into a blessed landscape.

The Tibetan herders sitting next to me in the truck stood and swayed and, facing Eternal Snow, shattered the frozen air with screams reminiscent of Genghis Khan's warriors charging to battle. "*Ki ki so so, lha gyalo, so so so so, lha gyalo!*—Victory and conquest to the mountain gods!"

As they sat down, one of my Tibetan travel mates threw the long arms of his woolen robe over my shoulder for warmth. It reminded me of how, in my youth in Wyoming, my father, grandfathers, and uncles taught self-reliance to me and my older brother and cousins. Preparedness was the key. But when others were not well equipped, you should always be ready to carry a bit heavier backpack or be ready to give up your own sleeping bag if someone was chilled in the Rocky Mountain night. And it was in the wilderness that my father offered us his own land-bound sense of place, having us train our vision to look in between the cottonwood and pine instead of at the trees themselves, for that is where you see the elk, deer, or ruffed grouse. And we crawled toward beaver ponds with our fishing poles because we knew the rainbow and brook trout scurried away when they felt the vibrations of our footsteps. On weekends and summers in the Wind River Mountains and on the sagebrush-covered Continental Divide, my brother, Mike, and

I refined our backwoods skills, emulating the heroes of our adolescence—Jim Bridger and other frontier trappers, the Indian chiefs Crazy Horse and Geronimo, and Butch Cassidy. Skills learned in the mountains and along the streambeds of my youth—how to read approaching weather, trail finding, or simply being able to withstand being bitterly cold—proved extremely useful in Tibet.

We soon passed the village of Shiwa, birthplace of Tertön Sogyal. I saw the mud-packed walls of the house where he was born in 1856. Most of the settlements in the Nyarong Gorge that are set above the banks of the roaring Nyachu (Chinese: Yalong) River offer little habitable land. Farming plays a limited role in Nyarong village life with cabbage and root vegetables cultivated in small gardens. Most of Nyarong consists of steep, south-facing spruce, juniper cypress forests, and high alpine pasture where the seminomadic herders move their yak and sheep in the warmer months.

Tertön Sogyal's birth in Upper Nyarong was prophesied in an ancient text. The scripture told how the eighth-century Buddhist practitioner Dorje Dudjom would reincarnate as Tertön Sogyal below Kawalungri Mountain, next to the Nyachu River. Dorje Dudjom was the minister of state for Tibet's king in the late eighth and early ninth centuries, just after Tibet's martial power had reached its apex, due in large part to an increasing confederation of tribes. Having seized control of China's then-capital of Ch'ang (Xian), overrun Arab armies in northern Persia, defeated Turks in East Turkestan, and left behind pillars of conquest as far south as Bodhgaya in the current-day Indian state of Bihar, the Tibetan mounted militia were as unyielding as they were feared. It was in the eighth century that Tibet's Yarlung monarchs decided to convert the Tibetans from their indigenous animistic beliefs to Buddhism.

It was not easy to establish Buddhism in Tibet. Despite the tribal confederacy that Tibet had become under the Yarlung kings, it was still a land of strong-headed chieftains, small kingdoms, and wide-ranging nomads, battling with one another or anyone else who might pass through their domain. They were rowdy and unaccustomed to taking orders. The whole of Tibet was thought to be the province of malevolent gods and demons, and innumerable spirits controlling the mountains, valleys, and lakes.

When King Trisong Detsen attempted to create a Buddhist monastic order and build the first monastery and temple, local shamans and magicians directed spirits and demons to destroy at night any construction that was accomplished during the day. They also caused a series of disasters, including drought and floods that brought famine and diseases. The elderly Bengali monk Shantarakshita, who was in Tibet on imperial patronage at the time, advised the king to search in India for the Buddhist master known as Padmasambhava, the Lotus-Born Guru, to come to the sovereign's aid. If the depictions we have today of Padmasambhava are accurate—heavyset, furrowed brow, and slightly wrathful grin welcoming challenges—then the king had found just the right master to accomplish the task. While the historical Buddha is known for his compassionate teachings on peacefully abiding, Padmasambhava was more of a tough-love teacher who offered powerful methods for removing obstacles to enlightenment. The king dispatched seven envoys with offerings of gold and silk across the Himalayas to invite Padmasambhava to Tibet. That group was led by Dorje Dudjom, the previous incarnation of Tertön Sogyal. Padmasambhava accepted their request and then, it is said, scattered their offering of gold in the air, with the words "Everything I perceive is gold."

Upon arriving in Tibet, Padmasambhava began subduing the myriad local spirits who were opposed to the Buddhist teachings. When he brought them under his command, the animistic forces and local spirits vowed to support Buddhist practitioners in the future. Padmasambhava bound the multitude of spirits and ghosts in the earth, sky, and water to their oath, setting the foundation for the dissemination of Buddhism in Tibet and throughout the Himalayas. In time, with imperial support and the blessing

Padmasambhava firmly established Buddhism in Tibet in the eighth century. This treasure statue of Padmasambhava was unearthed in 1891 by Tertön Sogyal and currently sits in Lhasa's Jokhang Cathedral.

of Padmasambhava, teams of scholars embarked upon the task of translating the vast corpus of scriptures from India's great Buddhist universities such as Nalanda, monastic colleges were established to study the inner science of the mind, and the community of lay vajrayana practitioners took root in every valley of the plateau.

Tibet, as a political entity, with the unifying social force of a shared religion, had been established. Tibet owes its spiritual and political foundation to the father of Tibetan Buddhism, Padmasambhava, which is why Tibetans still refer to him as the Second Buddha. The Dalai Lama has said of Padmasambhava, "It was because of his overarching power and strength that the Buddhadharma [e.g., Buddhism] was really established in Tibet, and then developed so that all the teachings of the Buddha, including the Mantrayana [e.g. tantric teachings] were preserved as a living tradition, and have continued down to the present day."

Dorje Dudjom served Padmasambhava as he journeyed across the Tibetan Plateau imparting spiritual teachings, engaging in meditation retreats, and advising on political affairs. Acting true to his name of Indestructible Subduer of Demons, Dorje Dudjom became spiritually accomplished through wielding the phurba while practicing the rites of the wrathful deity Vajrakilaya. It is said that he was able to slice solid stone with his phurba, as if the rock were warm butter; he could fly with the speed of the wind; and near Samyé he passed through a mountain unhindered. Dorje Dudjom was part of a small group of Padmasambhava's closest disciples. Demonstrating their spiritual accomplishments to the general populace in order to increase their faith in the teachings of the Buddha and Padmasambhava, they carried out such feats as bringing corpses back to life, walking on the rays of the sun, or passing bodily through solid objects.

Padmasambhava concealed innumerable treasures, or *terma,* across the Tibetan Plateau. Stored in the form of ritual objects or parchment of golden paper upon which mystical syllables were inscribed, these treasures were buried in the caves, mountainsides, lakes, temple pillars, and inside small stone caskets by Padmasambhava and his closest disciple, the Lady Yeshe Tsogyal. Additionally, Padmasambhava concealed teachings and prophecies in the very mind-streams of twenty-five disciples, so that when the auspicious circumstances converged in later incarnations, his instruction would spontaneously emerge from their minds and be written down on paper. Those who revealed the blessed physical objects and teachings are known as *tertöns,* or treasure revealers.

Padmasambhava used this unique method of concealment and prophecy because he knew that not all of his instructions could be utilized or be of benefit in Tibet in the eighth century. He foresaw some teachings to be more appropriate for future generations. He also knew that Tibetans would battle with other nation-states, so he concealed ritual manuals, including a number of phurba rites, with the express purpose of removing forces that would threaten Buddhism and the Tibetan state. With his concern for the development of future practitioners and to maintain Tibet as a container for spiritual development, Padmasambhava appointed future incarnations of his original twenty-five disciples as his own emissaries for revealing his treasure teachings and prophecies. In each of their successive rebirths, incarnations of these original twenty-five students perpetually reveal fresh spiritual instructions that were hidden by Padmasambhava in the form of liturgies, meditation manuals, and blessed statues. Dorje Dudjom's successive reincarnations in Tibet—for ten centuries—continued through Tertön Sogyal, and today to Khenpo and Sogyal Rinpoche.

I often wonder if the positive karmic seeds that Dorje Dudjom planted in the eighth century by serving Padmasambhava are ripening in the twenty-first century in Khenpo's and Sogyal Rinpoche's vast activities. No other Buddhist teacher in modern times matches Khenpo's accomplishments in Tibet and China. And in exile, except for the Dalai Lama, no other lama has connected to more Westerners than Sogyal Rinpoche has through his book *The Tibetan Book of Living and Dying*. Dorje Dudjom may have changed bodies to become Tertön Sogyal and then Khenpo and Sogyal Rinpoche, but their motivation and the vastness of their vision remains the same—to create the most generous and auspicious conditions for as many of us as possible to find the path to spiritual liberation and lasting happiness.

SPRING 1856, YEAR OF THE FIRE DRAGON

Shiwa Village, Nyarong, Eastern Tibet

Drolma leaned against a wall of bailed hay, her braids rolling off her slumped shoulders. Exhausted satisfaction beamed from her—her firstborn was a boy. Closing her deep eyes, she drifted into the memory of a dream she'd had the night she conceived her son.

"He shall not be with you for long," a sixteen-year-old girl with bejeweled hair in a topknot had told her. "Shower him with love while you can."

As the mirage figure faded, translucent bells, phurbas, and other ritual objects rained down, and dissolved into Drolma. Though feeling her body was blessed with the auspicious ritual items, she was anxious about the prediction that her child might not survive.

Her son's cry roused the new mother. Two cousins tightly swaddled the newborn while a third kicked at two dogs sniffing at the mother's feet. Blessed butter from the local monastery was rubbed atop the baby's head. With the traditional midwifery duties complete, they placed the infant on Drolma's breast to begin feeding.

"What is it, then?" the father bellowed from the room above.

"A beautiful boy," the youngest cousin shouted up the stairwell to the smoky kitchen.

The boy's father grunted and poured another round of rice wine for his gang of friends. Using his third finger, Dargye flicked the thick local brew in the air, as an offering to the spirit of the feared Nyarong chieftain Gönpo Namgyal, known simply as Amgon.

"By the power of Amgon, may my boy, born in the Year of the Fire Dragon, bring good fortune to this poor Shiwa village household."

"Shall we take him to Pema Duddul at the monastery for a blessing and name-giving ceremony?" asked one of his male cousins.

"No. I already sent some butter up to old hermit Palden at Purification Temple. He said the boy should be named Sonam Gyalpo. I don't want Pema Duddul of Kalzang Temple getting any ideas about having my kid chanting in robes at his place. My son, Sonam Gyalpo, is going to ride sidekick with me. Not be a monk."

Clan allegiance and matrimonial alliance were key to survival in Nyarong, where revenge and honor killings were the norm. While his newborn son and wife lay sleeping below, Dargye tried to wash away with alcohol the anger and curses that had been set upon him by locals.

Dargye's ancestors had been financially well off in Nyarong; however, he was an outcast and had only recently returned to Shiwa village to take the shy lady Drolma as his bride. The word around Upper Nyarong's pine-filled valleys was that before marrying Drolma, Dargye had been part of a small group of bandits known as the Sure Shots, who roamed the north-south trade route of the Nyachu River that flowed the length of Nyarong. The deep gorge requires slow travel on precariously narrow trails, making caravans easy targets for bandits. During a decade of late-night ambushes, mule-train holdups, and matchlock musket banditry, the Sure Shots had made off with considerable gold and silver, and in the process had left more than a dozen local traders and farmers dead.

Dargye claimed he had been a laborer in Dartsedo, a week's horse ride away—not one of the Sure Shots. He spoke of working for a shady Chinese tea trader and the herbal remedy dealers in the far western Chinese town of Chengdu. He told of working in the packinghouses, wrapping long bricks of aged *puerh* tea in bamboo wicker. Certainly his meager resources did not reflect years of high-revenue banditry.

"My boy is not going to pray in the temples," Dargye said, having no inclination to send his child to the Buddhist order as Nyarong tradition pre-scribed, especially his first son. "Sonam Gyalpo will be a crack shot, a shrewd trader, and marry a girl from Kandze. He'll carry on the spirit of Amgon."

Simultaneously feared and respected in Nyarong, the Nyarong chief-tain Amgon was a legend while alive, and his spirit continued to be invoked after his violent death. As a small-time chieftain in Middle Nyarong, Amgon subdued neighboring tribes in the mid-1830s, and by the winter of 1847, he had united Upper and Lower Nyarong. Amgon's commanders began steadily and aggressively subjugating the tribes in other provinces of Kham. The

Tibetan government in Lhasa and the Qing Dynasty in Peking wanted nothing to do with Amgon and his warriors and tried to ignore him. Finally, in 1863, the Tibetan government felt he had gone too far when Amgon established control of the southern tea-trade route to Lhasa, and dispatched troops with Commander Trimon. Two years of relentless fighting ensued. Finally, Amgon offered a truce, pledging his allegiance to the Dalai Lama and claiming that he had taken only those lands that the foreign Qing had occupied or were poised to control. Amgon demanded as part of the truce that Commander Trimon from Lhasa pledge never to betray him, and that Amgon's family would remain unharmed. Trimon agreed.

When Amgon returned to inform his commanders and family of the truce, Trimon and his central Tibetan forces laid siege to Amgon's massive fortress on the east side of the Nyachu River. Trimon's troops set the fortress ablaze and Amgon, his wife, other family, and close commanders were burned alive. To this day, acts of betrayal in Nyarong are known as "the Oath of Trimon."

During the attack on Amgon, when his fortress was engulfed in flames, the renowned Nyarong meditator Pema Duddul of Kalzang Monastery clairvoyantly saw Amgon and his family on the precipice of their fiery death. Seeing his teacher's unease, Pema Duddul's attendant asked if he was feeling unwell.

"It is indeed inauspicious to see the mighty Amgon's fortress ablaze, for his Nyarong rebels would have been the opponents to the Chinese demons who will soon arrive from the east," Pema Duddul spoke prophetically.

"Now I must transform myself into a great tiger, leap upon the battle scene, and disperse the soldiers from Lhasa to save Amgon. Amgon must be saved so he can fight the Chinese."

Pema Duddul's attendant was startled at his teacher's intention. Pulling at Pema Duddul's white shawl, the attendant said, "It only takes one rifle shot to bring you down, precious lama. You can't leave now."

When it later became known in Nyarong that the attendant stopped Pema Duddul from saving Amgon, it was taken as a menacing sign for the future of Buddhism in Tibet. Other learned lamas at the time contended that the Lhasa government should have left Amgon and the Qing to fight among themselves, and thus contain each other's expansionist efforts. This included the extraordinary and eccentric master Do Khyentsé, who wrote in his autobiography of a vision that he had experienced in the Year of the Earth Bird 1848. The mythological warrior Gesar told Do Khyentsé that there were imminent threats to the teachings of the Buddha in Tibet from both the Qing Dynasty and Amgon. However, the two warring sides must be left to fight between themselves and thus limit each other's capacity. Gesar had said:

When there is a war between devils,
The weasel-headed Chinese slaughterers and the red-faced Nyarong fiend,
They will gain victory or lose according to their own actions.
. . . There is no reason to assist or to harm them.

In the future when there is this war,
Should the Chinese devil gain victory,
The Buddha's teachings will certainly be harmed.
If the devil from Nyarong is triumphant,
Innocent sentient beings will face calamity.
Therefore, be neutral toward both.

Nyarong was forever scarred by the climate of fear and revenge as a way of life that Amgon had spread. Still today, blood feuds are rampant, and some can be traced back to Amgon's time. Such was the atmosphere into which Sonam Gyalpo, the boy who would become known as Tertön Sogyal, was born.

Chapter 5

Taking What Is Given

March 2002, Year of the Water Horse

Washington, D.C.

Stale air hung in U.S. House of Representatives' Rayburn Hearing Room. Maybe it was the tie and jacket, perhaps the central heating, or the fact that there was a ceiling where I was used to endless sky. Members of Congress took their seats in an arc that stretched the length of the room. Photographers jockeyed for position as they shot from the floor to accompany the next day's headlines. Hundreds of foldout chairs were jammed behind three experts testifying. A large group of congressional staff and the public waited impatiently in the hallway, trying to get in for the few standing-room-only positions.

The crowd was not gathered because all the congressmen on the committee were present at the hearing, an uncommon occurrence. Nor was it because this was a hearing on U.S. policy considerations on Tibet. Rather, the best-known Buddhist associated with Tibet, after the Dalai Lama, was present. Richard Gere had just flown in from a Toronto movie set to testify on religious persecution in Tibet.

During the rush to get the actor to Capitol Hill, I was asked by the International Campaign for Tibet to update him as to recent incidents in Tibet, something I had on occasion done in the past. Richard Gere knows the Tibet issue and uses his celebrity status not only to promote the Dalai Lama's message of compassion, but also to articulate how the Chinese government creates the façade of religious freedom. He wants to know all the details from inside Tibet. Returning from my trips to Kandze, Lhasa, and elsewhere, I would occasionally meet with Richard in India, Nepal, or New York to show him recent photographs and tell him what Tibetans were telling me. At times he was moved to tears.

On this occasion, I had only a few minutes with Richard. I pulled from his briefing folder a creased and slightly torn document in Chinese with a crimson stamp at the bottom; yet another incident of Chinese authorities ordering the destruction of monks' homes—this time at a place called Yachen.

"This is the poster I hid in the sole of my shoe and brought out of China."

Thirty minutes later, Richard held the document up as evidence during his testimony before the Committee on International Relations to demonstrate China's assertion that they guarantee religious freedom is baseless.

"They affixed this poster on the monastery's main prayer hall that reads, 'Monks and nuns who have *destroy* painted on their homes must demolish them. Otherwise work teams will destroy them.'" Richard continued to tell the committee what the monks and nuns had told me, that they were being expelled from their monastery, told to return home and stop practicing their religious faith, and to find a job that would contribute to the harmonious rise of China.

A few months earlier I had arrived at Yachen. Yachen is even more remote than Khenpo's monastic encampment of Larung. It is a sprawling community on the barren highlands of the eastern Tibetan Plateau, where monks and nuns lived in simple mud-walled houses, burning yak dung for fuel.

Above fourteen thousand feet in elevation, windswept and exposed, it offers few comforts. For the hermits, however, the infinite sky view and lack of distraction found in villages and cities make it ideal for meditation. The meditators here were, as an Italian scholar had told me, "Followers and disciples of Padmasambhava of extraordinary conduct; sons of the mountains, they chose mist as their clothes and contemplation as their food."

Despite the nonpolitical nature of the monks and nuns meditating at Yachen, trouble was at their doorstep. I had been told that Chinese authorities were planning a demolition of monastic quarters because Beijing feared there was too large a concentration of monks. My jaw was clenched as I made my way on bus and then motorcycle to Yachen in the hope of snapping before-and-after shots.

I arrived at Yachen too late. The government officials and police had left already in their four-wheel-drive SUVs. And in their wake, the dwellings of hundreds of monks and nuns lay in mounds of dirt, as if a massive graveyard. A monk would later tell me, "The authorities painted the character for *destroy* on our door and told us that we had two days to tear down our own house. If we did not take down our own house we would be beaten and fined. What else to do? We took the wood beams first and gave them to someone to store. Then we pushed and hit at the mud walls."

I traversed the ridge above Yachen to find a bird's-eye view of the area. I snapped photographs that showed large sections of the monastic community in ruins. The loudest sound was my heartbeat, but the stillness and peace in the mountain air bore no resemblance to the pain in the hearts of the monks and nuns at Yachen.

Later I walked into the community to find hot water and noodles. There were no visible security personnel posted at Yachen, though there would have been no way to conceal my presence. Through the muddy alleyways I found the shanty with the largest amount of smoke coming from a tin chimney. I took a seat on a rickety bench. As I changed the bandage on my knee from a motorcycle crash the previous day, three burly monks approached as if I were a strange zoo animal. I was accustomed to being stared at in China and Tibet, so I proceeded with the first aid. One of the monks sat next to my outstretched leg, and set a piece of paper on the wooden table. The red-ink stamp at the bottom of the page indicated it was official.

"This is the order from the police to tear down our houses. One of the houses you were taking photographs of was mine."

Other monks gathered to look at what had been placed before me. I felt uncomfortable. Even in far-flung monasteries the Chinese security bureau often placed spy-monks.

"Take it." The monk was not smiling as he pointed at the paper. There was no way for him to know that I was accustomed to spiriting information out of China.

"We cannot practice Buddhism with the Chinese here."

I decided I should leave at once, even though I'd wanted to speak to some of the Buddhist lamas at Yachen about meditation techniques. Now that I had what China would deem a "state secret" on my person, I knew it would be foolish to meet any of the teachers. Before getting on the motorcycle, I was able to slip away from the huddle of curious monks that followed me. I folded the demolition order, wrapped a plastic bag around it, and placed it under the insole of my hiking boot. Someone at Yachen who saw me take the paper in the noodle shop could call the police in Kandze and inform them, but no tail ever arrived. Though I had a false bottom in my satchel, I left the document in my boot. It stayed there for the next week of eastward travel back to China, and remained in my boot as I strode through the security in airports in Chengdu and Beijing.

SPRING 1870, YEAR OF THE METAL HORSE

Nyarong, Eastern Tibet

Sonam Gyalpo jumped off the back of the horse before his father, Dargye, dismounted. Drolma took the reins of the mare and led her to the feedlot next to their home. By the time Dargye ascended the staircase to the house, carrying his rifle into the kitchen, Sonam Gyalpo was already running up the side of the hill to tell his friends about his adventure.

"I spoke to Pema Duddul, the Buddha of Nyarong," Sonam Gyalpo proclaimed.

In the kitchen, Dargye slowly rubbed oil into the stock of his musket, bringing forth its deep auburn polish. Drolma was hanging strips of yak jerky from twine that ran the length of the smoky room when Dargye began to speak. He told Drolma of their son's matchlock musket target practice on the way back from Kalzang Monastery and how Sonam Gyalpo hit any target from the saddle—any target that was not alive, at least.

"Sonam Gyalpo tells me that whenever he aims at one of those pheasants, he sees female deities—*dakinis*—in the sights," Dargye lamented. "He tells me they are waving scarves. Then he says sometimes upright letters appear down the barrel of the gun. So the target is obscured."

As Drolma stoked the earthen stove, she hid her pleasure that her son's spiritual capacity was developing. She had always sensed a special quality in her son, though she never mentioned her intuition to Dargye.

"That boy said that Padmasambhava himself slapped him when he was aiming at a musk deer!" Dargye snarled.

Trying to calm her husband, she asked what had happened when they visited Pema Duddul at the monastery. She hoped that Dargye would not speak badly of the famous meditator.

"Typical." Dargye smirked. "The lama said that our boy must follow a spiritual life. We can't afford that. We need the boy to work the yaks here. Besides, he'll stop seeing those damn goddesses and be a fine hunter in no time." Dargye failed to mention to his wife that Pema Duddul had said their boy was an incarnate lama and that the old lama offered to tutor him personally.

That night Sonam Gyalpo fell violently ill. As Dargye drank barley beer, Drolma slipped out of the house to ask a mendicant camping near the Nyachu River for a divination on what course of action should be taken for her son's illness. With eyes rolling to the back of his head, the mendicant's lips murmured mantras, and then, blowing sacred syllables on his raksha-seed prayer beads, he pulled the prayer cord tight, and counted three by three along the oily beads until he arrived at a divined number. The mendicant's arcane divining technique, of which there are many varieties in Tibet, indicated that there was nothing immediately to be done, but once he recovered, the boy must be sent for a spiritual education. The mendicant took out his quill pen and ink and wrote out a quotation of the Buddha:

We are what we think.
All that we are arises with our thoughts.
With our thoughts we make the world.
Speak or act with a pure mind
And happiness will follow you,
As your shadow, unshakable.

We are what we think.
All that we are arises with our thoughts.
With our thoughts we make the world.

Speak or act with an impure mind
And trouble will follow you,
As the wheel follows the ox that draws the cart.

"Take heed of cause and effect, mother Drolma," the mendicant said. "Your son, Sonam Gyalpo, is ill because of handling rifles and weapons of violence. Instead, send him to walk in the footsteps of the Buddha and Padmasambhava."

It took a month for Drolma to nurse her son back to strength, during which time Sonam Gyalpo told her of his yearning to return to the Kalzang Monastery to see Pema Duddul. He wept continuously during his recuperation, not from his physical sickness, but out of despondence for the life his father was planning for him.

When Sonam Gyalpo had recuperated fully, Dargye told his wife that he was going to send their son to learn the ways of success in the rough-and-tumble world of highway robbery. Dargye knew a shadowy character in Tromge village with whom his son could apprentice. There, eight days' ride from Shiwa village across the Tromthar Plateau, he decided that Sonam Gyalpo would spend a season of banditry.

Sitting around a campfire his first night with the bandits, Sonam Gyalpo was told of the sacks of silver pieces to be gained from mule-train holdups, of women to bed after village raids, and of stolen stallions to ride. He was pained, knowing how his actions would cause others' suffering, but he could not say anything to the group.

One morning, he and the group of nine bandits took up a position above a gorge to raid a caravan of traders en route to Derge.

"No one is to shoot until Sonam Gyalpo fires," the leader of the bandits told the older Tibetan desperadoes.

One bandit held the reins of the other horses as eight rifles aimed at the caravan entering the gorge. When he tried to squeeze the trigger, Sonam

Gyalpo let out a yell and fell over, holding his nose. Blood flowed out of both nostrils. The commotion alerted the traders below, who kicked their heels and sped out to safety. Infuriated that Sonam Gyalpo had squandered their strategic position without gain, the eight robbers looked on in angry disbelief.

"He just punched me in the face," Sonam Gyalpo cried to his bandit friends, blood covering both hands.

"Padmasambhava came out of the barrel of my gun! He said to me, 'Until now you still haven't awakened your potential for enlightenment! You still behave like this.' And then he punched me!"

Scared that they might be the next to incur Padmasambhava's wrathful compassion, the bandits decided to head back to the dusty town of Tromge. After an hour on the trail, they spotted on the horizon the silhouette of a lone monk, prayer wheel spinning in his right hand.

"That pilgrim must have some roasted barley flour, and I'm starving," one of the bandits said to the group.

"Maybe he'll have some silver pieces he gathered from Tromge Monastery," another added.

As they approached the old man, Sonam Gyalpo saw a bundle of silk-wrapped scriptures tied atop his willow-framed backpack. Before any of his companions could accost the monk, Sonam Gyalpo jumped off his horse.

"O lama, bless me with your grace," he said, bowing to the dusty boots of the lama. When the old monk raised his walking staff above the head of Sonam Gyalpo, two of the bandits reached instinctively for their knives. The lama lightly grazed Sonam Gyalpo's braided hair with his wooden staff and recited the famous prayer:

> *May bodhichitta, precious and sublime,*
> *Arise where it has not yet come to be;*
> *And where it has arisen may it never fail*
> *But grow and flourish ever more and more.*

Then the monk added, "May you gain victory over all adverse conditions and obstacles to bring happiness and love to others."

The meaning of the lama's words pierced the young boy's heart and froze the other bandits in their tracks. When Sonam Gyalpo stood up, all he saw was the back of the lama, who had returned to spinning his prayer wheel and reciting mantras as he hobbled into the distance.

The next morning, the bandits pooled the little money they had to buy a bag of roasted barley flour. While they were waiting outside the general store in Tromge village, two of his companions decided to have a knife-throwing contest. Taking aim at a hitching post, one of the bandits launched his fourteen-inch hunting knife end over end. Flying past the wooden target, the sharp blade sliced the stomach of a pregnant mare standing in a feedlot. The group of bandits ran toward the scene to find a small foal lying halfway out of the mare's stomach. As the dying mother licked and tried to care for her young, the foal looked into the eyes of the man who had thrown the knife and, neighing slightly, died. The mare, close to death herself, continued to nuzzle the lifeless carcass.

When Sonam Gyalpo witnessed the dying mare still trying to care for her offspring, a profound understanding of the meaning of compassion welled from within. He mounted his horse and rode away.

During the week that it took him to ride home to Nyarong, Sonam Gyalpo experienced intense regret for his past deeds that caused harm to others. He thought about how much the mare had cared for her foal, and arrived at a deep conviction that his only reason to live was to help others by becoming enlightened himself.

Dargye was not pleased when he saw his son riding back into Shiwa village after having been gone less than a month. Within a fortnight of the boy's return, Dargye decided to try again to encourage his son to hunt. He handed him the home's musket, along with a leather satchel full of gunpowder and shot, and told him to bring back blue grouse or mountain pheasant for dinner. For sustenance on the day's hunt, Drolma poured yogurt into a bag fashioned out of a goat's belly and placed it in Sonam's shoulder pack. She hoped her boy would return empty-handed with more tales of dancing goddesses blocking his rifle's shot. Maybe then Dargye would finally understand that his son was no ordinary Nyarong boy.

Two hours' walk above the valley, Sonam Gyalpo passed by a long wall of stones chiseled with mantras and prayers and noticed a scrap of paper between two of the piled slate rocks. Thinking that it might be a page from an old prayer book, standing on his toes he took the scrap of paper and unrolled it to read the writing—but it was an ancient script that he did not recognize. Feeling the parchment was some sort of blessing, he placed the golden-colored piece of paper in the amulet case that hung at his chest. The amulet contained threads from robes of various meditation masters and other sacred relics that Sonam Gyalpo's mother had collected.

Sonam Gyalpo continued walking down the valley until he came to the small Chakpur Temple. Leaving his father's musket at the main temple's entrance, Sonam Gyalpo prostrated on the wood floor three times at the painted entrance and walked into the dimly lit temple. Six tattered maroon robes lay motionless, still warm from the monks who were taking a mid-morning break from their prayers. Proceeding to the shrine, Sonam Gyalpo gazed at the clay statues of Avalokiteshvara, Manjushri, and Vajrapani, representing the enlightened qualities of compassion, wisdom, and power. He wanted to offer something to the statues but he found only buckshot and gunpowder in his satchel, as he had already finished the yogurt. He remembered the parchment he had taken from the wall and decided to offer it to the Buddhas. Unrolling the paper and looking at the letters, he touched it to his forehead and placed the sacred paper on the altar.

Though feeling blessed from the temple visit, sadness welled within him as he walked away. Passing a series of precipices above the valley, Sonam Gyalpo decided to take rest under a small rock overhang. Just as he had dozed off, Sonam Gyalpo heard an ominous voice roll toward him like thunder. Blue-black clouds swirled as if he were being swallowed into a dark hole. A raging inferno vaporized the clouds, and from out of the whirling flames stepped the most ferocious-looking figure Sonam Gyalpo had ever seen—the Protectress of Mantras, the guardian of the innermost teachings of Padmasambhava's ancient tradition, the Great Perfection. The Protectress of Mantras stared at Sonam Gyalpo. "My mandate is not to be taken lightly," she roared. "Every treasure teaching has its time, place, and revealer."

Sonam Gyalpo had not realized that the parchment he had taken from the rock wall, and then left in Chakpur Temple, was in fact a key to a treasure teaching hidden by Padmasambhava many centuries before. And it had been intended for the young Sonam Gyalpo to use to reveal a teaching that would benefit others.

The terrifying figure swelled with fury, her turquoise-colored hair flowing out in every direction. Her single fang expanded to the size of the universe, as she flung herself upon Sonam Gyalpo and sank it directly into his heart, pinning him to the mountainside.

"How dare you reject the treasure map I offer?"

Writhing in pain, Sonam Gyalpo awoke in a pool of sweat, looking around the mountainside for someone, anyone, to help him. His upper body shook. It took all his youthful strength to drag himself back home to Shiwa village after night had fallen. Upon arriving, he collapsed, unconscious.

Weeks passed and Sonam Gyalpo did not rise. His fever and inability to eat had reduced him to skin and bones. Herbal remedies were sought from traditional healers, and fire rituals were done in the home to drive out the cause of the illness. Still, nothing worked. Drolma finally recounted to Dargye what the wandering mendicant had told her the first time Sonam Gyalpo had fallen ill. Dargye still did not tell his wife that he had heard the same thing from Pema Duddul. Instead, he told her that if she found the mendicant who had performed the previous divination, and if his second prediction was the same as the first, he would relent.

Drolma knew that the wandering mendicant was living in a nearby cowshed, so she sent her cousin for him. The second divination bore the same results as the first.

"Your boy must begin spiritual training."

Dargye sat silently by his son's side throughout the night. His wife's emotional request rang in his ears and Pema Duddul's advice ran its course in his mind. By morning, Dargye knew he no longer could keep his son bound to a yak herder's future.

Spring 2003, Year of the Water Sheep

Kalzang Monastery, Nyarong

I leaned my head out of the window and yelled to the driver that I wanted to get out of the truck. I was at the turnoff for the foot trail that leads to Kalzang Monastery. One of my nomad companions tried to convince me to come to his village farther south to meet his unmarried sister, not understanding why I was getting out in the middle of a gorge. I deflected his insistent offering that was accompanied with a dog-eared snapshot of a young lady. As the dust settled after the truck rambled off, I began trekking the four-hour distance to Kalzang Monastery.

Near Deer Horn Junction, I looked north to the inspiring Shangdrak Peak behind the monastery. The towering mountain is known as the "conch-colored crystal rock piercing the sky." Villagers tell pilgrims that merely hearing, seeing, or touching the mountain has the power to bring spiritual realization. Below this jagged granite arête the yogi Pema Duddul had a vision of a thousand Buddhas dissolving into the hillside one by one. In 1860, he built Kalzang Monastery on this very spot.

Walking with spirits high, I saw a monk on horseback approaching. We recognized each other from my previous visit.

"After your last trip to Kalzang, the police arrived," said the monk abruptly while dismounting. "They stayed for three days and bothered everyone at the monastery and around the mountain, investigating what you were doing. I know you were only meditating. But still, you shouldn't go back. I'll put your rucksack on the horse. We can walk back to the county town together and you can stay at my cousin-brother's house."

I apologized for any trouble I had caused at the monastery and asked him to give my regards to One-Eye Wangde. I thanked the monk for his offer to accompany me to town, but I told him to continue riding. I wanted to make my own way back.

A few weeks earlier a man in Chengdu had told me about his experience of a prison in Kandze. When I met the man, half Han and half another ethnic group I did not recognize, he was fixing a flat tire on my bicycle at a repair shop. He did not tell me the reason for his incarceration on the Tibetan Plateau. I thought he probably was busted for theft, but I had no way of knowing. He spoke matter-of-factly of what had happened inside the prison walls, the way only someone who has spent time in jail can do. He detailed the physical abuse in prison, even smirking at the way one particularly skinny policeman's punches did not hurt him. Beatings and electric shock, he said, were a routine part of interrogation. He was released after a month without explanation or charge. There were pink scars on his wrists above his greasy hands, not yet completely healed.

"Handcuffing our hands to our ankles with our arms behind our back, they made us squat all day in the blazing sun outside in the courtyard," he said while demonstrating the position. "If we moved, the self-tightening cuffs cut into our wrists. When they threw us back in the cells, there were no roofs. It was intensely cold at night."

I had read detailed testimony of the treatment prisoners receive in China and Tibet from Amnesty International, Human Rights Watch, and the International Campaign for Tibet. And I knew photographs of China's prisons were notoriously difficult for human rights organizations to obtain, as the Chinese government guards them as state secrets. China executes more of its own citizens annually than the rest of the countries in the world combined. And for all of the buzz of China's global rise, torture and abuse are tools used regularly in their judicial system.

The bike repairman encouraged me to see for myself the prison where he had been held. Drawing a map, he noted where the prison was located in Kandze and how the sign on the front of the building indicated a leather-tanning business, typical of the Chinese *laogai*, or prison-labor camps. Walking north of the prison, I was to turn west through a series of alleyways leading to a washed-out gulley. Walking along the gulley until an irrigation channel began, I was to bend southward around the hillside through a barley field, following a series of rock outcroppings that concealed the final approach to a hilltop perspective. The prison would reveal itself as I stuck my head over the edge of the cliff.

"Prison guards never look upward there. They are just waiting to give prisoners their next beating," the bicycle repairman had said.

After I was turned away from Kalzang Monastery, I decided to follow the repairman's suggestion to document the prison conditions at the so-called leather tanning shop. This was not what Khenpo had told me to do, nor what Sogyal Rinpoche had sent me to Tibet to find. Before leaving my Kandze hotel room, I took one last look at the greasy sketch the repairman had drawn in my Moleskine notebook. I strolled into the streets, hiding in plain sight, in this infrequently visited corner of Tibet. As I moved up the low-angled, parched hillside to the rock ledge that overlooked the prison, the clarity in my mind was more that of a bank robber than an attentive meditator.

Peering over the edge of the cliff, I saw the glass window of the sentry post of the cement-walled compound built above the single-story prison. Eight cement cells with prisoners inside were below, with open bars for a ceiling, just as I had been told. In the narrow prison courtyard behind the cells, two prisoners in faded green jumpsuits squatted facing the wall with their hands behind their backs at their ankles. I learned later in the week the two prisoners were Tibetan monks who had refused to denounce the Dalai Lama in the government-imposed "Patriotic Education" classes in their monastery. I retrieved my camera like a slow-motion gunslinger. Adrenaline pulsed as I fired off shots. I crawled backward from the ledge. Quickly taking the memory card out of my digital camera as I walked, I placed the electronic images inside the amulet I wore on my chest.

Chapter 6

Disappearing Bodies

Kalzang Monastery, Nyarong

Sonam Gyalpo and his mother tied the reins to a pine post at the side of Pema Duddul's monastery and unpacked the panniers. It was a typical morning, sun rising in the cerulean sky. Their arrival at the monastery was the same as for any other Nyarong shepherd who might come to pay his respects. Sonam Gyalpo's welcoming party comprised two chickens being chased by a stray dog, and three children who took no pause from their stick duel. Had the boy been recognized publicly as an incarnate lama, Kalzang Monastery would have ceremonially welcomed him.

"It has taken only a short time in this life for you, Sogyal, to loosen the ties to your worldly concerns," Pema Duddul said to his spiritual son, who was now known simply as Sogyal—the contraction of Sonam and Gyalpo, meaning King of Merit.

"You shall rekindle the fire of your enlightened potential, and if the auspicious conditions ripen, a treasure house of teachings buried deep in your mind will burst open like a shattered beehive."

Pema Duddul chose not to have Sogyal ordained as a novice monk nor to keep him at Kalzang Monastery. Rather, Sogyal was sent to a remote encampment where the ascetic Yogi Thayé oversaw a group of lay practitioners. As Sogyal rode westward to the encampment, mother Drolma's tears flowed from a deep reservoir of joy for her son's future.

When he arrived at Yogi Thayé's Buddhist encampment, Sogyal was put into strict retreat to contemplate the preciousness of human rebirth, the impermanent nature of everything in life, the nature of cause and effect, and the inevitable suffering found in birth, old age, sickness, and death.

First, contemplate the preciousness of being free and well favored.
This is difficult to gain, easy to lose; now I must do something meaningful.

Second, the whole world and its inhabitants are impermanent;
In particular, the life of beings is like a bubble.
Death comes without warning; this body will be a corpse.
At that time, the Dharma will be my only help;
I must practice it with exertion.

Third, when death comes, I will be helpless.
Because actions bear their inevitable effect,
I must abandon evil deeds
And always devote myself to virtuous actions.
Thinking this every day, I will examine myself.

Fourth, attachment to home, friends, wealth, and the comforts of samsara
Are the constant torments of the three sufferings,
Just like a feast before the executioner leads you to your death.
I must cut desire and attachment and attain enlightenment through exertion.
Recognizing this, may my mind turn toward spiritual practice!

Month after month, again and again, Sogyal sat in formal meditation sessions either in his wood hut, in remote caves, or on the cloud-covered cliffs that rose above the encampment. Well before the sun had risen, throughout the day, and into the night, Sogyal contemplated his teacher's instructions to realize their most profound meaning. Soon, Sogyal received instructions from the deepest source of wisdom within the Tibetan Buddhist tradition—the Great Perfection, recognizing what already is present—the mind's luminous and cognizant nature.

During the fourth month of the Water Monkey year of 1872, Sogyal was continuing his retreats under Yogi Thayé. Early one morning, Sogyal had a brief vision of his first teacher, Pema Duddul. Pema Duddul was seated in meditation posture with his hands in his lap and a single thin cotton shawl draped around him. As if Pema Duddul were spiraling into his own heart, the old lama's body dissolved into light and vanished. Sogyal awoke to a feeling of joy tinged with a sense of loss. It would be a few months before Sogyal realized the significance of his vision.

I read many times the story of Prince Siddhartha, who became known as the Buddha, the Awakened One. The prince had renounced his throne at twenty-nine, leaving a life of luxury and power, to wander as a mendicant in the jungle searching out spiritual teachers of the day. Siddhartha was trying to understand the source of pain and anguish that is found in old age, sickness, and death, for no comfort or authority can overcome these realities. He wanted to discover the way to be free of the suffering that everyone experiences. Siddhartha was instructed to practice intense austerities, which included eating only what blew into his lap while meditating for months on end, and spending month after month twisted in yogic postures. Yet, after years of mastering asceticism, Siddhartha realized such methods would not transcend suffering. Later, he equated the spiritual path to the manner in which one tunes a violin. If the strings are too loose, as in a life of luxury, nothing will come from any attempts to play the instrument. And if the strings are drawn too tight, as from practicing extreme austerities, they will break and the instrument will not be able to be played. Instead, one has to know how to perfectly adjust the tuning pegs so that the strings are not too loose or too tight.

Siddhartha eventually came upon a bodhi tree near the hamlet of Gaya. There he vowed not to move from his meditation seat under the tree until he had seen the Truth of reality and understood the source of suffering. That evening, deep in meditation, he saw how all suffering has a cause. This cause is ignorance, similar to the dimming of the light of our awareness. When our awareness is dimmed, we are ignorant that our existence is in a constant state of flux and that all of our emotions ultimately result in suffering. Continually being in the dark that everything, including ourselves, is impermanent results in an endless cycle of suffering. But, Siddhartha logically understood, if the cause of suffering is removed, then the effect will not arise—the cycle of suffering will be severed. While he sat in meditation, Siddhartha conquered the self-centered ego that veiled his indwelling light of wisdom. Realizing that the whole of existence is played out in a web of cause and effect, Siddhartha saw reality as it is, and became the Awakened One. The Buddha did not receive anything when he became awakened; quite the contrary, he got rid of what was obscuring his potential for enlightenment. What's more, he asserted this was possible for all of us.

On my long road trips across Tibet, I often wondered, *Is Buddha's enlightened state really possible?* I studied and meditated upon Khenpo's and Sogyal Rinpoche's instructions, but I could not deny my uncertainty about their central premise that asserts all of us are enlightened, but we are just obscured. I knew that enlightenment is not just about being calm, concentrated, or serene. It is the revolutionary notion that we can rid ourselves of our hang-ups, our distractions, what holds us back from knowing all that is possible to know, and thus make us as beneficial to others as it is possible to be. But could this be achieved through meditation?

SUMMER 2003, YEAR OF THE WATER SHEEP

Lumorab Monastery, Upper Nyarong

A cargo truck carrying a load of boxed karaoke all-in-one microphone-speaker-TVs dropped me off a few miles from a hermitage near Lumorab Monastery in Upper Nyarong. The truck was en route to Derge. I was just a few hours' horse ride from where Tertön Sogyal's teacher, Pema Duddul, spent his last days.

Pema Duddul's itinerant lifestyle reflected the Buddha's teachings on impermanence, setting up temporary encampments and then moving on before any routine was established. His unelaborated demeanor was a manifestation of his beatific realizations. Wherever he went, white-robed, longhaired hermits and meditators gathered around him like bees following the bloom of mountain flowers. They sat in the open alpine meadows, in caves, or in large nomad tents and listened to Pema Duddul's teachings on the methods for revealing Buddha nature, the ultimate love and compassion that dwells within.

I walked to Lumorab Monastery with a backpack of provisions, as well as a short biography of Pema Duddul. With sustenance and inspiration, I was ready to spend several weeks in retreat. One of the monks remembered me from a previous visit and, after tea, showed me to a cabin beyond the confines of the monastery. On the first afternoon, I spoke to a middle-age monk in the monastery's open-fire kitchen. A cauldron the size of a bathtub was heating water for the assembly who were chanting in the main hall. The monk had a round face and a soft voice. He told me how five years before he had attended his elderly uncle as he demonstrated the same profound accomplishment as Pema Duddul had displayed when he dissolved into rainbow light at his death. It was just the kind of inspiring story, whether I could believe it fully or not, that I needed to hear before I went off to meditate for a few weeks.

"I helped Uncle Achung lie on his right side as he breathed his last breath," the cook told me. "He had not really been sick but he just stopped breathing, after which his facial complexion began to shine, getting brighter."

Those attending Uncle Achung wrapped his corpse in an outer monastic garment and left the body untouched for some days, as is the custom in Tibet. When they opened the door to the room after four days, it was apparent that the body was shrinking.

"For the week that we prayed beside Uncle, his shrinking body smelled of mountain flowers, and we all heard music from the sky," he said. "Then when we finally looked under his monk's cloak, we found that only his nails and hair remained."

The monk put a few strands of Uncle Achung's white hair into a small envelope for me to place in my protection amulet with the other relics of Tertön Sogyal and Pema Duddul that I carry on my person. Another monk pulled a rumpled magazine from a bookshelf. A headline in *China's Tibet*, an English propaganda magazine published in Beijing by the Communist Party's United Front, read "A Demised Lama Shrinks." Even the most skeptical of sources, the atheist Communist Party, reported in the *Kandze Daily* that Uncle Achung had attained the rainbow body:

An 80-year-old abbot of . . . the Lumorab Monastery in Nyarong County passed away on September 13. His remains, laid open in a hall for seven days according to Buddhist rituals, shrank to the size of an ink bottle on the afternoon of the sixth day, to the size of a bean on the eighth day, and disappeared on the tenth day. What remained are hair and nails.

During my stay at Lumorab Monastery at the head of Half-Moon Valley, I spent my evenings with an elderly Tibetan doctor, Chime, talking about the history of his monastery and about his main teacher, Chöpel Gyatso, Tertön Sogyal's grandson. One evening, while the howl of wolves ricocheted off the valley walls, Dr. Chime told me the story of Pema Duddul's attaining the rainbow body.

Pema Duddul had gathered his closest disciples in the deserted Nyin Valley in Lower Tromthar. When the teachings were finished, they shared a ritual feast together for many days. Then, Pema Duddul asked his students to help him walk farther up the hillside. There, he gave his students his last advice: "Be determined and have courage on the spiritual path." Pema Duddul then instructed his disciples to "sew up the door of my tent, and do not come near for seven days."

"Some say that it rained heavily all that week, and rainbows appeared in the sky. Others say that when the seven days were coming to an end, the earth shuddered three times, the sky was streaked with iridescent spheres of light, music was heard, and a fragrance of unearthly beauty filled the air. Others say a rainbow arched from the tent all the way to his throne at Kalzang Monastery," he continued.

"As his disciples climbed the slope on the eighth day, most of them must have known that when they cut open their master's tent, nothing but Pema Duddul's hair, ten fingernails, and ten toenails would remain. Pema Duddul had attained the rainbow body, the supreme realization."

Dr. Chime told me how Tibetan medicine asserts that the process of dying begins when one's breathing stops and the five inner elements of earth, water, fire, air, and space, which comprise the corporeal body, progressively dissolve into one another. The person is not dead when the breathing stops, as the complete death process takes anywhere from a few hours to a few days.

"While the death process of the body is occurring, the consciousness is suspended between death and the next rebirth. During these in-between states, the person's consciousness will likely experience different kinds of intense, visionary experiences that are seemingly real," he told me.

I was wondering how Tibetan medicine comes to this conclusion, since the person who is having such visions is dying and most likely not able to report. The doctor continued to say how these visions tend to be very disturbing to the person's consciousness because the physical constituents of the body, for which we have a strong attachment, are disintegrating. Furthermore, our sense faculties with which we engaged the world of sensation are ceasing to function. Finally, the consciousness departs the corpse and is "blown" by karmic wind into its next rebirth, entering the mother's womb at the time of conception. Where the karmic wind takes the consciousness to be reborn—whether among the blissful gods, humans, animals, or the extreme suffering of the hell realms—depends on one's previous actions.

For a normal person, the process of death and the in-between states causes great trepidation. As the process unfolds, the consciousness experiences an array of acute inner visions that we are unfamiliar with, and these visions tend to create fear in the dying person's mind. I had read accounts, however, of accomplished meditation masters who, rather than being disturbed by the turbulent death of the body, remained in a state of meditation while the body's elements dissolved. The disorienting inner experiences happening at the time of death are said to not disturb them because they train for the moment and have the power to exert control over death's process as their consciousness departs their body. Then, they themselves consciously direct where they will be reborn.

"This is how the Dalai Lama, Tertön Sogyal, and many other meditation masters have in past centuries reincarnated to continue their work from their previous life. They choose where to go."

For supreme meditators such as Pema Duddul or Uncle Achung, who attained the rainbow body, it is said that their consciousness does not depart the body at death, as in an ordinary person. Rather, because of the power of their meditation, as their consciousness remains in the vast and luminous essence of the mind itself, the material elements of the body dissolve into light and the body itself disappears, leaving behind only hair and nails. In such cases, the consciousness is said to merge into the luminous expanse of pure awareness.

It was easier for me to believe the story of Pema Duddul, which happened more than a century before, than it was to accept the account of Uncle Achung's rainbow body. I saw photographs of Uncle Achung, and he seemed normal, reminiscent of so many of the lamas and monks I had met on my travels in Tibet. In the photo he looked worn, with a crooked neck and aged eyes. The story of Pema Duddul was the raw material of saints—asceticism, visions, and miracles. Pema Duddul was a mystic; Uncle Achung seemed like any grandpa. While I was unable to verbalize my skepticism, I tried telling Dr. Chime my doubt about the ability to dissolve one's body into light at the time of death. Chime listened, and told me to return before sunrise the next morning.

When I awoke, the valley was still except for the hum of the river below. Stars hung in the last of the night. Dr. Chime's attendant was thumbing his prayer beads, sitting on a log outside his teacher's cabin waiting for me. We entered the doctor's cabin together and as I took my seat in front of his prayer table, the attendant filled his teacher's wooden bowl with thick butter tea.

"Look at this man," he said wasting no time. He showed me a black-and-white photograph of a seated older lama, cane in hand, hunched over. "His name is Ol' Penam, and nobody knew while he was alive how deep his spiritual realizations were."

"Ol' Penam was a meditator from this valley who died in 1980 in his seventy-second year. He was cantankerous and feared because of his furious outbursts that sometimes even resulted in physical abuse of others. Because most people thought him to be mad, he was left alone. He took the opportunity to meditate in solitude during the Cultural Revolution. He even managed to teach and quietly give empowerments in the wooden cabins around Half-Moon Valley. Despite his outwardly fierce demeanor, at the time of his death, Ol' Penam displayed a high degree of meditative accomplishments by partially dissolving his body.

"My monk's vow prohibits me from ever telling a lie, my American friend. So I will only tell you this—what you are going to see is Ol' Penam, and is clear evidence that he dissolved his body into light at death."

After Dr. Chime's brief remarks, the attendant took me out of the cabin to another small cottage. It was still dark as we made our way across the mountainside. Two monks were waiting inside for us. Smoke from juniper powder hung in silence. Three butter lamps on the shrine illuminated the room just enough to let us see one another's faces. In the middle of the room's shrine at eye level was what appeared to be a statue covered in brocade and silk wrappings.

As the attendant and I sat down on the wooden floor, he whispered that I was going to meet Ol' Penam. Perhaps his cremated relics were inside a stupa, a traditional conical container for saints' remains? Maybe Ol' Penam's personal belongings had been enshrined for the devoted? Two monks began unwrapping the silk and brocade with slow, measured movements, as if not wanting to wake what was underneath. I quickly realized that it was a body.

The monks continued to unwrap white and blue silk strands from the head area. Ol' Penam's body had shrunk to the size of small child within a few days of his death, dissolving part but not all of it into light. Then, as if allowing the corpse to speak for itself, they removed the last coverings and stood back in a deferential bow and hands in prayer.

Ol' Penam's presence filled the entire valley, though his body was the size of a month-old infant. I noticed the distinct features of an elderly man with large ears and a flat nose; but these features were on a body not sixteen inches long. Ol' Penam's desiccated hands resembled those of an old man, but were also the size of an infant's hands. The similarities of the corpse to the photograph that Dr. Chime had just shown me were undeniable. It was as if the doctor, and the deceased Ol' Penam himself, were prodding me with the question, "What more evidence do you need?"

With Ol' Penam's motionless eyelids open as if in meditative equipoise, and wrappings of yellow, blue, and white silk bunched under his legs like a multicolored lotus, I sat with the three monks in silent meditation in front of the body until the morning's orange light entered the room.

Autumn 1872, Year of the Water Monkey

Tromthar Plateau, Eastern Tibet

The accounts brought in by the pilgrims and nomads of Pema Duddul's attaining the rainbow body confirmed Sogyal's early morning vision. Pema Duddul's attainment spurred Sogyal more than ever to strive to realize the profound Great Perfection teachings. He decided to search out the renowned Dzogchen master Nyoshul Lungtok.

Donning his threadbare robes and white shawl, and carrying a few texts, his prayer beads, and a wooden bowl, Sogyal walked alone for well over a week to Dzongkar Nenang on the Tromthar Plateau, not far from where he had spent his days as a bandit. As he stopped to beg among the very outlaws he used to run among, Sogyal's poverty protected him from harm.

Master Lungtok quickly accepted Sogyal as a student. He imparted meditation instructions and sent him away to practice in solitude. Every few days Sogyal returned to relay his experiences, have his dreams interpreted, and receive more teachings. They repeated this process, month after month, while Sogyal's meditative realizations deepened.

During this intense period, Sogyal had only one robe, and nothing on which to sleep. He lived among the forest animals, sleeping on the ground or flat rocks just as they did. He had no pans to cook with, so for his daily sustenance he ate small amounts of roasted barley flour mixed with water from a nearby spring. When Sogyal's austerities became known to Master Lungtok, the teacher ordered him to take up residence next to the kitchen tent. When Sogyal was not receiving meditation instruction or practicing in solitude, he attended to Master Lungtok's needs, cutting firewood, bringing tea and food, preparing for his daily rituals, and escorting pilgrims and local nomads into the private meditation chamber of the sagacious lama.

For more than two years, Master Lungtok sent Sogyal into uninhabited forests, where the call of wild animals kept him alert throughout the night, and to charnel grounds to meditate where the stench of death was palpable. There, Sogyal cultivated increasingly subtle states of awareness. Following his teacher's instructions to the letter, Sogyal performed the meditations, rituals, and yogic postures day and night until exhaustion overwhelmed body and mind and he collapsed. Then, lying as if a corpse, Sogyal rested in thought-free awareness, allowing his lucid mind to meet face-to-face what is present when thinking is not.

Early in 1875 in the Year of the Wood Pig, Sogyal was ready to leave the care of Master Lungtok and strike out on his own. Master Lungtok called Sogyal into his tent, where they were camped below Katok Monastery. Holding an eight-inch phurba in his hand, made of meteorite and blessed by meditation, Master Lungtok offered it to Sogyal.

"You will reveal many phurba treasure teachings in the future. Now, take this; wield it in the world, but do not be of the world," he said, blessing Sogyal with his wisdom mind. "Use the phurba to destroy the self-cherishing ego and its many demonlike guises."

Sogyal did not know at this time that the demonic forces his teacher was referring to would be military threats to the nation. Nor could he have fathomed that Tibet's most dangerous demons would emerge from within the government's own ranks.

WINTER 2003, YEAR OF THE WATER SHEEP

Eastern Tibet

My regular sojourns to Tibet usually lasted a month to six weeks. I was rarely in a hurry, because things happened in their own time. Waiting an extra few days so that I arrived at a temple with the appropriate monk or local official who had the right connections guaranteed a blessing from a temple's most sacred statues that were behind lock and key. Or waiting a week for a hermit to return to his cave from a village ceremony meant that I received instructions on the proper smoke offerings to make to the local mountain deities. While moving between pilgrimage sites or in retreat, or in these in-between waiting periods, I worked to stabilize my meditation, not losing sight of my hope to learn the phurba ritual. This was the fuel that drove my spiritual engine toward what I now felt I owed myself, enlightenment itself.

Outside meditation caves and prayer sessions in sacred temples, however, I continued to be shaken by the stories of torture and abuse of Tibetans. Waiting for situations to play out fully did not always yield a pleasant ending.

Once, in the middle of a trip in eastern Tibet, I needed to extend my visa, which was nearing expiration, so I returned to the provincial capital.

While I was filling out the paperwork for the application at the local public security bureau, a policewoman stepped forward to fill in my forms in Chinese. Her ink-black hair was wound into a tight bun, exposing her slender neckline that dove into the blue uniform. In her official attire I could not tell if she was Tibetan or Chinese. I asked her name, in Tibetan. She lifted her gaze from the paperwork, and a slight smile emerged. There was an uneasy pause as our eyes connected. She responded in English, informing me the waiting period was forty-eight hours for the visa to be processed, and said, "My name is Ming." As if forgetting that I was in the branch of the security forces that tortures monks and nuns and that coordinated the destruction at Khenpo's encampment, I spontaneously asked, "Shall we have tea tonight after you get off work?"

Her response was as smoothly casual as it was surprising. She wrote on a piece of scrap paper a street address and said, "Practicing my English would be wonderful. Meet me at this teahouse tonight at seven P.M."

Ming and I met for the next six evenings, and a mutual attraction soon developed. She became more comfortable with my physical way of being, from brushing aside her hair when it fell into her face to holding her hand in taxicabs. Such innocent acts of affection raised the stakes considerably. The locations where we met were increasingly more intimate, from teahouses to walks in the city parks to dinner at her apartment, where she lived alone. Sitting in her kitchen the first time she prepared a meal for me, I caught myself looking down the hallway toward her bedroom. An uneasy tension bound us to keep meeting, and steadily tightened. I felt it in her embrace each evening when we said good-bye.

A mixture of motivations had been behind my initial invitation to Ming for tea. The physical attraction was there, but I also had motives based upon collecting human rights information. I knew the city had many *laogai* prisons, and I had been asked to take photographs of them by a Chinese dissident living in Washington, D.C. I was also uncertain of Ming's intentions behind our repeated meetings. Perhaps she did want to practice her English, which the government had sponsored her to study in Shanghai a decade earlier. She could have had a genuine interest in me, but she could also have been spying on me. I could not rule out a honey trap.

A week after my visa extension in my passport was stamped, I was again having dinner at Ming's home. As the meal was simmering on the stove, we talked about when we would meet again. We consulted calendars and her work schedule. We talked of meeting on the Chinese coast, or maybe a beach in Thailand. As we dreamed of unrealistic holidays together, Ming leaned toward me and placed her lips on mine. No sooner had I felt her warm breath and her hands in my hair than a knock came at the door. Ming jumped up and led me to a closet, silently motioning for me to enter. She closed the door.

My heart raced in the darkness. My backpack was in her bedroom with *laogai* prison notes hidden in the foam of the arm strap. I tried to follow my breath but it was no use. I began to berate myself for my carelessness. Slowly, I replayed events from the previous ten days—the chain-smoking man who sat at the table next to us in the tea shop; the cabdriver's inquisitive look when he heard us speaking English; the hotel cleaning lady's odd arrival times in my room; and then, Ming herself. Why did she always arrive ten minutes late for our appointments? Did I ever leave my backpack unattended? And why did Ming ask to see my passport at home a day after I had been given the visa extension? But then, I came to the moment just after our lips met and the knock at the door—her fearful look of shock was real.

After nearly an hour in the darkness, with the sound of Ming's conversation in Mandarin coming from the kitchen and the departure of whoever had come, she opened the closet.

"It was my uncle. It is not proper for me to have you here, for my family or for my job. I could not bring you out. I'm sorry." Ming pulled me to her, and began to cry on my shoulder.

We made a pot of tea. Ming said her uncle likely sensed something odd about her behavior. She feared he read her anxiousness. I could not leave her house, as her uncle, also a policeman, probably had asked neighbors to report any visitors to his niece's home. Neighborhood watch committees are well-honed information-gathering units. The last thing I wanted was the police investigating me—even if it was because I was romantically involved with one of their own.

"I am trapped," Ming said, in what became a cathartic conversation that lasted into the night. Growing up in China one is encouraged to doubt everyone's motivation, even family members'. Tibetans do not trust Ming because she works for the police, and Chinese do not trust her because she is half Tibetan. I held her tightly as she tried to escape, even for just a night, from her fractured, divided life.

"I don't expect anything from the Tibetans I help through my job. I don't expect payoffs or gifts, but Tibetans don't realize how I help them. I am doing it for my nation. There are decisions in my job where my choice can change someone's life. Many Tibetans who work for the government have these choices to make—not every day, but every once in a while. That decision can make the difference between a girl staying in the village without education or the possibility of a scholarship to study English in the city."

She was speaking from personal experience. Because a Tibetan Communist Party cadre pushed through her application, Ming had received a scholarship to study English.

"We all know if a Chinese person has the choice, they will first think of themselves and their own wallet, and second how they can keep or strengthen their own position of power. I think about Tibet."

Ming had excelled in her study in public administration and had dreamed of being assigned a clerk position at a foreign embassy. Instead of an embassy job, she was sent back to the provincial security bureau, where she was then dispatched to a small county police department. Ming was a caged bird—her language skills could give her flight away from China, but she was trapped inside the system.

"I will never forget the screaming on my first night of duty at the police station. I learned very quickly how we 'close a case,'" she continued, while crying.

Ming's police work was not to enforce the law, but rather it was to fulfill a conviction quota. Whether it is for gamblers, thieves, prostitutes, or even murderers, the police were given the task of convicting a specific number of criminals each month. The number of monthly convictions each police station needed to achieve was decided in Beijing, even in this outpost on the edge of the Tibetan Plateau. "Closing the case" was another way to describe extracting a confession, with the usual methods being beatings and electric shock, sometimes while suspending the person from a rafter in the confession room.

"None of the police bosses or officers like lawyers because the lawyers are educated. The police won't let the lawyers see the criminals before the criminal makes a confession. So really the lawyers aren't allowed to see them until the case has been closed."

"What happened that first night?" I asked, returning to what Ming had said about never forgetting the screaming.

"I was told to report to the interrogation room. There was a man sitting on the floor with his hands bound. One policeman held an electric baton. The other cop had his shirtsleeves rolled up. The man on the floor was accused of stealing a motorcycle. He cried out that he had stolen nothing.

"After they started punching him, I was sick to my stomach. Then, they actually broke a chair over his head. The man's face was unrecognizable. It was so bloody. The way he screamed, he had to have been innocent. I will never forget that scream. Innocent men cry out differently than criminals."

"And you? Did you ever have to take part in extracting confessions?"

I was unable to imagine the petite woman lying next to me in bed striking, beating, or electrocuting another person.

My question was met with silence. Then, uncontrollable sobbing.

I left the provincial city two days later on a night bus. Ming came to the station to see me off. Exhaust fumes mixed with burnt cooking oil from the nearby noodle shop. Thousands of people swirled around us in a light rain, finding their bus to board, as we stood silently looking at each other.

"I don't know what to say," I truthfully admitted.

I wanted to hold her, even to take her with me, and tell her everything was fine; but that was not the case. Her life, her future, her country, everything about this woman, was anything but fine. Behind her small figure, her gentle touch, her mixed Buddhist and Communist heritage, lay a self-perpetuating confused world of suspicion and violence.

"Forget about me, please. For yourself and for me, just forget," she implored.

Ming rubbed my hand against her cheek, and then, without another word, turned and walked away.

My home in Nepal had become a place of rejuvenation, or at least a diversion. I could meditate and study the life of Tertön Sogyal without being pulled into accounts of atrocities. There were other human rights monitors in the city but I could choose when to visit them. I spent much of my time on the outskirts of the city, at the hermitage of Yangleshö, to study with Khenpo Jikmé Phuntsok's primary student living outside of Tibet, Abbot Namdrol. Abbot Namdrol is a humble sixty-year-old monk, unrivaled in his scholarship in the Tibetan Buddhist world today. In the 1980s and 1990s, he journeyed periodically to Tibet to study with Khenpo at the Larung Encampment, and also acted as a messenger between Khenpo and the Dalai Lama in India, paving the way for Khenpo's visit to Dharamsala, India, in July 1990.

I considered Khenpo one of my teachers, even though it was nearly impossible to receive meditation instruction from him in Tibet. Therefore, while in Nepal, I sought out the learned Abbot Namdrol, telling him how I wanted to gain stability in my own meditation practice, to reconnect with the experience I'd had when Khenpo revealed nakedly the thought-free, pure, and pristine nature of mind. My Western mind was looking for a quick-fix method, which undoubtedly indicated to Abbot Namdrol how little I understood about the spiritual path.

Abbot Namdrol is a preeminent scholar-meditator who resides at a hermitage near Yangleshö Cave, south of Kathmandu.

He decided to explain the meditation techniques found in a manual from Khenpo's revealed treasure teachings. The manual's techniques progress from contemplations on the impermanence of the human body to esoteric rites involving yoga in solitude in the wilderness. These were the very kinds of instructions that Tertön Sogyal had received from his teachers.

Abbot Namdrol taught me slowly, word by word, over the course of three years. As I passed through each of the text's progressive stages, I would report to my teacher various experiences from my meditation.

The structure of every teaching session was the same. Arriving at Abbot Namdrol's room after sunrise, I found him meditating on his low bed, wrapped in his favorite woolen shawl. I prostrated three times at his feet and took my seat on the floor. He began the sessions by having me renew my bodhisattva vow, telling me to pray strongly that others might benefit through my study and practice. Closing his eyes and folding his hands in prayer, he invoked his lineage masters by reciting their names. Turning to the text, Abbot Namdrol read a few lines, and then taught on the meaning for an hour or so, quoting Khenpo at length from the instructions he had received decades earlier. At the end of each session, Abbot Namdrol answered my questions, and then sent me into my retreat room or away to the forest above the sacred Yangleshö Cave for a day or two, sometimes a week. This was the manner in which Khenpo had taught him at Larung, and the way that Master Lungtok had taught Tertön Sogyal.

Each time I returned, usually enthusiastic to report minor experiences in meditation, Abbot Namdrol deflected my excitement with comments such as, "Do not attach importance to good or bad experience. Simply remain aware, Matteo. Loosen your habit of reacting."

"Fully aware, what is there before thinking begins?" he once asked. After a few moments of pregnant silence, he nodded to my nonresponse, and said, "Yes, rest there, naturally."

Chapter 7

In the World but Not of It

After a couple years of my Tertön Sogyal pilgrimage, I was becoming increasingly nervous about being caught with the human rights abuse evidence
I carried. With each conversation, each photo I snapped, or each report
passed to me, the stakes were growing higher. I had smuggled documents out
of China in the sole of my shoe, in the straps of my backpack, and in the false
bottom of my satchel, sewn in by a Thamel alleyway tailor in Kathmandu. I
also handed off parcels to willing Western tourists, who then mailed them to
the International Campaign for Tibet in Washington, D.C.

The cost for trafficking state secrets in China is high, retribution is
swift, and the punishments exacted are severe, often meaning death—not
for an American, but for any Tibetan or Chinese who gets caught. Even a
single e-mail containing what the Chinese government deems "state secrets"
will bring with it years of imprisonment and torture; the toll on family and
friends will include police harassment, surveillance, work bans, and public
humiliation. The Communist Party of China broadly defines "state secrets"

as anything that harms state interests. Commonplace information such as land use development plans, environmental quality reports, data on public health risks, and statistics on those harmed by natural disasters can all be considered state secrets by the Party. Writing poems about Tibetan history, photographs of some Buddhist teachers living in India, or a mobile phone ring tone if it has the Dalai Lama chanting are also are of criminal nature. Images of prisons I had taken, the reports on changing the medium of secondary school instruction in Sichuan Province from Tibetan to Mandarin, or any of the numerous personal stories of Tibetans that I obtained, the Chinese government also consider state secrets. The trepidation I felt in 2003 was confirmed a year later in an incident I watched with dread.

In 2004, the Chinese government released a document banning media coverage of the fifteenth anniversary of the Tiananmen Square massacre. Chinese journalist Shi Tao forwarded the memo through his Yahoo! e-mail account to a pro-democracy group outside China. Bowing to pressure by Chinese authorities, Yahoo! China revealed Shi's identity to Internet police. In a secret trial lasting a mere two hours, Shi was convicted of "leaking state secrets" and sentenced to ten years in prison. When the U.S. Congress held hearings on the case, representatives of Yahoo! eventually admitted responsibility for Shi's arrest and conviction through their complicity with Chinese censorship law. Subsequent appeals on Shi's behalf have yielded nothing. In 2010, Shi is still in prison for that single e-mail.

China operates the most sophisticated Internet censoring system in the world, a project begun in 2001—Operation Golden Shield—in which it continues to invest hundreds of millions of dollars and a wealth of new detection and censoring technologies annually. Although Yahoo! admitted their moral error in the Shi case, Cisco Systems, Microsoft, Nortel Networks, Sun Microsystems, and Skype and other companies continue to supply the Chinese government with technology to maintain their iron grip on the flow of information, while maintaining perhaps the most robust hoard of malware trojans in cyberspace. As one commentator put it, "President Clinton warned Beijing that controlling the Internet would prove as tough as 'trying to nail JELL-O to a wall.' Well, consider the JELL-O nailed."

In the late 1990s, when I began traveling in Tibet, the Internet was just arriving. By 2002, Internet connectivity could be found in remote villages in eastern Tibet, but I still had to wait for sometimes a day while connections were established just to send a single e-mail. A year later, Internet cafés had sprung up across the entire plateau, serving Chinese migrant workers' children, who spent day after day immersed in online gaming. I wanted to use the Internet to my advantage, to unload my political baggage so I could meditate without fear of the police appearing at my hermitage looking for me.

Back in Washington, I sought experts in Chinese Internet censorship and detection techniques and methods. I needed to move sensitive information through China's "Great Firewall" without detection. Cyberpolice deploy data mining applications known as "frame grabbers" and "key loggers," loaded and operating on every five-yuan-per-hour computer used in the smoke-filled Internet cafés. Frame grabbers take snapshots of the computer screen when activated; key loggers record keyboard strokes at specific instances, such as logging into an e-mail account or a password-protected Web page. These small, virtually undetectable applications are highly effective in gathering large amounts of data from publicly accessible computer systems, and are some of the most prolific applications to be found infecting systems today—or so the experts told me.

It was risky to step into Chinese cyberspace to communicate with human rights counterparts in Washington. If the Chinese government connects the dots between a Western human rights monitor and a Tibetan or Chinese national with the dissemination of information the government labeled "state secret," imprisonment or death are the likely outcomes for them.

"Don't think you can work in the shadows in China and Tibet," my friend Richelle told me one day. "If you want to work within China's Internet firewall, your information must not exist to them."

Richelle came from a long line of intelligence specialists, the world's second-oldest profession. We talked extensively about her tradecraft, including the range of protective measures designed to preserve operational security. Though our discussions were focused on the more technical aspects of information trafficking, invariably the conversation would descend into the moral and ethical implications of doing what, in the eyes of many, was deemed theft and deceit.

"Doesn't stealing violate your basic Buddhist tenets?" she questioned, positing that by silently smuggling government secrets by border police, I was both stealing and lying.

"Perhaps there is an element of taking what was not given, but it is for a just cause," I countered. Her green eyes glinted as she returned a smile. Richelle excelled in intellectual combat. She was attempting to equate my covertness as a courier of information with espionage, a theory I disputed. The tradecraft might be similar between spies and what I was doing, but espionage is state-sponsored and thus did not have moral or ethical ground upon which to stand, I replied.

"It depends on one's perspective," Richelle quipped as she updated the encryption on my laptop. "You use the privilege that comes with a U.S. passport to take photos of Chinese prisons and maybe get your paws on some secret documents. You give it to your friends who are advocates for Tibet in D.C., who in turn shop it around State, NSC, or send it over to friends in the EU," referring to the International Campaign for Tibet, the Department of State, the National Security Council, and the European Union.

"China calls that spying. You call it Buddhist pilgrimage!"

"It is a moral responsibility to share the stories I am told by Tibetans!" I blurted, feeling exposed.

"The Chinese, they see you as a spook. You are an enemy violating their laws. That is a fact. For you, you see yourself as a pilgrim, who also happens to expose the realities of an authoritarian state. That is also a fact. Facts depend on one's perspective."

Within weeks of my request for assistance from Richelle, a package arrived for me in Kathmandu. Richelle had found the necessary technologies I needed to operate with complete anonymity, a ghost in the machine. She reminded me of the Buddhist metaphor of a lotus flower; the lotus lives within the muck of the dirty swamp but is not sullied by it; similarly, the Buddha lives within the world but is not of it.

"Though you will move information out of China, it will be untouchable."

Richelle provided a compact disc that, when inserted into a computer system at a cybercafé, rebooted the machine into a secured operating environment, circumventing the installed operating system on the computer itself. Any memory needed for computing was stored in cyberspace, not the computer on which I worked. This allowed me to work invisibly to any data mining applications installed on the PC, or detection systems deployed on the Chinese Internet infrastructure. When I ejected the disc, all my activity vanished, like writing in water.

"Don't forget to take the CD out of the computer when you are done!" Richelle instructed. "I can only tell you to follow the directions; you have to carry them out."

SEPTEMBER 2003, YEAR OF THE WATER SHEEP

Chengdu, Sichuan, China

On my next trip to Tibet, I carried the CD Richelle had given me between the pages of my prayer book. I had flown straight to Chengdu from Sogyal

Rinpoche's retreat center in France, where I had stayed for a month receiving teachings.

Sogyal Rinpoche had taught about the phurba practice of Vajrakilaya. Sitting with a few hundred fellow students in front of an enormous scroll painting of Vajrakilaya, Sogyal Rinpoche explained how meditating upon Vajrakilaya is a means to develop wisdom within so that we may emanate compassionate activity. In this age, when war and aggression are very intense, Vajrakilaya is thought to embody the compassionate activity of all the buddhas—Vajrakilaya is the Buddha's troubleshooter. I was beginning to experience how, by identifying with a deity such as Vajrakilaya, reciting a mantra within a deep state of concentration, and using the creative aspect of our mind to perform virtuous activity, we can change the way we react to what arises in our minds and the challenges in life.

Sogyal Rinpoche taught from a treasure text of Vajrakilaya that Tertön Sogyal had revealed at Katok Monastery in eastern Tibet. After Padmasambhava taught this phurba rite in the eighth century, he concealed the teaching in Dorje Dudjom's mind-stream so that it could be recalled in the future. When Tertön Sogyal discovered a parchment scroll that had mystical syllables inscribed, the writing was a reminder of that treasure teaching. Such a mnemonic aid kick-started Tertön Sogyal's memory of his past life as Dorje Dudjom receiving the phurba teachings from Padmasambhava. Tertön Sogyal wrote down the teaching, and that is what Sogyal Rinpoche was teaching in southern France more than twelve hundred years after Padmasambhava first gave it in Tibet.

As in other Vajrakilaya texts, the phurba is a "great weapon of compassion" and it is wielded to destroy demonic and negative forces, the obstacles to being able to act compassionately in the world. There is a particular emphasis with such Vajrakilaya practice to cut through and annihilate forces, such as anger and vengeance, which obstruct compassion and love. Of the myriad deity yoga practices in Tibetan Buddhism, which have their origins in

India's ancient vajrayana Buddhist tradition, the phurba-wielding Vajrakilaya practice is central to the tradition of Padmasambhava's teachings.

Many deities of the Tibetan Buddhist pantheon are depicted as peaceful, sitting on lotus thrones with flowing silk robes, hands positioned in meditative equipoise, eyes softly cast low or inspiringly open. Deities such as Avalokiteshvara, Manjushri, or Tara represent the Buddha's qualities of compassion, unexcelled wisdom, and giving protection from fear. Vajrakilaya, on the other hand, is anything but serene. He is depicted striding out of a raging firestorm with bulging eyes, mouth agape, and fangs bared. Between his hands he rolls a three-bladed phurba the size of the universe. He is roaring terrifying noises, clothed in skins and animal parts, and stepping on two corpses that symbolize attachment and aversion, hope and fear.

"Vajrakilaya subjugates and transmutes," Sogyal Rinpoche taught one stormy evening in southern France. The crash of lightning rumbled across the Languedoc Plateau.

"In this age, when negativity is very intense, it is necessary for compassion to be accompanied by power. This is the practice to destroy obstacles to compassion."

Sogyal Rinpoche had already taught us how compassionate wrath is differentiated from anger. While the intention behind ordinary hatred and anger is to inflict pain and do harm, the intention behind Vajrakilaya's wrath is quickly and decisively to remove the obstacles and delusions that hinder spiritual progress and cause suffering. Wrathful enlightened activity may appear in some ways akin to anger, but its motivation is the opposite, as it is driven by compassion.

Autumn 1884, Year of the Wood Monkey

Dzongsar Monastery, Eastern Tibet

In the eighth month of the Wood Monkey Year, Tertön Sogyal traveled to Dzongsar Monastery to see the greatest master of the day, Khyentsé Wangpo. Khyentsé and another eminent lama, Jamgön Kongtrul, were the primary forces fueling a Buddhist ecumenical movement that was reinvigorating Buddhist scholarship and practice across Tibet in the middle of the nineteenth century. This movement emerged in stark contrast to the sectarian polity that was prevalent in central Tibet, and to some degree in the eastern regions. Sogyal's years in retreat practicing the esoteric rites of his treasure revelations proved to be a preparation for the cutthroat politics that he would encounter among orthodox monks and sectarian government officials in Lhasa. But for now, Sogyal had his Vajrakilaya treasure revelations to discuss with Khyentsé, as the elder teacher was prophesied to be the custodian for most of these treasures.

From Dzongsar Monastery's hilltop perspective, Sogyal saw the path leading north toward the holy pilgrimage sites around the Crystal Lotus Cave. To the southwest, barley fields stretched toward the Drichu River. Hundreds of tents were pitched in the fields below, with pilgrims and disciples of Khyentsé awaiting an audience. When the attending monks saw Sogyal, they escorted him immediately into Khyentsé's room. Sogyal prostrated himself before the sixty-four-year-old master. The time had come to tell of his treasure revelations.

Khyentsé was filled with joy to hear of Sogyal's Vajrakilaya revelation. He spoke briefly of how he and Sogyal were connected in their past lives

in the eighth century—when Khyentsé was the Dharma king Trisong Detsen, who had tasked Dorje Dudjom, Sogyal's previous incarnation, to invite
Padmasambhava to Tibet to establish Buddhism. With his unrivaled spiritual authority, Khyentsé proclaimed Sogyal as an authentic treasure revealer,
confirming him as a representative of Padmasambhava. From that moment
on, Sogyal took the formal title of *tertön,* or treasure revealer.

Before the evening rituals were concluded, Khyentsé told Tertön Sogyal, "To the southwest in the province of Gonjo, in the house of Khangsar,
there is a dakini, a lady of unparalleled beauty, who possesses enlightened
qualities.

"When the time is right, venture there with this letter," Khyentsé said,
handing Tertön Sogyal a note with his seal affixed. "Ask the father for the
hand of his daughter Pumo. Should she become your spiritual wife, the door
to your storehouse of treasure will be flung wide open."

Khyentsé's prophetic statement about the young woman in Gonjo highlights one of the most significant factors contributing to a treasure revealer's
achievements—the connection with a spiritual consort. Similar to a muse,
a treasure revealer's consort arouses the inspiration necessary for the discovery and decoding of treasures. It is through this auspicious link with the
consort that the treasure revealer's work to benefit the world can meet with
full success.

"Consorts embody wisdom. They provide the treasure revealer keys
to open the doors," Wangchen, a treasure revealer from eastern Tibet, explained to me while thumbing his worn prayer beads.

I had never met anyone in my life as spontaneous and utterly natural as
Wangchen. As we visited different pilgrimage sites together, it seemed that

he was never separate from a calm and joyful state of equanimity. Whether on a cliff top meditating or in a noisy Sichuan noodle café, he emanated a profound natural serenity. Wangchen's disposition was the same after a twenty-hour backbreaking bus journey as it was when he was sitting in a mountain field teaching his disciples. His very being was so spacious that one felt enveloped in the cool shade of blessing.

I felt comfortable enough with Wangchen to ask him anything. One evening I asked him for the instructions on practicing with a consort. I did not have a steady relationship, but any romantic encounters that might flare during my travels from Kathmandu through Delhi, Washington, D.C., and Colorado would provide an opportunity to put Wangchen's instructions into action. Besides, I thought that if, by associating with a consort, a tertön can benefit many beings, perhaps even I could benefit a few.

Wangchen grinned, and instead told me stories of how Tertön Sogyal had trained—alone.

Tertön Sogyal manifested outward signs of development, such as being able to hold his breath for more than ten minutes, or levitating a few inches off the ground. He sat in the frozen winter landscape, wearing only a cotton shawl, and melted snow around him in a ten-foot diameter. But his ability to abide continuously in the direct recognition of the nature of mind, whether awake or while sleeping, was his supreme attainment.

The next day, Wangchen and I went to circumambulate a local sacred peak in the Dzachukha Mountains. The sky was cloudless and in the early morning sun, our shadows extended more than twenty feet. After an hour of walking, we paused in the thin alpine air. Suddenly, there were rumblings from a large rockslide in a steep gully across from us. Wangchen's hands slowly lowered to his knees, and breathing out, he held his body steady. His eyes pierced the space between the rockslide and us. As the resonance of the boulders crashing below faded, all thinking evaporated. Tranquility pervaded the mountainside as we sat unmoving.

"Do you see the red syllable *hrih* there?" Wangchen pointed to discoloration in the granite stones far above where the rockslide had started.

"Behind the red syllable, there is a treasure in the form of a small *dorje*—waiting there for me to extract it from the rock," he said. The dorje, a ritual scepter, is symbolic in vajrayana Buddhism of the masculine, skillful means of compassion. Its ritual counterpart, the bell, symbolizes the feminine aspect of pristine wisdom.

"The local protector deity is shaking in excitement that I am here to retrieve the dorje," he declared, explaining the cause of the rockslide.

I saw the vermilion-colored marking on the rock some four hundred feet aboveground. "Well, then, are you going to go and get it?" my words stumbled out.

"Now is not the time. I must return later with my wife, Lhamo, to offer prayers," he humbly acknowledged. "There is a time and place for every treasure revelation. Without Lhamo, there are no treasures.

"And as for your practice with beautiful consorts," Wangchen concluded, "you still have a few years' worth of meditating before that!"

1887, YEAR OF THE FIRE PIG

Dzongsar Monastery, Eastern Tibet

For three years Tertön Sogyal was on the move, revealing treasure teachings and studying philosophical treatises and vajrayana liturgies with the learned masters residing in eastern Tibet. His travels and interactions were guided by his dreams, prophecy, and vision of the Protectress of Mantras. In the Year of the Fire Pig, the thirty-three-year-old tertön told his teacher, Khyentsé, that he had been having signs that it was the right time to search out his prophesied spiritual consort. Khyentsé confirmed the signs were correct and offered a celebratory feast before Tertön Sogyal departed.

Tertön Sogyal traveled to Gonjo with a group of Nyarong cohorts. They moved with ease on horseback through the deep valleys and high passes. Twice a day, they stopped to brew tea. As a few members of the party collected kindling and yak dung from the hillside for the fire's fuel, Tertön Sogyal would set up a three-rock tripod on which to balance their blackened and dented kettle. Every so often, as the fire was boiling the tea, Tertön Sogyal poked one of the rocks with his phurba, whereby an aperture would appear from which he extracted small treasures that had been concealed inside— sometimes a small statue of Padmasambhava or Buddha, or simply a blessed stone. As the group passed through mountain hamlets and nomadic tent communities, Tertön Sogyal blessed the locals with these objects, often leaving the treasure in the village shrine.

By the time the group arrived at the Khangsar estate after weeks of travel, their vagabond appearance was evident.

"How could you possibly ask for our daughter?" the matriarch of the influential Khangsar household said to the dust-covered Tertön Sogyal after he had handed over the letter from Khyentsé. "We know this letter comes from master Khyentsé, and we have heard stories that you may be a treasure revealer. But, if you are just a charlatan with long hair and white robes, you certainly won't be the first."

"For my daughter's hand," Pumo's father bellowed, "you must prove yourself."

Tertön Sogyal took up the challenge.

The group from Nyarong erected a few lean-to tents. The Khangsars were generous with butter, jerky, and roasted barley flour, sending large portions to the gang from Nyarong each morning. Before the sun rose, and in the dying hours of the day, the beautiful Pumo and her family could hear Tertön Sogyal's drum and bell as he summoned local protectors. In the late afternoon, when beings from the hungry-ghost realm are said to roam in search of sustenance, a burnt-food offering of roasted barley flour, butter, and dried cheese smoldered outside of Tertön Sogyal's tent. Days turned into weeks in Gonjo as Tertön Sogyal waited for auspicious omens indicating it was time to prove himself to the Khangsar household and fulfill Khyentsé's instructions.

Finally, on the morning following a prophetic dream, Tertön Sogyal told his attendant to gather Pumo and meet him at a granite cliff by the river. She was to carry a ritual long-life arrow decorated with colored silken tassels. Word spread around the village quickly that the Khangsar daughter might soon take the hand of the Nyarong tertön. By the time Pumo went to meet Tertön Sogyal, a few hundred people were at the cliff, including Pumo's family.

A ceremonial cup was set on a flat boulder and filled with rice wine, an offering to the local spirit protectors. Tertön Sogyal threw blessed barley seeds into the water and against the rock wall as a prepayment for the treasure object he was going to take from the spirit's possession. As he made his way through the crowd, Tertön Sogyal stopped to gaze into Pumo's eyes. The arm-length tassels from the long-life arrow she held upright waved with the flowing tresses of her black hair. In that moment, both of their perceptions were transformed.

Tertön Sogyal took his seat on the ground. Pumo followed, kneeling close enough behind him that Tertön Sogyal smelled her skin. Everyone's hands were together in prayer to Padmasambhava while Tertön Sogyal chanted. Tertön Sogyal prayed that, if taking Pumo as his wife was the proper course of action to benefit beings, he might be able to prove his worth to the family. At the end of the silent prayer, Tertön Sogyal raised his eyes to see a gap slowly being stretched open in the granite. Villagers held their breath in awe.

Approaching the hole, he reached into the rock and retrieved several treasures, including a phurba and a small statue and liturgy of the Buddha of Compassion. He handed the blessed objects to his attendant, who wrapped them in blue silk scarves. Then, reaching into his wool overcoat, he took his own teacup and placed it where the treasures had been so as not to leave the land empty. Backing away, he nodded his head toward the rock wall, communicating to the local earth and water spirits to reseal the rock.

"Padmasambhava is still before us," members of the crowd gasped. "Treasure revelations in public are as rare as a white yak," praised another.

Handing over the freshly revealed phurba, Tertön Sogyal told Pumo's father to enshrine the treasure in the Khangsar family's temple room. Pumo then approached Tertön Sogyal and offered him the long-life arrow, symbolizing their spiritual union. Before sunrise the next day, Tertön Sogyal, Pumo, and the Nyarong congregation had broken camp and headed back to eastern Tibet.

November 2003, Year of the Water Sheep

Larung Encampment, Eastern Tibet

For the fifth time in three years, I returned to the Larung Encampment. I needed to see my teacher. But my hopes of meeting Khenpo were soon dashed when I ran into police posted at the base of the valley. They did not recognize me from before, but were irritated by the presence of a Westerner nonetheless, and told me, as in years previous, that the Larung Encampment was an area closed to foreigners.

"Don't try to sneak into Larung over the mountain," the policeman snapped as we were walking out the door of the station. "You won't be the first rat we have caught and kicked out!"

There were still reports of the ongoing demolition of monastic housing, which I had been asked to confirm by photographing the gutted huts.

Khenpo's health had not improved in the last year and his continual requests to travel abroad on medical grounds were denied by the Chinese government.

I decided not to don monastic robes and a thick woolly hat in Serthar town and slip by disguised into the encampment. I walked away to the road in disappointment, swallowing dust while waiting to hitch a ride to town. On the way I met a Tibetan businessman, who had brought dry cheese to the monks and nuns at Larung. He gave me a small booklet of Khenpo's poems and advice. In one of the last poems, entitled "Drops of Advice from My Heart," the poet-mystic urges his students to rely ultimately on themselves and meditate diligently, rather than continually searching out instructions from teachers but never actually applying them in practice. One of the last verses in the poem stressed what Khenpo had told me when we first met and he sat with me in meditation.

> *Whatever arises, in pure awareness, unaltered and unconfined,*
> *Look into the mind that is settled by itself, resting naturally.*
> *If you recognize the mind's natural clarity, utterly free and unbound,*
> *You will instantly traverse all stages of the path, seizing the stronghold of*
> *enlightenment.*

Two months after being turned away from the Larung Encampment, I was in Kathmandu trying to follow the contradictory reports coming out of Tibet of Khenpo's deteriorating health—diabetes, high blood pressure, and the stress of seeing the destruction of his Buddhist institution. Sogyal Rinpoche was also closely following the situation.

In mid-December 2003, I began receiving reports at my home in Kathmandu that Khenpo had been taken to receive medical care in the small Serthar town, then transferred to Barkham, and then again to Military Hospital

363 in Chengdu, some two hundred miles from the Larung Encampment. This was a worrying sign.

When we confirmed the reports of Khenpo's transfer to a military hospital, we knew Chinese officials were controlling his movements. None of my Tibetan or Chinese friends who had traveled to Chengdu were able to see him. There were rumors the Chinese authorities intended to poison Khenpo, as many believed China had done to important lamas in the past. With Chinese security hovering outside his hospital room, Khenpo's entourage was apprehensive about speaking to anyone and it was impossible to confirm any details in Nepal. I received telephone calls from *Washington Post* and *Time* reporters in Beijing asking about current developments with Khenpo, as they had reported fully on the destruction at the Larung Encampment in 2001 and 2002, and the restrictions on Khenpo's travel thereafter.

"Phone the Sichuan authorities and ask them what is happening to Khenpo." I told the reporters to go to Chengdu. "Let them know that the eyes of the world are watching."

On January 7, 2004, I received the telephone call at my home in Kathmandu. On a crackling telephone line from Beijing, a reporter spoke.

"Matteo, Khenpo Jikmé Phuntsok has died."

I froze. The image of my teacher's body lying in a bare concrete room in a Chinese military hospital in Chengdu flashed in my mind. Not knowing whether to give the reporter background information, go weep in Pharping with Abbot Namdrol nearby, or contemplate Khenpo's teachings, I remained silent, telephone in hand.

"Matteo, are you there?" the voice on the other end said. "Matteo? I have to file a story in the next few hours. Can you e-mail me a quote? What he did in his seventy years . . . the impact that will be felt? If you think Beijing will react . . . Just two or three lines . . . E-mail it straightaway to me, would you? And do you have a high-resolution photo we can use?"

I felt a contradiction in being asked to get online to write a few sentences about my meditation teacher—my dead teacher. How to squeeze a saint's life into a few sentences? Why am I writing *about* Khenpo's life rather than heading to a mountain retreat to follow his yogi example? Distressed, I sat, shaken.

Dogs barked in the alleyway as I opened my laptop. The illuminated screen was the only light in the house. I placed the small phurba that Khenpo had given me on top of one of my notebooks. After hovering an hour between thinking about Khenpo and typing something I thought useful to the newspaper reporter, my duty for the evening was complete.

Great masters such as Padmasambhava state that there is in fact no separation between teacher and disciple, for the heart connection is beyond death. Khenpo once told me at Larung that one of the qualities of authentic teachers is that they are committed to maturing their students until complete enlightenment is attained, no matter how many lives that may take. The students' devotion is striving to embody the essence of the teachings whether the teacher is with us or not. But for now, in the Kathmandu night, I felt alone, sadly alone in the silence of loss.

Major news outlets in the West and Indian subcontinent reported Khenpo's death. Later, a Tibetan friend from Serthar phoned to say, despite China's continual attempts to jam the frequency, he had heard the Dalai Lama talking about Khenpo on Radio Free Asia and Voice of America. The Dalai Lama had taken the unusual action of broadcasting into Tibet via radio a message to Khenpo's students at Larung Gar.

"At this unfortunate time," the Dalai Lama said, speaking as a student of Khenpo, "it is extremely important for us, as Khenpo's grief-stricken disciples, to pray one-pointedly to our great teacher and to make an offering of our practice by diligently applying ourselves continuously and without hypocrisy, as well as by keeping in our hearts his essential instructions that distill the essence of Buddhist scripture and tantra, and not forgetting them."

Abbot Namdrol told me later how Khenpo's attendants had whisked his corpse away on a stretcher from the hospital, hoisted it into a four-wheel-drive SUV, and sped off to his mountain retreat hut at the Larung Encampment, despite the Sichuan provincial authority's attempts to block them. Barreling through roadblocks in Barkham and with four police cars following the SUV, they drove throughout the day and night to reach the Larung Encampment, where tens of thousands of students had gathered in disbelief.

After the Larung monks finished wrapping the body, they carried it to the main temple hall. Over fifty thousand devoted pilgrims and students managed to file by the body to pay their respects, offering white scarves and prayers.

The *Washington Post* reporter found a way into Larung and filed a report. After a week, early in the brisk morning, while nearly five thousand monks and nuns recited traditional prayers, Khenpo's body was ceremonially placed upon a cremation pyre and set alight. Three monks from Larung, who had smuggled lengthy descriptions through me in previous years of the political turmoil, sent me a note in English a day after Khenpo's body was cremated:

> *Before burning time, body get very small*
> *Body shrinking, we see our eyes*
> *At burning time, many rainbows above us in sky*
> *Also we see our eyes. Good Buddha sign.*

At the last public teaching Khenpo gave at Larung, he told his monks and nuns, "After I leave this present body, do not look for my reincarnation but spend your time practicing what I have taught." My initial reaction to his instruction was that Khenpo foresaw how his reincarnation would be co-opted by Chinese authorities for political gain, like their attempts with other young reincarnated lamas. Yet, Abbot Namdrol indicated that Khenpo's instruction not to look for his reincarnation was not so much political, but rather he wanted his disciples to concentrate on that which is most critical—practicing and realizing the essence of the Buddha's teachings. Khenpo's instruction reiterated the Buddha's final words whispered before passing into Nirvana over two thousand five hundred years ago. "All compounded things pass away," the Buddha said. "Strive for enlightenment with diligence."

Khenpo's death was itself a direct teaching for me. Thinking of his body burning in the cremation stupa seared the reality of impermanence into my mind—we can only be sure in this life of this—*we will die, and when death will come, we cannot know*. Khenpo's passing was an insistence to live with the awareness of death, for then we will not cling to past experiences nor hanker after a future that has not arrived.

A week after the cremation of Khenpo, I began to think ill of the Chinese government for not having allowed Khenpo medical treatment in the West. Abbot Namdrol told me soon thereafter what Khenpo's last words were from his hospital bed.

"Never to disturb the mind of others; look upon them with love and compassion. My disciples, you must never abandon this vow."

Part III

Though my view is higher than the sky,

My respect for cause and effect is as fine as grains of flour.

PADMASAMBHAVA

Chapter 8

In Service to the Dalai Lama

JANUARY 1888, YEAR OF THE EARTH RAT

Lhasa, Central Tibet

Word had spread to Lhasa of Tertön Sogyal's spiritual power. His enigmatic reputation was circulating among the three great Gelugpa monastic universities of Sera, Drepung, and Ganden. Traders and pilgrims from eastern Tibet brought tales of Tertön Sogyal's treasure revelations to the marketplace and teahouses of Lhasa. And Tibet's State Oracle had proclaimed the tertön must connect with the Dalai Lama to deal with the most pressing dilemmas of the day—strengthening Tibet's borders against invasion—especially as the British India forces were facing off with Tibet's weak army at the Sikkimese border.

At the beginning of the Year of the Earth Rat, Tertön Sogyal received a communiqué from the XIII Dalai Lama stating he must come to Lhasa right away, because Tibet was on the verge of war with the British. He was being called to perform rituals intended to push back the foreign troops, as well as to protect the life of the young Dalai Lama. This summoning of Tertön Sogyal was the precursor to his effective appointment as chaplain to the Dalai Lama, charged with special responsibility to use his mastery of the vajrayana for the defense of the realm.

Tertön Sogyal's summoning to Lhasa to meet the Dalai Lama was a reenactment of the spiritual dynamism between Padmasambhava and Tibet's imperial rulers, a time thought of by Tibetans as a golden age. Because the nation was established in support of Buddhism, to reconnect with the obstacle-removing activity of Padmasambhava and Tibet's kings would, it was believed, drive away threats to the nation. The Dalai Lama, like Tibet's imperial kings, was responsible for maintaining the nation-state as a political entity. And Tertön Sogyal, Padmasambhava's emissary, was responsible for protecting the country so her spiritual practitioners might flourish. Padmasambhava, and the treasure caches he concealed, are to be drawn upon in times of crisis. Extremely powerful practices, such as phurba rites, and the building of strategically placed temples and stupas, could, it was believed, repel invaders, whether from British India, or later the Qing and the Chinese from the east. The biography of the XIII Dalai Lama highlights the relationship of Tibet's rulers to vajrayana adepts:

> In particular, just as the abbot [Shantarakshita], Acharya [Padmasambhava] and the Dharma King [Trisong Detsen] had once joined forces to found the great temple at Samyé and perform works of inconceivable benefit to the advancement of Buddhadharma, so now this great ruler [the XIII Dalai Lama], endowed with skillful means and great compassion, together with Tertön Padma Lingpa Hutuktu and Tertön Sogyal and other noble masters of the old and new schools joined together following prophecies that the time had come to greatly expand altruistic activity for the benefit of the teachings and sentient beings.

As Tertön Sogyal departed for the six-week journey to Lhasa to meet the Dalai Lama for the first time, he knew the situation was but a continuation of his bodhisattva promise he had vowed to accomplish many lifetimes before.

The Dalai Lama, nearly twenty years Tertön Sogyal's junior, had yet to assume political rule of Tibet and was acting through his regent. Regent Demo, who was in charge of the country's political affairs, was chosen by Tibetan government ministers from one of a handful of prominent and historically influential monasteries in central Tibet. Though charged with overseeing the nation with the same Buddhist principles that the Dalai Lama embodied, some of the regents of the past were responsible for religious sectarianism, corrupt cronyism, and in some cases, it is believed, the premature death of the Dalai Lama.

Regent Demo changed the ways of incompetent regents, directing the young Dalai Lama's education so that he would simultaneously develop his spiritual and political skills. Regent Demo also took the State Oracle's pronouncements very seriously, including how critical it was that the Dalai Lama connects strongly with Tertön Sogyal. For the regent, the oracle, and the tertön, the highest priority was to remove obstacles to the Dalai Lama's health, and secure the nation so that the teachings of the Buddha in Tibet would flourish into the twentieth century.

But militant threats in the south from British India and from the Manchu Qing Empire in the east were threatening the security of the Dalai Lama, and placing the Tibetan nation and the life force of Tibetan Buddhism in peril.

MARCH 2004, YEAR OF THE WOOD MONKEY

Lhasa, Central Tibet

My late-night arrival was announced by the growling of a Lhasa Apso. I stood momentarily at the metal entry gate to one of the many new cement-housing compounds that have replaced nearly all the historically significant buildings in Lhasa. A dim streetlight illuminated the painted five-colored silk exterior bunting that used to decorate houses in the Barkhor area. Painting cement apartment blocks with a Tibetan façade demonstrates Beijing's policy to retain Tibet's "national characteristics" for the Barkhor, the last surviving traditional quarter in Lhasa. I wondered how Beijing reconciled such a pledge with the oversize polka-dotted mushroom parking barriers close to Jokhang Cathedral, or the small forests of fifteen-foot plastic coconut palm trees near the Dalai Lama's Potala Palace.

As I waited I could smell the juniper smoke that had permeated my jacket, having made offerings to the local protectors earlier in the evening in preparation for this meeting. The clanking of the gate startled me. "Did you bring the package?" I gave a silent nod and was hurried up two flights of stairs. I carefully found each of the metal steps with my foot in the darkness; a hand on my back directed me into an apartment with a single lightbulb hanging from wires. Steam was rising from a paper cup of jasmine tea.

"Have tea. She won't be long."

I had brought the parcel of medicine from Kathmandu, sent by Osel, a Tibetan who regularly supplies current and former political prisoners in Lhasa with medicine and cash.

"Some of the Drapchi Fourteen need this medicine," Osel told me, referring to a group of fourteen nuns being held in the notorious Drapchi Prison. "They were given multiyear term extensions for singing devotional songs to the Dalai Lama while in prison.

"The person you give the medicine to in Lhasa will know for whom it's intended. You need not say anything."

Drapchi Prison is regularly cited by European governmental councils on social justice and the U.S. Department of State for its egregious and consistent use of torture. Whoever I was meeting on this evening had connections with prison guards at Drapchi, and could deliver medicine and food. The person would inevitably have up-to-date information on prison conditions and term extensions—information nearly impossible to obtain by human rights groups.

Most of the political prisoners in Lhasa in 2004 were monks or nuns arrested in the late 1980s and early 1990s, when political activism and peaceful demonstrations against China's rule in Tibet were violently repressed. One of the Drapchi 14 told me how during the interrogation sessions, she and her fellow nuns were hung "in airplane" position, hands and legs tied together behind the back, and suspended from the ceiling. That was after they had had electrical wires attached to their tongues, a method prison guards know sends scorching charges throughout the entire body. The Drapchi 14, nuns ranging in age from their early teens to early thirties, were among this group. Some of the nuns had been released already on medical parole after their bodies were unable to withstand the brutality of Drapchi's torture chambers.

I regularly passed through Lhasa en route from eastern Tibet back to Nepal. Firsthand reports of torture victims and prison sentence extensions often came to me, as in eastern Tibet. But in Lhasa, where Tibetans fear being seen with Westerners, sometimes unmarked envelopes were slid under my hotel room door while I slept. Still other times I met former political prisoners in secret locations.

Once I was taken to meet a man who had been in Drapchi Prison for over five years. He had yelled in a public square for the Chinese government to allow the Dalai Lama to return to his homeland. Within minutes, plain-clothed policemen tackled him and threw him into a van. He was convicted of colluding with forces intent on splitting Tibet from China. He had been released on medical parole. Electrical batons, and beatings with heavy, sand-filled rubber tubing do not leave external scars, but they destroy prisoners' internal organs.

"The shocks felt like a fire in my chest. They told me to admit the Dalai Lama had ordered me to demonstrate in the streets—and then shocked me, over and over. I have never even seen the Dalai Lama in person!"

The man's head ticked involuntarily when he spoke, not an infrequent symptom in victims of head injuries. My video camera recorded his pain.

"The first month in prison, every other day I was taken to a room where I was hung by my wrists and given electrical shocks. I was told to admit my crimes of trying to split Tibet from China, and that I was supported by the Dalai Lama. I am a simple person. I have only ever seen photographs of the Dalai Lama. I want to see the Dalai Lama in my country, Tibet—that was all I was yelling for that day in the street."

I had to force myself to remain composed, though tears filled the eyepiece of the video camera.

He had been kicked in the stomach and urinated blood for ten days afterward. He was put in solitary confinement for mumbling mantras during prison work, accused of inciting others to believe in the Dalai Lama. The first year of his prison term, he was punched and hit with a baton more often than he was fed. But for him, the most difficult part was the years of humiliation, political indoctrination sessions, and being forced to denounce the Dalai Lama, day after day.

The face of this man was as determined, and sad, as any I had ever seen. This is what the Chinese government is most afraid of—this power, this resolve for freedom—and it is this fear that causes the Chinese state to shove electric cattle prods into the mouths of those who call for the Dalai Lama's return.

After forty-five minutes, he was too tired to keep talking. His bloodshot eyes, head bobbing and ticking, watched as I closed the camera lens. He had only enough energy to bid farewell with a long blink. Less than a year later, the man died of kidney and liver failure.

It was such interaction with Tibetans that led me to begin to work more directly with human rights groups in Hong Kong, London, and Washington, D.C. In the first years of my travels in Tibet, I gave my photographs and documents of human rights abuses only to them. They, in turn, used them in campaigns and to lobby governments. After two years, however, I began speaking directly to individuals in Washington who wield some political power—these were people in the U.S. National Security Council and State Department.

During one of my trips to Washington, a man who had seen copies of my photographs of Kandze Prison contacted me. He did not work for an advocacy group, but wanted to talk. I did not know much about him except that he had returned recently from a U.S. government assignment as an information technology consultant in the Middle East. He told me that he had contact with individuals who would pay for such photographs. Satisfied that the prison photographs proved helpful to the human right groups, I declined his encouragement to call him before my next journey to Tibet to discuss other "useful images."

I had sidestepped employment offers before by professionals in the business of collecting information. The first time had been by an Indian intelligence officer based at their embassy in Kathmandu.

"Kind sir, knowing Red China's road capacity near our northern borders will indeed help us evaluate their intention, economic and military," the Indian spy said, trying to lead me to offer him my observations from time spent in Tibet. I was inquisitive enough to meet with the Indian officer a second time, but when I realized that they were interested in paying me for information, I was out the door before the second cup of masala chai was poured.

I initially believed that the United States and various European countries could provide real political help to the Tibetans inside Tibet. It did not take me long to see this as overly optimistic. Maybe believing that any state can pressure the Chinese government to respect human rights is simply not in accordance with the political realities of the Communist Party. Tibetan leaders and activists outside Tibet will argue that it is more significant that the Tibetan movement emboldens Tibetans inside Tibet with hope—that to lose hope is the greatest danger. Prominent Western scholars have told me that the West's lauding gestures to the Dalai Lama, such as the Nobel Peace Prize and the Congressional Gold Medal, have made the situation worse for Tibetans inside Tibet because it has created unrealistic expectations that the Dalai Lama has real political clout with China. I disagree with these scholars—the world should stand next to the Dalai Lama in solidarity—but, still, I had to believe more could be done.

Beijing is confounded by the Tibetans' hope in the Dalai Lama and by the Tibetans still maintaining after sixty years a firm belief in a historic narrative that includes the Chinese invasion of their homeland and the forced flight of their leader into exile—this strikes at Communist China's legitimacy in Tibet. As long as Tibetans are separated from the Dalai Lama and the question of legitimacy remains, China will have a Tibet issue to be resolved.

After nearly twenty-five years of activism, the Tibet issue is more prominent than ever in the West. And despite the indefatigable hope of Tibetans, it is difficult to measure the political benefit that the campaign for Tibet has brought for Tibetans inside Tibet. Outside Tibet, the campaign has created tangible support for the Tibetan refugee communities and the Dalai Lama; and the U.S. government has led Western governments with funding and policy on the Tibet issue. But the focus must remain on Tibetans inside Tibet. The inability to show clearly how human rights organizations, and Western governments' pressure on China, has had practical political benefits for Tibetans in Lhasa, Kandze, and elsewhere, I found distressing.

When the Dalai Lama accepted his Nobel Peace Prize in 1989, he said, "I accept the prize with profound gratitude on behalf of the oppressed everywhere and for all those who struggle for freedom and work for world peace. I accept it as a tribute to the man who founded the modern tradition of nonviolent action for change—Mahatma Gandhi—whose life taught and inspired me. And, of course, I accept it on behalf of the six million Tibetan people, my brave countrymen and -women inside Tibet, who have suffered and continue to suffer so much. They confront a calculated and systematic strategy aimed at the destruction of their national and cultural identities. The prize reaffirms our conviction that with truth, courage, and determination as our weapons, Tibet will be liberated."

"You smell like curry spice and Kathmandu's dust," the president of the International Campaign for Tibet said, handing me a black blazer at Dulles Airport. Though I had not slept for over twenty-four hours, we sped off toward the U.S. Capitol. He had borrowed a pair of shoes from his office's media director to replace my hiking boots. I changed in the car ride into Washington. He dropped me off a few blocks from the White House, at the massive office buildings that house key policy decision-makers, including those in the National Security Council and vice president's office. It was there I met another advocate from the International Campaign for Tibet. We ducked out of the rain and entered a marble lobby.

The first thing that caught my eye was a large emblazoned seal hanging above our heads: a Roman cuirass surrounded by unsheathed swords, crossed bayonets, and other artillery, and a rattlesnake with a scroll unfurling from his fanged mouth that bore the inscription *This We'll Defend*. We were in the former Department of War building. The seal above us is still used today, with its blades and swords—not unlike the wrathful weaponry used in Tibetan Buddhist iconography to symbolize destroying the self-cherishing ego. But what is the difference between common weapons of war and wrathful weapons such as a phurba? The difference lies in the motivation behind their use. The Dalai Lama draws the same conclusion when discussing the use of science.

"Science and technology are powerful tools, but we must decide how best to use them. What matters above all is the motivation that governs the use of science and technology, in which ideally heart and mind are united. . . . Unless the direction of science is guided by a consciously ethical motivation, especially compassion, its effects may fail to bring benefit. They may indeed cause great harm."

As I stared at the fangs of the snake above my head, I said to my colleague, "Gandhi believed once the venom of war is waged, a policy of an eye for an eye makes everyone blind."

"Photo ID, sir. Place your bags here," the bulletproof-vested security officer ordered, bringing me back to the present task.

We were escorted down enormous hallways into the director's office of the department tasked with affairs in China. My colleague reminded me quietly, "Just present your photos of the prisons and tell them what the Tibetans relayed to you."

A handful of senior staff formally introduced themselves. They slid their business cards across the table; I did not have one to return. I took enlarged photographs out of a manila folder and laid them out on a coffee table, which included the pictures of Kandze Prison, as well as more recent images of another prison where two highly publicized political prisoners had been jailed in Dartsedo.

"See these two solitary confinement cells—this is where Tenzin Delek Rinpoche and Lobsang Dhondup were held," I said, pointing to a small prison in Dartsedo in Sichuan Province. A few assistants took notes.

The Tibetan Buddhist teacher Tenzin Delek Rinpoche and his colleague had been arrested on trumped-up charges of setting off a series of small explosives intending to incite "separation of the state."

"Both of these men were in the prison at the time I took photographs of their cell. A day after I took this photo, Lobsang Dhondup was executed by a bullet in the back of his head."

Before what I said resonated with meaning—that an innocent man had been summarily executed—one of the staff quipped, "Any connection to Falun Gong?"

I shook my head briefly, attempting to use silence as an ally.

"Did anyone in Congress make any noise about the execution?" another person quickly asked, presumably weighing how strong the blow-back from the Hill would be if the administration failed to act on my reports. Someone mentioned a U.S. trade mission to Beijing, and I waited as various acronyms were batted around the room. I interrupted their discussion.

"Look, Tenzin Delek Rinpoche was framed by the Chinese. He was trying to be a force for good in his community. Lobsang Dhondup was shot in the head. Neither of these guys were saboteurs or separatists. Can we please focus on the human rights principles involved here and on the U.S. reaction?" I said, searching for support in the room.

"Yes," I continued, "Tenzin Delek met with the Dalai Lama in India a long time ago. Since when is it a crime to meet with the Dalai Lama? Presidents Bush one and two and President Clinton all met the Dalai Lama right here in the White House."

"Do you have any GPS coordinates on these prison shots?" someone interrupted, taking his turn to ask whether I happened to travel with a global positioning system unit. "We might want to take a closer look and update our maps."

Tibetans had risked their lives to collect information that I could pass on to the outside world, and now someone was at least going to take a look, albeit from a satellite. Perhaps this was as good as it was going to get on this occasion. Earlier on the way to the meeting, the radio in the car had been playing Bob Dylan and his words rang frustratingly true. *I heard ten thousand whispers and nobody listening.*

After a week's worth of meetings with various U.S. government officials, my mind was weary and my heart was heavy. I agreed with what one fellow at the Council on Foreign Relations later opined, "Today the lack of interest in human rights has been virtually institutionalized in Washington and other capitals. A decade ago, policymakers could move up the ladder within bureaucracies like the U.S. State Department, the British Foreign Office, or Germany's Foreign Ministry by focusing on human rights, but today advocating for global freedom will get you nowhere." I had met a handful of individuals in the State Department and Congress who were skilled and experienced practitioners of human rights diplomacy within their institutions and with Chinese officials. However, it was also clear that their hands were tied by an entrenched U.S. policy approach where human rights concerns were "of necessity" placed well below other pressing bilateral concerns. Moreover, I was told, Chinese officials were upping their own skills in batting down U.S. human rights diplomacy. In a twisted way, human rights was becoming a higher priority for China in the bilateral relationship, and they were prepared to proactively shut down any sanction or censor brought against them for their human rights offenses. I was becoming convinced that China is just plain tougher than the United States in using the issue of human rights to their advantage. After all, I had seen China's handiwork in Tibet.

In Washington in 2007, I sat in the U.S. Capitol Rotunda and watched President George W. Bush present the Dalai Lama with the Congressional Gold Medal, the highest civilian honor bestowed by an act of Congress. The president and congressional leadership, Democratic and Republican, extolled the Dalai Lama for his nonviolent leadership of the Tibetan struggle and his international work to advance religious tolerance and human dignity. The message was clear, "We support you," and it was directed at Beijing. But would such gestures move beyond the ceremony?

When Americans voted Barack Obama into office the next year there was every hope for a more just and peaceful world. I wondered how Tibet would fare under a foreign policy based on "mutual interest and mutual respect" when it came to the U.S.-Chinese relationship. Like many Americans I was deeply disappointed when Secretary of State Hillary Clinton on her first official trip to China in February 2009 told the press that human rights would not knock her off her economic and security issues agenda. And, the following October, President Obama sidestepped a much anticipated meeting with the Dalai Lama so his November summit in Beijing would be free of the typical Chinese histrionics attached to presidential meetings with the Dalai Lama. The two leaders eventually met in February 2010 and, according to the White House, "the President stated his strong support for the preservation of Tibet's unique religious, cultural and linguistic identity and the protection of human rights for Tibetans in the People's Republic of China. . . ." Still, I kept hearing the Bob Dylan song in my mind.

I was too nervous to drink the tea in the paper cup while waiting for my meeting in Lhasa. The silence in the night amplified the hazards that lurked. Anyone spotted with me this night could be marked as a "splittist" because of collusion with what Beijing would call an anti-Chinese operative. I placed my hand on the bag of medicine next to me for solace. As my other hand felt for the protection phurba around my neck, I wondered why Khenpo had told me to come to Lhasa on pilgrimage in Tertön Sogyal's footsteps. I only seemed to get angry in Lhasa.

"Greetings." A female voice startled me from behind.

As I stood and turned, a nun walked toward me. The graceful manner in which she tossed her monastic shawl over her left shoulder slowed the thump in my chest.

"Next Wednesday. Meet me at seven sharp. Mani Temple on the Bark-hor route, behind the Jokhang Cathedral," she said, stretching both of her hands to me.

I handed the medicine over as I repeated mentally the time and place of our next meeting. Before I could say anything, she bowed slightly and re-turned to the adjacent room. I was quickly escorted down the chilly stairwell and sent silently into the dark.

As I laid to rest that night in my hotel room, I saw a Bible next to the night table. I had not noticed the book before, though I had been in the hotel for a few days. It had a scrap of paper marking a page. Maybe it was from the previous tenant. Perhaps the hotel staff had placed the Bible in my room. I opened it to the bookmarked page and there read Ephesians 6:12:

> For we wrestle not against flesh and blood, but against principali-ties, against powers, against the rulers of the darkness of this world, against spiritual wickedness in high places.

Before turning off the room's buzzing fluorescent light, I copied the verse and wrote next to it my own commentary:

Absence of violence is not peace,
Absence of protest is not agreement.
In this city of pain
Virtue is bound & honesty beaten.
Fear of the truth is the fuel
Driving these occupiers' actions.

Through the light fog in the early Wednesday morning, I spotted the nun. She was walking among the crowd of pilgrims and devoted residents circling the eighteen-hundred-year-old Jokhang Cathedral on the Barkhor circumambulation route. As the nun approached, I fell into step ten feet behind her. She did not acknowledge me. I matched her quick pace as she turned the copper prayer wheels that surrounded the temple. In her left hand she thumbed prayer beads, and over her right shoulder she carried a small pannierlike cotton bag sewn of fabric with a cartoon surfboard and the words "Joe Cool Surfing Company." In one side was powdered juniper incense and in the other, barley flour. Both the incense and flour are scooped out and offered into the large outdoor incense burners that surround the Jokhang. I stood at her left as the urns sent fragrant smoke into the mist outside of Meru Nyingma Temple. We continued around the devotees' route before entering the large courtyard of Jokhang Cathedral.

Inside the ancient temple, locals and pilgrims jockey for space to make religious offerings and prostrate themselves before the many sacred statues in small alcoves and tucked away in ancient shrines. I fought my way through the crowd of pilgrims, keeping an eye on the brown woolen hat of the nun and the Joe Cool surf logo on her shoulder. Passing the wooden door entrance to the inner sanctum of the Jokhang, we continued clockwise around the inside of the cathedral, where we found more dense crowds queued to enter each of the chapels. The sweet fragrance of sandalwood and juniper incense mixed with the toasted smell of burning butter lamps.

As we approached the far side of the route past the last small chapel, the crowds thinned and the nun took a seat near a group of tired pilgrims. She continued to roll her prayer beads, as did every pilgrim I saw. They all recited *Om Mani Padme Hum*, the six-syllable mantra of the Buddha of Compassion, of whom Tibetans believe the Dalai Lama to be a manifestation. The mantra represents the deity's speech, and is both an invocation and prayer to the deity to bless them so that they may embody the Buddha's compassion. She recited each syllable with rapid-fire precision.

Beijing views Tibetan Buddhism as a threat to the state. Tibetans who work for the Chinese government have told me that they and their children are banned from wearing traditional Buddhist amulets and pendants or from going to the temples to pray. On numerous occasions, Tibetan monks and nuns, wiping tears from their eyes, have admitted to me that they were forced to sign documents denouncing the Dalai Lama during Communist Party "Patriotic Education" classes in their monasteries. And I have met both novice monks and elder teachers whom the Chinese government no longer allows to stay in the monasteries, thereby effectively severing the life force of traditional pedagogy.

China believes the Dalai Lama wants an independent Tibet, though the Dalai Lama has since 1988 repeatedly stated he is only seeking genuine autonomy for Tibetans within the People's Republic of China. Still, the Chinese government considers Tibetans' religious devotion to him a political act of attempting to split Tibet from China. Local governments enforce strict regulations on sensitive dates such as the Dalai Lama's birthday or International Human Rights Day and the anniversary of the Dalai Lama's Nobel Peace Prize on December 10. I once read a public announcement posted by the Lhasa city government days before the Dalai Lama's July 6 birthday, which banned, among other actions, throwing handfuls of barley flour into the air, a traditional celebratory gesture often done on hilltops or mountain passes:

> The People's Government . . . forbids any person, any group, or any organization, in any form or in any place, to use any situation to represent celebrating the Dalai's birthday, to pray to the Dalai for blessing, to sing prohibited songs, to offer incense to the Dalai, or to carry out illegal barley-flour-throwing activities.

While the Chinese government unsuccessfully tries to control the Dalai Lama's influence in Tibet today, they are also planning for the Dalai Lama's reincarnation. Reiterating the Communist Party's past assertions that they will select the next Dalai Lama, in March 2009, Jiao Zai'an, an official in the Communist Party–led United Front Work Department, said that the Communist Party must "decide what kind of person is allowed to be reincarnated," because such approval is essential to "ensure the political soundness of reincarnate lamas." As they have done with the Panchen Lama and other prominent Tibetan Buddhist teachers, China has found Tibetan Communist Party cadres' children to use as puppets and install them as reincarnate lamas. The incongruity that an atheist government is involved in the mystical process of finding a reincarnate lama is ignored by Communist officials.

The Communist Party of China argues that they are the sole authority on knowing whose body the Dalai Lama will choose to reincarnate. The current Dalai Lama has repeatedly stated publicly that he will never be reborn inside territory controlled by the People's Republic of China.

"If the Tibetan people want another Dalai Lama, then I will be reborn outside of China's control," the Dalai Lama told me in a private meeting in Benares, India. "The purpose of reincarnation is to continue our duty, our work from before. The Chinese don't like my work today, so why would they want it again in my next reincarnation?"

After the Dalai Lama dies, the situation will likely unfold like this: The entire Tibetan Plateau will be in lockdown martial law to suppress any outpouring of emotion by Tibetans. Authorities will be caught off-guard by thousands of Chinese publicly expressing their sadness and sympathy as well—though they will be successful in suppressing it. The Chinese Ministry of Foreign Affairs spokesman will report, "The selection of the Dalai's reincarnation will be overseen by the Religious Affairs Bureau in conformity with China's constitution, which guarantees religious freedom of it citizens." After a "search" that will last for a few years, the government will select a boy born to a Tibetan Communist Party cadre, or perhaps a village family, to be named as the XV Dalai Lama. A few months later, in front of the Jowo Buddha statue in Lhasa's central cathedral, the preselected boy will sit together with a few other reincarnation candidates. The bogus scene will take place with the temple full of monks in wine-red robes in rows on the carpeted floor; government leaders in dark suits will sit in chairs. A golden urn, supposedly containing each of the candidates' names written on paper taped to ivory sticks, will be on a high table. There will be a row of young men whom Beijing has already approved as reincarnate lamas, such as the Gyaltsen Norbu, wearing yellow ceremonial robes. As the CCTV cameras roll, an elderly monk from the cathedral, certainly coerced into the role, will step forward to chant auspicious prayers before the golden urn. Official Chinese media and the likes of Sky TV will be invited to cover the mockery, but the BBC and CNN will be kept out. The elderly monk will place a ceremonial hat upon his head and select one of the eight-inch ivory lots from the urn with the name of the next Dalai Lama. One of the Chinese Communist Party leaders will step forward and, over a crackly microphone, read in Mandarin, not Tibetan, the name of the boy the government already knew was going to be selected. Applause by Party members may occur, despite the fact that Tibetans only clap in a temple when they are driving away evil spirits. The Communist leader will confirm all has been done in accordance with ancient Tibetan tradition and will praise Beijing for its enduring support of all minorities including the Tibetans. The next day, the Ministry of Foreign Affairs spokesman will say at the press briefing that this is how all Dalai Lamas have been selected in the past, a patently untrue statement, as the Dalai Lamas of the past have been discovered by reading mystical signs or relying on religious prophecy and confirmed by the Tibetan religious authority, not by the Chinese.

"The young Dalai Lama will soon know that only under the Chinese Communist Party's leadership, only in the embrace of the Motherland's family, only firmly on the road of socialism with Chinese characteristics, will Tibet enjoy a prosperous today and a better tomorrow. We look forward to a patriotic fifteenth Dalai Lama," the Ministry of Foreign Affairs in Beijing will conclude.

In mid-2006, Zhang Qingli, the Communist Party Secretary of Tibetan Autonomous Region, announced the government's "Fight to the Death" campaign against the Dalai Lama. The policy prohibiting possession of the Dalai Lama's photograph in Tibet, which began in 1995, is emblematic of how much the Chinese government fears the Tibetan leader. Singing songs about the Dalai Lama or reciting poems that praise his qualities is also a criminal offense. Banning the Dalai Lama's photo—though difficult to enforce across the Tibetan Plateau—made his face an even stronger symbol of resistance. Despite the ban and the legal reprimands for displaying the Dalai Lama's image, pictures of him can still be found in some monasteries, especially in eastern Tibet. I once watched a group of nuns place a large scroll painting over a life-size photograph of the Dalai Lama in order to hide it from the view of a Communist Party work team that was due to arrive.

"Just because we turn the frame around and display a picture of a Buddhist deity doesn't mean that the protection given by His Holiness's picture isn't still in the temple," a nun in central Tibet told me while dusting a photograph of the Dalai Lama with President George H. W. Bush in the White House.

Despite the ban on images of the Dalai Lama, Tibetan religious ingenuity gives ample opportunity for his face to appear across Tibet. From monks and nuns hiding the Dalai Lama's photograph behind the silk lining on the back of a throne in a temple hall, to sewing his photograph inside the top of nomads' cowboy hats, to having a string long enough so that a Dalai Lama pendant is not visible, the Dalai Lama's face, and the courage and resistance it represents, continues in Tibet today.

Continuing to observe devotees around the Jokhang, I noticed that my Joe Cool nun next to me was gathering herself and getting ready to move. We were all seated on the ground, leaning against a wall. It seemed that she had not found the appropriate opportunity to pass whatever information she had brought for me. She looked at the pilgrims next to me and said, *"Kalay shu—* stay well." The pilgrims responded to the nun, *"Kalay pheh*—go well."

The nun looked at me and said the same thing, meaning not so much to sit well but not to follow her. Perhaps the secret police were onto us? Perhaps one of the Jokhang's monk spies was peering around the corner? I watched as she disappeared into a wave of pilgrims.

I allowed time for her to exit the temple grounds. As I stood up, I noticed the nun had forgotten her Joe Cool incense pannier at my side. When I took the bag in my hands, I realized a safety pin attached the bag to the tail of my own coat. The information drop had occurred and I had not even been aware of it.

Back in my hotel room, I found folded folios wrapped in plastic inside the incense bag. The juniper-dusted paper contained handwritten lists of ailing political prisoners, the dire conditions they were subjected to in prison, and what medicines were critically needed. In the other pocket with the barley flour, she had slid a booklet entitled *Handbook for Education in Anti-Splittism; Tibetan Autonomous Region Patriotic Education for Monasteries Propaganda Book no. 2.* This was one of the many propaganda textbooks that monastics in central Tibet are required to study and memorize, but such documents are difficult for human rights groups to get their hands on.

I felt some sense of accomplishment for having acquired a dossier of materials for the International Campaign for Tibet. But this could not have been why Khenpo told me to come here as one of the four pilgrimage places. I was still trying to figure out why he had told me to come to Lhasa.

Chapter 9

The Merging of Politics and Spirituality

APRIL 1888, YEAR OF THE EARTH RAT

Lhasa, Central Tibet

Government representatives in full regalia and the Medium of the State Oracle from Nechung formally greeted Tertön Sogyal a few hours outside of Lhasa and began escorting him toward the Potala Palace. With more than a thousand rooms of living quarters, chanting halls, reliquaries, shrines, libraries, ceremonial reception areas, and government chambers, even at such great distances Tertön Sogyal could see the towering white-and-red fortress. The Potala Palace was home to the Dalai Lamas and the Tibetan government, with several hundred courtiers, monks, bureaucrats, attendants, and civil servants. Tertön Sogyal would, in time, come to know well the Potala Palace, as well as the Dalai Lama's summer residence of the Jewel Garden.

As the small procession with honor guard made its way into Lhasa, residents of the Shol neighborhood below the Potala Palace stopped chit-chatting and milling about to take notice of the warrior lama. Tertön Sogyal was ushered up the thousand stone-carved steps that lead into the Potala

Palace to meet the young Tibetan ruler. The significance of the Dalai Lama's reconnecting with Padmasambhava's ambassador in Tertön Sogyal was so powerful, it is said, that their minds merged like water being poured into water. With the specter of war hovering over their first meeting, Tertön Sogyal could not have arrived at a more opportune time.

Since 1816, Tibet had watched British India progressively gain control over Nepal, Kashmir, Ladakh, and Sikkim, and now in 1888, they had their sights set not only on Bhutan, but the entire Tibetan Plateau. The British wanted to establish and control the trade route between China and India through Tibet. Britain had already signed various trade compacts with China, treating Tibet as a colonial spoil. Furthermore, the British had successfully sent spies disguised as a pilgrims to Tibet to map the region, hiding completed maps and notes in their hand-spun prayer wheels and amulet boxes.

Tibetans knew the British wanted to control trade into Tibet, but they also believed their Christian missionaries wanted to destroy Buddhism, and had fears they would bring smallpox. So in 1883, the National Council of Ministers banned all foreigners in central Tibet. When the Tibetans sent a small force in 1887 to inspect the British trading outpost at the Sikkim border, the English threatened retaliation. The Dalai Lama and his regent conscripted all able-bodied men into the army, ordered the commencement of prayers at the three great monastic universities of Lhasa, and yogis were instructed to ritually support the effort. One battle had already been fought with the British, with more fighting to come.

Tertön Sogyal's ceremonial welcome was short and he was soon escorted through narrow passageways to Jokhang Cathedral in the center of town. Lhasa, with its population of fifty thousand and a constant stream of pilgrims and nomads, Nepali craftsmen, and Chinese and Indian merchants, was as cosmopolitan a city as Tertön Sogyal would ever see.

Tertön Sogyal's duty demanded that he begin without delay ritual activity to strengthen the Tibetan nation. Monks for the Dalai Lama's personal monastery of Namgyal were dispatched to support the tertön. With the monks seated in facing rows and Tertön Sogyal presiding on a throne, thunderous chants rolled out of the same temples that Padmasambhava had blessed. The phurba was wielded. The Medium of the State Oracle also joined in, at times becoming possessed and issuing forth additional prophecies and directives to protect the Dalai Lama's life. The rituals would last for weeks.

The Tibetan forces suffered losses during the six-month battle, though, as Tibetan vajrayana practitioners contend, the British were still unable to penetrate into Tibet because of their protective shield and Tibet's storehouse of positive merit. If Tibet's depot of positive karma had somehow held back the English on this occasion, it was being quickly depleted back in Lhasa. The challenges for the Dalai Lama were not only from the external threat of the British—there were internal sectarian fights as well that were draining Tibet's spiritual reservoir.

While the Dalai Lama, Regent Demo, and the State Oracle welcomed Tertön Sogyal's involvement, the tertön also met with opposition. The overarching conservative attitude that pervaded the monastic government officials in Lhasa was resistant to change. The conservative elements had especially strong reservations about the Dalai Lama's intimate relationship with an idiosyncratic, mystical lay master like Tertön Sogyal. Given that Tertön Sogyal and other yogis like him had no direct connection with any particular monastery in Lhasa, and that they were likely to question the status quo, their presence in Lhasa was perceived by many as a challenge to the

monastic hierarchy. Any influence on the Dalai Lama beyond the monk officials' tightly controlled circles was seen as a threat to the economic control
they held through vast monastic estates, corvée, and the taxes they collected.
In addition, Tertön Sogyal ran head-on into influential monks who held sectarian biases against Padmasambhava. They contended that only the teachings propagated within the reformed Gelugpa school were authentic, and
that treasure revelations in particular were nothing more than fabrications
by swindlers like Tertön Sogyal.

The Dalai Lama and his regent Demo soon became aware that there
were some in the Tibetan government and aristocracy who objected to Tertön Sogyal. Regent Demo had also heard that some monks had even begun
conducting their own rituals—filling a yak horn with spell-laden black mus-
tard seeds, small pebbles, and the name of Tertön Sogyal, which, when sealed
and then shaken, were believed to cause debilitating headaches—trying to
drive Tertön Sogyal away from central Tibet. Not wanting such esoteric duels
to get out of control, Regent Demo requested the Dalai Lama to command
Tertön Sogyal to display his spiritual accomplishments by publicly revealing a treasure text from within Jokhang Cathedral. The Dalai Lama agreed,
believing that such a rare event could correct the flawed view of misguided
officials, and increase public confidence and devotion for Tertön Sogyal, despite his unconventional demeanor. Tertön Sogyal was commanded to reveal
a treasure from within the hallowed temple walls, to which both the public
and government would be invited.

A date was set when the stars, planets, and elements were deemed in
favorable alignment, and the time of day when the treasure discovery should
take place was announced. The disciplinarian-monks of Jokhang Cathedral
and Demo's police force made sure there were no disturbances. An elaborate throne was set up for the Dalai Lama on the day of the revelation, and
cushion seats were arranged for the Medium of the Nechung Oracle, rank-
ing monastic officials, as well as some of the foreign ministers and honored

lamas who happened to be in Lhasa at the time. Lhasa residents knew a momentous event was being planned as lamas and dignitaries began filing into the cathedral.

The scene was set. The Dalai Lama presided over the large gathering of lamas and monks, brocade-clad government ministers with their long, single turquoise earrings and hair tied in oiled topknots, and aristocrats in richly attired silks. Tertön Sogyal sat in a deep state of meditation. The chant leader began the invocation prayers, followed by lengthy liturgical recitations in guttural multitonal chants. When the hundreds of monks joined in, it was as if the earth were rumbling below Lhasa. After an hour, no extraordinary signs had occurred. Some of the government ministers began to nod to one another that Tertön Sogyal was a fraud. Whispers spread outside the Jokhang among the shopkeepers that Tertön Sogyal was ashamed because he sat unmoving with his eyes lowered. It was not difficult for Tertön Sogyal to read what was on the weak minds of the cynics in the crowd. Just the day before, Tertön Sogyal had confronted some of the government ministers in the Potala and told them that they had better follow to the letter all of Padmasambhava's prophesies to avert danger from outside Tibet.

"You must build the requisite reliquaries and temples, sponsor the specified rituals that Padmasambhava presaged, and desist from using the monastery's finances for personal gain," Tertön Sogyal said, wagging his finger at the lavishly attired monk.

"Ah, you smelly so-called treasure revealers from eastern Tibet are a scourge to the Buddha's teachings," a government monk-official said. "Move out of the way. My assembly of two thousand monks needs me to guide them in prayer."

"If you don't follow the great guru Padmasambhava's clear prophecies," Tertön Sogyal shot back, "I will hold you and those with similar views responsible for the death of our nation."

WINTER 2004, YEAR OF THE WOOD MONKEY

Dharamsala, India

Thick Coke-bottle spectacles magnified Khamtrul Rinpoche's eyes to twice their normal size as he welcomed me into his home. His wife served a cup of tea. I welcomed the caffeine, having taken the overnight Jammu Mail train from Delhi. I had come to meet the venerable seventy-year-old lama for the third time in two years.

Khamtrul Rinpoche and his family live within walking distance of the Dalai Lama's private residence. He is frequently summoned by the Dalai Lama to preside over ceremonies conducted on behalf of the Tibetan government-in-exile at Namgyal Monastery, and consulted for divinations daily by local Tibetans. He experienced visions of Padmasambhava early in his life while still in Tibet, and his uncle, a disciple of Tertön Sogyal, oversaw his religious education. Khamtrul Rinpoche is a master of the phurba ritual. He works hand in hand with the Medium of Tibet's State Oracle who lives just down the road at Nechung Monastery. They assist the government-in-exile and the Dalai Lama in using prophecy on matters of state and religion. Like Tertön Sogyal, Khamtrul Rinpoche is a vajrayana master of the highest caliber who has been called upon to use his spiritual power for political purpose.

"Tertön Sogyal was a rarity in Lhasa. There was so much partisan and sectarian politics at the time in the Lhasa government and the monasteries. Tertön Sogyal was above all a spiritual practitioner, and this allowed him to effectively navigate the sectarian politics in Tibet at the end of the nineteenth century. He had no choice, actually, because he was ordered to come to Lhasa by the Dalai Lama!" Khamtrul Rinpoche said, understanding exactly Tertön Sogyal's duties set upon him by the XIII Dalai Lama, for he, too, is commanded by the current Dalai Lama to conduct rituals at a moment's notice.

"Not unlike Gandhi," I commented, "whose political action was founded on his own spiritual understanding of the Truth."

"Yes. But it is not just about bringing politics and religion together. We just have to look at the world today and see how mixing the two can result in violence and hatred. There are abundant examples of how this mixture can go terribly wrong—mainly because those political causes are not founded on *ahimsa,* nonviolence."

Khamtrul Rinpoche used the Sanskrit word *ahimsa,* which equates with the first Buddhist precept of nonharming—a notion that is extended not only to humans but to all living beings. Nonharming was the foundation of Mahatma Gandhi's political movement of *satyagraha,* truth-insistence. It was these two spiritual pillars—nonharming and truth-insistence—around which Gandhi effectively built his social activism that contributed significantly to India's gaining independence from Britain in 1947.

"The Dalai Lama is the modern-day example of insisting on the truth in politics and on carrying out a nonviolent struggle. His efforts are but a continuation of the great efforts of the thirteenth Dalai Lama and Tertön Sogyal, who worked hand in hand trying to strengthen a nation so our religion could be practiced freely."

Khamtrul Rinpoche fell silent. This was not uncommon among this older generation of Tibetan lamas with whom I spoke—they are inspired by talking of times in Tibet's past, but then realize that they will likely never see their homeland again.

"There were dark forces," Khamtrul concluded. "Very powerful forces that rose up against the Dalai Lama, Tertön Sogyal, and the Tibetan nation. And we still have not been able to get rid of them."

Tertön Sogyal rose to his feet, then prostrated three times to the Dalai Lama. Approaching the altar, on which were set elaborate butter sculptures and ritual offerings, the tertön took a cone-shaped offering cake in his right hand and a skull cup overflowing with barley beer in his left. He walked toward a wall painting of Palden Lhamo, the wrathful protectress of Lhasa and the Dalai Lamas. Palden Lhamo rides a mule and carries in her two hands a club and a skull cup of blood. With a tiger skin tied around her waist and human skin over her shoulder, she arrives with a storm of flames behind her. The saddlebags of the mule contain a skull, poison, and two divination dice.

Tertön Sogyal stared at Palden Lhamo, circling the skull cup in front of the image on the wall. One of the ministers jabbed his portly sidekick, chuckling that Tertön Sogyal was sure to fail. Tertön Sogyal's eyes bulged and his stance widened. He let go of the ritual cake in order to seize the phurba from his belt. Staring eye to eye with the mural of Palden Lhamo, he reminded the deity of her oath to protect Tibet and the Dalai Lama. Immediately, the mule on which Palden Lhamo rode brayed loudly and kicked its right hoof toward the open space of the courtyard. In the space where the hoof had landed, suspended in air, seethed a vicious black snake, coiled twenty-one times. And in each of its slithery coils rested a small treasure casket.

"Cover your eyes, nose, and mouth," the Dalai Lama shouted from his throne. As the snake hissed, a commotion shook the entire congregation as monks covered themselves with their red shawls. Two of the cynical ministers were so frightened they ran out of the temple, shaking with panic.

"If you ingest any of the poisonous vapor of this serpent, you will certainly meet your death!" the Dalai Lama warned.

Tertön Sogyal stood holding the skull cup on high, barley beer dripping over the edge. The phurba in his right hand pointed in a threatening manner. The chanting had stopped. There was a pregnant silence. The snake's fangs dripped silvery venom as Tertön Sogyal walked ever closer. An attendant ran to the tertön's seat, took a silk scarf from his shoulder bag, and, returning, unraveled it and draped it over Tertön Sogyal's outstretched wrists.

The assembly began to peer over each other again, still keeping their shoulders hunched and heads lowered as if the snake were going to spit at them. Hissing and writhing, the serpent widened its eyes and then, snapping its body, it pitched an emerald-colored treasure casket toward Tertön Sogyal, which landed in the middle of the open silk scarf. He quickly wrapped the treasure with the scarf, stepping backward in deference. He nodded to the treasure-protecting serpent in gratitude, and the snake dissolved into light.

Tertön Sogyal presented the treasure casket to the Dalai Lama at the throne. It was marked with the personal seals of the ruler and treasure revealer, and placed in the inner sanctum of Jokhang Cathedral. The stunned monks began reciting auspicious prayers to Padmasambhava as Tertön Sogyal walked back to his seat. The devotion that welled from the hearts of the faithful caused the treasure casket to open by itself. It was then again presented to the Dalai Lama, who took out an exquisite statue known as Blazing with the Glory of Auspiciousness, as well as five small golden treasure scrolls, along with a crystal capsule of holy substance, with which he blessed the government ministers and congregation.

Tertön Sogyal stayed in Lhasa more than a year, performing rituals for the Tibetan government and deepening his connection with the young Dalai Lama. In late 1889, Padmasambhava and the Protectress of Mantras were visiting the tertön in visions and dreams, telling him of additional treasures to be revealed in eastern Tibet, so he prepared to depart Lhasa. Tertön Sogyal's position in the inner court of the Dalai Lama had been firmly established, even though some resentment of his influence on the Dalai Lama still remained within orthodox elements in the Tibetan government. When Tertön Sogyal met with Regent Demo before departing, he told the regent about a treasure statue Padmasambhava had hidden in eastern Tibet that, if placed in Lhasa's Jokhang Cathedral, would be an exceptional means to prevent invaders from entering the Land of Snows.

"Endeavor with all your efforts to find this statue," Regent Demo pleaded, offering Tertön Sogyal one hundred pieces of turquoise and coral with the request, before sending the tertön off with a government escort.

Returning to eastern Tibet in a small caravan, Tertön Sogyal first visited his teacher, Master Lungtok, to pay respects and present him with the jewels, silver, and gold he had been offered in central Tibet. The tertön was then led by visions to a sacred mountain in the region of Derge, where he unearthed the Wish-Fulfilling Jewel Guru statue that he had told Regent Demo about. The Medium of the Nechung Oracle in Lhasa was immediately possessed and called for the statue's presence near the Dalai Lama. The Tibetan government sent an urgent message via horseman to the Nyarong governor to track down the wandering tertön, who had not even had a chance to visit his wife before he was ordered back to Lhasa.

Tertön Sogyal brought the Wish-Fulfilling Jewel Guru statue into Lhasa during the ninth month of 1891, which coincided with the festival commemorating the Buddha's descent to earth from the Joyous Tushita Heaven. Thousands of nomads with thick overcoats lined the road to Jokhang Cathedral as shop owners locked their doors to come out on the street, pushing one another aside to get a glimpse of the sacred image. Monk security guards with wooden staffs cleared the way, while all government officials made their way to the event. As the statue and Tertön Sogyal proceeded toward Jokhang Cathedral, led by twirling parasols and monks playing the high-pitched short oboe, plumes of juniper incense filled the sky above the Barkhor areas. From the cathedral's rooftop boomed the drone of long horns and the crashing of symbols, and monks played the conch shell in the ten directions, invoking the blessings of enlightened beings to descend. It was as if Padmasambhava, in the flesh, had returned to Lhasa. The Wish-Fulfilling Jewel Guru was taken into the inner sanctum and offered a throne to the right side of the most sacred statue in all of Tibet, the Jowo Buddha.

Whenever I returned to the United States after my extended stays in Tibet and Nepal, one of my first stops was to visit Lodi Gyari, the Special Envoy of His Holiness the Dalai Lama, who lives outside of Washington, D.C. Lodi Gyari has held many senior posts in the Tibetan government in exile and thirty years ago was among the founders of the Tibetan Youth Congress, an organization of Tibetans in exile that still adheres to a pro-independence stance. In his early sixties, Lodi Gyari has been the Dalai Lama's diplomat-at-large and chief negotiator with Beijing for much of the past two decades, carrying the Dalai Lama's messages to Chinese leaders, including, principally,

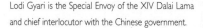

Lodi Gyari is the Special Envoy of the XIV Dalai Lama and chief interlocutor with the Chinese government.

that he is seeking genuine autonomy—not independence—for Tibet. Lodi Gyari is also a quiet phurba practitioner, and a blood relative of Tertön Sogyal. Since I began my pilgrimage to Tibet in the 1990s, he has been a mentor in both my spiritual and human rights monitoring work.

When we met at his home, his wife always welcomed me with the finest Darjeeling tea. I usually arrived carrying time-sensitive information: photos of the destruction at Buddhist encampments or monasteries, updates on political prisoners in Lhasa, or even messages for him from lamas or officials living in Tibet or Beijing. Oftentimes, I carried personal messages or sacred offerings for the Dalai Lama from elderly lamas in Tibet that I gave to Lodi Gyari.

Yet, handing over the latest communiqué or showing him photos of the destruction in his homeland, or other political news, always came after the first order of business. Lodi Gyari is most concerned about the state of Buddhist practice in his homeland, firing off specific questions about little-known temples, asking if an aging hermit was still practicing there. Or he would ask if the collected writings of a nineteenth-century lama, which he had directed to be reprinted, were being distributed to small monasteries in a remote corner of eastern Tibet. He checked on prophetic visions that contemporary hermits in Tibet had told me, making sure that I had made appropriate monetary offerings to care for the hermits' basic needs. Or he asked about big-picture issues, such as to what extent the Communist Party's obligatory "Patriotic Education" was implemented. Just as Lodi Gyari moves pieces around the political chessboard in negotiating with Communist officials on the Dalai Lama's behalf, I witnessed how he was simultaneously supporting more esoteric endeavors among the monks, nuns, and lay Buddhist practitioners in Tibet.

"When I think about the future of China, I think about the story of Rudra," Lodi Gyari told me in late 2004 at his home. He was relating a traditional story that tells how the ogre Rudra, the embodiment of the negative self-cherishing ego, after carrying out many atrocious crimes, was subjugated by a powerful Buddhist deity from whose body protrudes the head and neck of a horse. In the story, the Buddhist deity entered Rudra's body and, through powerful and skillful compassionate means, destroyed Rudra's anger and aggression from within.

"When the deity went inside and finally emerged from Rudra's body, the horse neighed loudly in a victorious cry. This is what is slowly happening in China, with the teachings of nonviolence and compassion emerging as the victor."

I saw a disconnect between cultural mythology and the political reality of the day, saying, "Yes, but the Chinese Communist Party are co-opting Tibetan Buddhism to their advantage, and certainly the most egregious act will be when the Communist Party identifies and enthrones the next Dalai Lama, as they have said they will."

"This is my point. Until China changes, nothing will substantially change in Tibet," he said, connecting the dots. "The lives of Tibetans and Chinese are interdependent, and shall remain so. This is a reality, whether the Communist Party is ruling, or when the Dalai Lama's vision of brotherhood and peaceful coexistence prevails. After all, we are neighbors.

"Did you make the incense offerings to the mountain deities of Eternal Snow while you were there?" he asked, changing the subject to his ancestral protector in Nyarong.

I told him that we had placed juniper branches, barley flour, sugar, and yogurt in a ritual fire, as well as a jug of local wine that was ceremonially offered with a prayer composed by Lodi Gyari himself.

"Thick cumulus clouds quickly dispersed during the middle part of the ceremony, revealing an intensely blue sky," I reported, "and a local farmer walked nearby carrying two full buckets of water."

"These are all very auspicious signs indicating clarity and abundance—and were indeed timely," Lodi Gyari said, nodding affirmatively.

The last word—*timely*. I knew *timely* meant it was connected to his political work, likely the negotiations with Chinese officials, the details of which he always kept confidential. I also knew that the timeliness he spoke of was beyond a specific situation. I was struck by how Lodi Gyari, incarnate lama, Washington political strategist, and chief interlocutor with the authoritarian Communist regime in Beijing, moved so quickly between the spiritual realm and current-day politics, between vajrayana practice and political action, between his attempts to bring the Dalai Lama's message to the world, as well as to specific Chinese government leaders who influence the Communist Party.

For Lodi Gyari, like his boss the Dalai Lama, politics and spirituality emerge from the bodhisattva commitment to strive for enlightenment so that they may be beneficial to others. Social activism is one and the same with spiritual practice. There is no separation—so long as the commitment to benefit all beings never wavers. Bodhisattvas teach by example, not by simply quoting scripture. And of the many elements at that particular time that Lodi Gyari chose to employ for both his spiritual aims and political ends was a Wyoming Buddhist quietly chanting a sacred Buddhist text next to a pile of smoking juniper branches, sending plumes of dense white sweet-smelling smoke to the ethereal beings living atop a snowy mountain peak in eastern Tibet. It was a link in a matrix of interconnections, a small trigger in a larger mechanism trying to manifest the Dalai Lama's vision for real autonomy and religious freedom in Tibet through nonviolent means.

Lodi Gyari took me to his shrine, which occupies one entire wall of his living room, with the other three walls covered in traditionally brocaded scroll paintings of Buddhist deities. Rows of ancient Buddhist statues, some carried out on his back from Tibet when he fled at the age of nine, looked down from the shrine. A butter lamp flickered among the water offering bowls and the bowl of chocolate Hershey's Kisses arranged on the shrine. Lodi Gyari reached to the back of the top row of statues, behind a copper image of Padmasambhava, and removed a phurba about seven inches in length. As he unrolled it from an indigo-colored silken cloth, he told me how he used to carry this phurba to all of his meetings with prime ministers and presidents the world over, and also when he met with the Chinese. After the September 11, 2001, attacks in America, when airport security tightened, he chose not to wear it on his person, so for now it remains on his shrine.

"Whenever I used to feel physically ill, a kind of blackish crimson oil would discharge," he said in his matter-of-fact tone, pointing to the edge of the phurba. "This is a most sacred phurba, which I have a very strong connection to.

"It used to belong to Tertön Rangrik," he continued, speaking of the elder spiritual brother of Tertön Sogyal, who hailed from Lumorab Monastery in Nyarong. Tertön Rangrik was not only close to Tertön Sogyal but was Lodi Gyari's great-grandfather. As I bowed my head to the shrine, he placed the ancient phurba on the crown of my head in blessing and recited a quiet prayer.

> *All forms that appear are the wisdom deities,*
> *All sounds are mantra,*
> *All thoughts are the wisdom mind of Vajrakilaya,*
> *This whole existence is the play of thought-free perfection.*
> *In the confidence of this recognition,*
> *We vow to work always for the benefit of beings.*

WINTER 2004, YEAR OF THE WOOD MONKEY

Cave That Delights the Senses, Near the Jewel Cliff of Tsadra, Eastern Tibet

When Padmasambhava began to give the vajrayana teachings in Tibet in the eighth century, one of the first instructions to his "heart disciples" was the phurba practice of the deity Vajrakilaya. One cycle of the Vajrakilaya teach-ings that was hidden at that time is known as *The Razor of the Innermost Essence*. Nearly two volumes of Padmasambhava's instructions are found in *The Razor* treasure, which include complex rituals believed to remove obstacles to one's spiritual development, to thwart attack by enemy invaders, and importantly, to protect the Dalai Lama. In the autumn of 1895, Tertön Sogyal received the key to *The Razor* treasure at a remote cave in eastern Tibet. Within a de-cade after being written in liturgies, the rituals found within *The Razor* were employed in the nation's spiritual defense, and with it Tertön Sogyal became Tibet's Tantric Defense Minister.

In the first months of 2004, Antonio, an Italian scholar with whom I had traveled across Tibet on numerous occasions, and I were in the vicinity where Tertön Sogyal had received the key for *The Razor*. Antonio and I had met years before while we both were traveling near Serthar, and after a month of grueling travel from Golok to Lhasa—where on two occasions, we had to get out of our transport and hike a wide detour around the police check posts undetected, before returning to the main road to hitch another ride—we became close friends. His pensive personality checked my emotional flares. My gregarious manner brought him out of his sometimes somber moods. We both thrived on trekking to remote hermitages in the deep of winter, as much as we took pleasure in making coffee before dawn. And in the evening, wrapped in our sleeping bags with woolly hats pulled low, we would take out our pens to journal both the sadness of political injustices in Tibet and the joy of our pilgrimages. We each understood the other's needs, and we relied on each other, which is essential as travel partners on the Tibetan Plateau.

Antonio and I met up with Wangchen, the contemporary treasure revealer from Golok whom I had traveled with earlier in Dzachukha. We planned a pilgrimage to Tertön Sogyal's treasure site of *The Razor* near the Jewel Cliff of Tsadra. The evening before we departed on horseback, Wangchen spoke to us about pilgrimage and the mind.

Sitting in a Sichuanese spicy noodle café, Wangchen explained that the Tibetan term for pilgrimage is *nekor*; *ne* meaning "abode" or "sacred place" and *kor* meaning "to encircle" or "circumambulate." Outwardly, nekor may be a journey to a frozen crag, across windswept plains to solitary hermitages, or around mountain peaks, the home of enlightened deities and past saints. It pushes the limits of one's endurance, strains the physical senses, and tests one's resolve to walk on sacred ground. But that is only the outer journey.

Wangchen had literally walked the talk. He'd prostrated himself to Lhasa from Nangchen in eastern Tibet—a journey of a thousand miles, which is roughly equal in distance and similar in mountain terrain from the Rocky Mountains of Wyoming to the coast of California. Facing west toward the Potala Palace in Lhasa, Wangchen placed his hands together in prayer, touched his forehead, neck, and heart area, and then bent forward and lay prone on the ground with his hands outstretched and his forehead touching the earth. Standing upright, he would take three steps forward, the length of his body, and then drop down again for another prostration. During each prostration, Wangchen brought his teacher to mind, recited the mantra his master had empowered him to recite, and rested in the pure awareness of his actions. Mud-covered, enacting this repetitive gesture of pure devotion of body, speech, and mind thousands of times a day, for more than nine months, straight to Lhasa—Wangchen accomplished this feat on two different occasions, leaving a callus on his forehead the size of a quarter.

"When you truly experience the meaning of pilgrimage, you will see the dirt you are treading on as a sacred abode," Wangchen told us. "The outer, physical pilgrimage is but a support, a container, for the spiritual practitioner who journeys to the innermost essence of their own mind.

"This is the pilgrimage mind without concepts, without thinking—a mind that is indeed resting in the open spaciousness of wisdom."

Sitting back in the noodle café's plastic chair as a Jackie Chan kung fu movie blared on the television, Wangchen might as well have been on a teaching throne.

"Free from distraction, each step around the mountain leaves the grasping mind in the dust; each prostration on the ground keeps us pointed toward our inner wisdom; each icy breath is another concept that is frozen in midair and dissolves into the day; and each prayer is a proclamation of the all-pervasive truth of interdependence."

We traveled on horseback and by foot south from Derge, heading toward Palpung Monastery and on to *The Razor* treasure site at the Jewel Cliff of Tsadra. We crossed four inhospitable sixteen-thousand-foot mountain passes, navigated pine-dense valleys, and traversed high-altitude glens. Local herders let us camp next to their yak-dung-pasted huts, and we offered almonds and cashews in exchange for hops porridge thickened with yak butter. Nearly every day, the high cirrus clouds whisking into the shape of a mare's tail suggested snow later in the afternoon. By evening, hunkering down in our sleeping bags with a hot drink in hand, I consistently found a sense of exhausted satisfaction. *Free from distraction, each step around the mountain leaves the grasping mind in the dust,* I recalled as I went to sleep.

As we walked the Tsadra pilgrimage circuit an hour from the monastery, we found wooden panels staked in the ground with written instructions for the pilgrim to recite specific prayers or mantras, invoke particular deities, or make offerings meant to be effective—an interactive booklet, carved with devotion, to assist the pilgrim's transformation. With muddy boots, we stepped over orange and green moss-covered scree and around willow trees, then, at an exposed rock face, Wangchen stopped us to offer a glimpse of his blissful reality.

"See those five rivers flowing below us," Wangchen pointed out. "And look how these five ridgelines surround us—we are standing in the heart center of a massive lotus flower."

On the south side of Jewel Cliff, Tertön Sogyal's biography told us, was the Cave That Delights the Senses—the cave where Tertön Sogyal received the key for *The Razor* treasure. I had brought a few pages of the biography, which held cryptic suggestions and descriptions of the cave for which we were searching. Wangchen kept the pages securely at his chest under his thick sheepskin coat, pulling them out to consult occasionally as a kind of esoteric Lonely Planet guidebook.

We found a fifty-year-old hermit on the mountainside who showed little interest in our arrival and even less when Antonio asked him to take us to the cave somewhere along the Jewel Cliff. It seemed impossible to find the cave through the thick juniper and rhododendron shrubs and granite crags. Pulling his skirt up to reveal his swelled ankles and bulging veins, a result of having sat still in his meditation box for decades, he could hardly walk. But, he said, if we had accumulated enough positive karma in our past lives, we would find what we were looking for regardless of his directions. A smiling Wangchen nodded. Antonio and I were not so convinced. We urged the hermit to at least send us in the right direction.

"Below the last cabin, go into the steep ravine, across the protectors' stream near the large boulder with one hundred and eighty cracks; up past the Lady Yeshe Tsogyal's Cavern with the large thorny bush, you will see a row of tall pine trees that recite mantra in the wind. Walk in the direction in which the sound of mantra begins in the trees and you will come upon a greenish boulder with a self-emanating image of the protectress Drolma. Once you are at the rock, look up and you will see the Cave That Delights the Senses above you."

"Topography, botany, and a bit of pure vision." Antonio chuckled. "Classic Tibetan directions."

As we trekked down the ravine, heeding the inspired directions of the hermit, it seemed as though only marmots and hares had used the so-called route we were following. In the shadows of the narrow gorge, we came across two etched wood panels set among the birch trees:

Descend to what is known as Raven Valley. Wash in the nectar of
the stream while reciting wrathful mantra. Walk along the precipice to distinguish Virtue and Nonvirtue until Tiger's Lair Gorge.
It is here that a dakini manifests in the form of a leopard and
devours people of ill will. To other pilgrims, she growls or shows
frightening fangs; maintain awareness of the rising fear and this
will cleanse the obscuring effects of your past negative deeds.

We followed Wangchen in rinsing our mouths to purify our speech and
rubbed our eyes with the blessed water. He instructed us in the appropriate
mantra to recite.

The second faded sign farther on told us:

... don't be intimidated by terrifying things such as narrow
passages, rain, wind, densely forested gorges, hungry animals,
lightning, or hail: Pray to your teacher, chosen deity, and dakinis and offer ritual cakes and libations to the mountain's lords
of the land and command their protection. Regard any fear and
anguish that arise in you just as you will the period between
your eventual death and rebirth; pray one-pointedly to be liberated at the moment between death and rebirth.

"Let your own fear of death sharply spur you to grasp the need to realize here and now the absolute state—the nature of mind. Don't try to understand this with your intellectual mind, but realize deeply in your heart!"
Wangchen blissfully said while staring into the sky.

I kept the instructions in my mind as we continued bushwhacking.
After passing the cracked rock, the speaking pine trees where Wangchen
heard the recitation of mantra, the wrathful bushes, and the rock that indeed
had an image of the deity Drolma seemingly growing out of it, we saw the
cave above us. Clinging to mossy bushes and short grass to pull ourselves up

the fifty-foot incline to the cliff wall, Wangchen said, "Padmasambhava will not allow us to fall."

An old hemp rope hung down from the last pilgrim who had dared to scale the cliff wall. We used the tattered rope for balance as we climbed the last twenty feet of nearly vertical rock.

The Cave That Delights the Senses turned out to be a ledge that was just large enough for three people, jutting precariously from the southerly end of the Jewel Cliff. Two griffon vultures circled by, wind whistling off their wings, as we caught our breath on the ledge. A slight overhang of gray-white rock arched above our heads. Wangchen pointed at thigh level to the door from which the treasure *The Razor* had been taken. An upside-down U-shaped portal, fifteen inches in height, was clearly visible, with silky vermilion dust seeping out around its edges. The portal was warm to the touch. Concentric circles of the dust spiraled into the center of the entrance, which Wangchen said was indication that more than one treasure had been taken from this location in the past. The vermilion powder was a blessing substance that still remained in the rock.

Tertön Sogyal and Jamgön Kongtrul had come to this ledge in the autumn of 1895. As they approached the location, red dust began flowing profusely from the edge of the door. It was the sign Tertön Sogyal needed. He raised his phurba in a threatening gesture, reminding the local spirits that he was a representative of Padmasambhava, then hurled a stone at the red-dust door. The earth shook as if the whole mountain were crumbling beneath their feet. A small aperture where the rock had hit opened and a fragrant smell burst forth like a rain of perfume. Tertön Sogyal plunged his hand into the opening of the granite rock and withdrew a statue of Padmasambhava, in a striding posture holding a phurba and dorje scepter. With the treasure door open, Jamgön Kongtrul stepped forward and took a golden scroll with a string of syllables, the mnemonic key to *The Razor*. It was from this scroll that Tertön Sogyal eventually decoded the Vajrakilaya rites and practices of *The Razor*.

The significance of *The Razor* treasure discovery for the Dalai Lama and Tibetan state cannot be overemphasized. In addition to guaranteeing the health and longevity of the XIII Dalai Lama, its practice would quell the internal strife in the Dalai Lama's court, as well as within the influential monasteries in Lhasa. Many of the leaders of these monasteries held senior posts in the Tibetan government. If *The Razor* rituals were carried out in the specified manner, including strategically protecting Lhasa by placing a phurba before the sacred Jowo Buddha statue in Jokhang Cathedral, then, as a prophecy within *The Razor* states:

> The Yellow Hat [Gelugpa] teachings will remain firm and not decline [and] in particular, the successive sovereign masters [the Dalai Lamas] will henceforth be assured uninterrupted life spans. The sovereign master named Thubten [Thubten Gyatso, the XIII Dalai Lama] will surely live to his sixtieth year. The vicious elemental spirits promoting internal conflict at Sera and Drepung [Monasteries in Lhasa], and promoting the inroads of foreign armies, will be subdued. The ruler will not face opposition from his subjects [and] Tibet will be at peace, and the ruler's command be strengthened. Of this there is not the slightest doubt!

As with all treasure revelations, the tertön himself must practice it for a period of time to reignite the blessing and power before it is spread. It would still be three years before Tertön Sogyal would offer *The Razor* to the principal individual whom it was meant to protect, the XIII Dalai Lama.

Wangchen began reciting prayers to Padmasambhava and Vajrakilaya on the cave ledge. Antonio fanned the embers below a burnt food offering of a barley flower and Milky Way chocolate bar, sending smoke into the late afternoon air for the local spirits who sustain themselves on such smells. We had bought two bottles of Pabst Blue Ribbon beer from a farmer the previous day to offer to the protectors of this area. As Wangchen chanted supplication prayers to the mountain spirits living in the trees and rocks, the rattling of his hand drum resounded down the valley, calling the ethereal beings to the cave. I filled a golden libation cup from the twenty-ounce beer bottle and tossed the fizzing alcohol into the air, and then filled and tossed again, and again, with each of Wangchen's offering prayers. As we continued offering and chanting in front of the treasure door, clouds rolled in on either side of us. With our concluding prayers came heavy snowflakes, as ravens took cover under wide pine branches.

"Frozen flowers falling from the sky; an auspicious sign that the protectors of Tertön Sogyal's treasures are pleased with our offering today." Wangchen nodded.

"This is the exact place Khenpo told you to come," Wangchen reminded me. "That was over five years ago when you were with him in the Larung Encampment. Feel extremely pleased that you have finally accomplished your teacher's instruction. Never, never leave your guru's instructions unfinished or incomplete."

I had visited three of the four places where Khenpo had told me to go on pilgrimage—Kalzang Monastery in Nyarong, Jokhang Cathedral in Lhasa, and this cave. Now, only the Nyagar Encampment in Golok remained.

"After I visit Nyagar, I think it might be the right time to stop traveling, stop the human rights work, and enter a multiyear meditation retreat," I said to Wangchen.

I had wanted to broach the subject with Wangchen in the previous days and the cave seemed an appropriate place to seek his advice. I was still angry when I worked in the political realm, I told him, feeling like I was losing spiritual ground.

"Who will be the object of your compassion if you are alone in a hut or cave?" Wangchen pointedly responded.

"Just like the warrior Tertön Sogyal, you must take your responsibilities seriously. You must not think you have the power to effect change with prayers only. Prayer is important—but when combined with wise action, prayers become manifest."

He then quoted the seventh-century Indian saint Shantideva:

Whatever joy there is in this world,
All comes from wanting others to be happy.
Whatever suffering there is in this world,
All comes from wanting oneself to be happy.

What need is there to say a whole lot more?
Buddhas work for the benefit of others,
Ordinary people work for the benefit of themselves,
And just look at the difference between them!

Pointing to my chest, Wangchen continued, "The protection phurba Khenpo gave you should remind you of this.

"Wielding this phurba means you work to destroy your self-cherishing and ego-grasping by working for the benefit of others. The more violence and anger in the world, the greater the responsibility of all those who follow this practice."

Pushing down on his own phurba in his belt, Wangchen began to stand up.

"Always remember, there is no Vajrakilaya, no Buddha, no Tertön Sogyal, if there are no suffering beings to be helped!"

Chapter 10

Trouble on the Path

1896, YEAR OF THE FIRE MONKEY

Lhasa, Central Tibet

The XIII Dalai Lama ascended the throne in 1895 and assumed control of Tibet's political reins. The Nechung Oracle issued a prophecy shortly afterward that Tertön Sogyal must return to the capital to bless the Tibetan leader with his latest treasure revelations. When the tertön returned to Lhasa, he conducted ceremonies to remove impediments to the ruler's long life, and specifically, to carry out the rituals in front of the Wish-fulfilling Jewel Guru Statue in Jokhang Cathedral. He did not, however, offer *The Razor* to the Dalai Lama. As with all treasure teachings, the tertön needs to completely decode and practice the rituals himself before passing them on to another. The Dalai Lama, and Tibet, had to wait for *The Razor*.

Tibet had not improved its relations with any of its neighbors since battling the British in 1888 on the southern border with Sikkim. British India, the Qing Dynasty in China, and Tsarist Russia were positioning themselves to control Tibet through treaties. These countries were ready to take advantage of Tibet's vulnerability in their greater effort to control Central Asia. Tibet ignored most communiqués from the British, and chose their own terms concerning when to communicate with Russia and the Qing. All the while, the British, Manchus, and Russians were negotiating trade and suzerainty treaties involving Tibet. Eventually, both British India and the Qing calculated that if Tibet would not come to the negotiating table on its own, they would force the issue militarily.

In the Tibetan worldview of the late nineteenth century, the ability of an enemy to wage successful warfare, such as the British did in 1888 and 1904, or later the Chinese, is understood to mean not that Tibet was necessarily a weak military force, but that its spiritual core was compromised.

"Sectarian rivalry between monasteries was a chronic disease. The use of money donated to monks for illicit activities was morally decadent. This behavior collectively weakened the power of the nation to guard against itself," Lodi Gyari once told me. "The treasures and prophecies that Padmasambhava concealed in the eighth century addressed the issue of a weakened nation-state at the end of the nineteenth century."

Tertön Sogyal's principal duty as a treasure revealer and representative of Padmasambhava at the end of the nineteenth century was to support the Dalai Lama in his effort to protect Buddhism and a cultural atmosphere meant to be of benefit to all beings. "Spiritual practice and social action came together in Tertön Sogyal," Lodi Gyari went on to say. "Though Tertön Sogyal was not political himself, much of his ritual activity and treasure revelations were expressly for political purposes. He consistently tried to support the Land of Snows as a conducive place to become enlightened."

Tertön Sogyal returned to eastern Tibet in January 1897. But the tertön's time in Kham was brief, as he was summoned back to Lhasa. While in eastern Tibet, Tertön Sogyal made sure to exchange teachings and empowerments with the elderly Jamgön Kongtrul, with whom he had revealed *The Razor* treasure. Tertön Sogyal also discovered a number of treasures in the summer of

1897, including a phurba known as the Life Force Phurba of the Dharma King. The Life Force Phurba was meant for the reigning Dharma King—the Dalai Lama—so that its full effectiveness to pacify conflict could be utilized.

Tertön Sogyal took a less traveled southerly route back to Lhasa through the area of Kongpo on the advice of the Nechung Oracle, using horses provided by the Office of the Tibetan High Commissioner in Nyarong. At his campsites in the lush forests, Tertön Sogyal took time to decode additional liturgies of *The Razor,* writing them down in his own hand or dictating them to Kongtrul's scribe, who was traveling with the group. Along the banks of the Three Cliff Lake, Tertön Sogyal called upon the Protectress of Mantras and the local guardians to assist him.

The smoke rising from the smoldering juniper reflected in the deep green waters of the lake and then blew northward to the mountain deities. Local guardians soon delivered a treasure to Tertön Sogyal's hands, which included a prophecy entitled *Garland of Sunlight* that Padmasambhava had originally given to King Trisong Detsen. The prophecy told of additional methods to repel harmful demon spirits. Part of the prophecy called for the construction of various temples on the Tibetan Plateau. These temples were believed to ward off demons who invite military incursions that are bent on destroying the Buddhist teachings in Tibet. Additionally, the prophecy warned that if the temples were not built at the specified time, "then immediately afterward the Tibetan ruler and Bodhisattva incarnation [the Dalai Lama] will be killed by the Chinese and the life spans of kings and ministers both Chinese and Tibetan will become short." If, on the other hand, the temples were built, "law will be established and invaders repulsed, and the sun of happiness will shine in Tibet for a long time to come."

Tertön Sogyal arrived in Lhasa for the fourth time in 1898, his penultimate visit to the capital. He offered the Life Force Phurba, as well as the *Garland of Sunlight* prophecy, to which the Dalai Lama listened intently and then ordered that every detail be attended to straight away, including the strategically placed temples. Preparations were made for Tertön Sogyal to bestow upon the Dalai Lama *The Razor* phurba teachings. It took more than a month of empowerment ceremonies and complex explanations. Both the Dalai Lama's personal monastery of Namgyal and the temple of the State Oracle began the practice of *The Razor*. Woodblocks were carved so that texts could be distributed to initiated yogis.

The morning after *The Razor* empowerments, the Dalai Lama experienced a vivid dream in which he found himself before the palace of Padmasambhava, where two celestial beings met him, singing prophetic verses that referred to the empowerment he had just received. The celestial beings told the Dalai Lama that if he performed specific ritual offerings according to *The Razor*, the three poisons—desire, anger, and ignorance—would be eradicated and profound spiritual realizations would unfold.

Nevertheless, threats to the Tibetan nation and dangers to the Dalai Lama's life persisted. Indeed, the foreign menaces that were intent on driving the Dalai Lama from his home were coalescing and gathering strength. But Tibet's internal dark forces would strike first.

January 1899, Year of the Earth Pig

Lhasa, Central Tibet

In the Year of the Wood Sheep in 1895, Regent Demo of Tengyeling stepped aside when the Dalai Lama was enthroned as the spiritual and political ruler of Tibet. Demo had held the influential regency for nearly a decade, looking after not only the Dalai Lama's spiritual education, but indeed the country's political affairs during a challenging period. Demo was the head of Tengyeling Monastery, and its estate was the largest in Lhasa. Given the regent's prestigious position, his monastery and estate increased its already substantial wealth. When the Dalai Lama ascended the throne, many at Tengyeling Monastery were not pleased with their regency's loss of political and economic power. In particular, Norbu Tsering, Demo's nephew and manager of the estates, was most upset at the sudden reduction in Tengyeling's political clout.

The wealth of Tengyeling in the late 1800s was testament to Nephew Norbu's proficiency in the worldly ways of banking and real estate. He not only employed astute financial skills, but he also relied heavily on vajrayana practitioners to perform wealth rituals. But now, Tengyeling's influence was on the wane. Increasingly discontented with Tengyeling's lot, Nephew Norbu believed the regency would be returned to his uncle Demo if the Dalai Lama's life should come to a tragic end. Unable to gain access to anyone who worked with and served the Dalai Lama's food, Nephew Norbu felt that poisoning, a common political tool at the time, was not an option. On the occasion of hosting a ritual in their family home in the western part of Lhasa, Nephew Norbu hatched a plot with a black magician to take back the political control of Tibet for Tengyeling.

Nyagtrül hailed from Shayul village in Nyarong, close to Tertön Sogyal's home village, and had come to Lhasa with the tertön and his entourage in 1896. With Tertön Sogyal's engagement with the Dalai Lama and the Tibetan government, he had no time to look after the young man from Nyarong. Some said Nyagtrül was an incarnate lama, but as the saying goes in Nyarong, "A mother with a skilled tongue can turn any child into an important incarnate lama."

Given that Nyagtrül had arrived at Lhasa in Tertön Sogyal's company, many believed the young Nyarong lama was the tertön's protégé. Nyagtrül played on this impression, displaying minor spiritual accomplishments by reading people's thoughts in order to seduce aristocratic families to invite him into their homes. He rose quickly in aristocratic circles in Lhasa and began to fantasize about ruling over a monastic estate, where thousands of students bowed at his feet.

Just after dusk one evening Nyagtrül agreed to assist Nephew Norbu in a conspiracy to stop an unnamed person who had to be vanquished in order that Tengyeling might regain their power. Nyagtrül set about the task.

On thin rice paper, Nyagtrül sketched the body of a man, bound with chains at the neck and pinned down by two large scorpions. He drew an esoteric diagram encircling the scorpions and man. As he inscribed a spell on the paper, he slowly enunciated each syllable, meant to deplete an individual's life force. He strengthened the spell by visualizing scorpions and snakes and then dissolving the essence of their venom into the sketch. Burning poisonous plants on a small ember, Nyagtrül waved the diagram over the bluish smoke, saturating the paper with noxious fumes. At the conclusion of the ritual, Nyagtrül called Nephew Norbu into the dark chapel where the wicked diagram lay on the table. "Give me the name and birth year of the person," Nyagtrül said, coughing from the smoke. "I will write it on the paper."

"Thubten. Thubten Gyatso. Born in the Year of the Fire Rat."

Nyagtrül paused. The bamboo pen in his hand hovered above the paper as the butter lamp fizzled out.

"You want to kill the Dalai Lama?" Nyagtrül questioned.

"Do it. I've backed you this whole time in Lhasa, and provided you with whatever you wanted. Now, just write what I have told you!"

"You write it. I am not writing his name," Nyagtrül said, thrusting the pen toward Nephew Norbu.

"I don't care who is the scribe or the sorcerer. I just want what is due to me," Nephew Norbu rebutted, grabbing the pen and writing, "SUPPRESS THUBTEN GYATSO, BORN IN THE YEAR OF THE FIRE RAT."

Nyagtrül hung his head, not wanting to look at the Dalai Lama's name. As the ink dried on the agent of death, a slow grin pulled Nephew Norbu's eyes into an unblinking stare.

"I'll take it from here."

When the Dalai Lama was twenty-four years old, he began having recurring ominous dreams. Tertön Sogyal interpreted the dreams as life-threatening, and suggested rituals to drive away the source of the aggression. Years later in 1899, the Nechung Oracle began to warn of similar dangers to the Dalai Lama's life.

Before the Great Prayer festival in 1899, although the Nechung Oracle strongly warned of threats to the Dalai Lama and cautioned against his being in any public space, the ruler still took part in ceremonies at Jokhang Cathedral with Lhasa residents. Days after the ceremonies were complete, the Dalai Lama complained of dizziness and nausea. Potala Palace doctors were summoned to assess the Dalai Lama's weakened condition. That evening, the Medium of the Nechung Oracle went into a trance at his small temple on the outskirts of Lhasa. The medium's attending monks knew something serious was in the offing because the oracle rarely entered the medium outside of a formal ceremony. The message mentioned death, the Dalai Lama, and a pair of boots.

A messenger was dispatched by horse to the Potala with the warning in writing for the Dalai Lama. As soon as the oracle departed from the medium's body, the exhausted monk prepared to go to the Potala. A separate runner was sent in the dead of night to fetch Tertön Sogyal.

By the time Tertön Sogyal arrived at the Potala, the Dalai Lama's attendants and advisors were trying to decipher the meaning of the Nechung Oracle's enigmatic warning of spells, ill will, jealousy, and footwear. The group had made no headway as they spoke in hushed voices. All present bowed their heads and bent at the waist when a disturbed and tired Dalai Lama walked into the room.

"What, then, is this about?" the Dalai Lama questioned the group. His query was met with silence.

Turning toward Tertön Sogyal, the Tibetan ruler said, "Rinpoche, you must tell me!"

Tertön Sogyal, still breathing heavily from running up the many stone steps to the Potala Palace, asked chamber attendants if a new pair of boots had recently been given to the Dalai Lama. One of the attendants ran to retrieve the footwear in an adjacent room.

Some weeks before, Tertön Sogyal had visited ex-Regent Demo at Tengyeling Monastery. While at the monastery, Nephew Norbu had asked Tertön Sogyal to try on a pair of boots that, he was told, had recently been delivered from an expert boot maker. Tertön Sogyal did not know that Nephew Norbu had sewn the heinous diagram that Nyagtrül had empowered into the heel of one of the boots. Nephew Norbu wanted Tertön Sogyal to wear the boots, because when a powerful tantric practitioner like Tertön Sogyal stomped on the black magic diagram, it would kick-start the curse. As soon as Tertön Sogyal pulled on the knee-high boots, blood started to drip from his nose. He took the boots off at once and departed from Tengyeling. Failing to get Tertön Sogyal to wear the boots, Nephew Norbu arranged for the cursed boots to be offered to the Dalai Lama during a ceremony that took place during the Great Prayer festival two weeks before the Dalai Lama fell ill—precisely when the oracle had warned of dangers.

The sound of the scurrying steps of the chamber attendant grew louder in the hallway. Two separate pairs of boots had been given to the Dalai Lama during the offering ceremony and the attendant held both. Tertön Sogyal recognized the pair he had placed on his own feet a fortnight earlier. The Dalai Lama almost vomited simply being in close proximity to the boots.

"Give me those," Tertön Sogyal yelled while grabbing a single boot with both hands.

Tertön Sogyal's body surged with wrath. He tore at the boot's leather and brocade, slamming the sole to the floor until the dense insulation in the heel broke open. The cursed talisman was ejected from the boot's heel and fell to the cold flagstone floor. The Medium of the Nechung Oracle reached forward to grab it, but Tertön Sogyal pushed him away. Dark shadows slid around the room as wind pushed at the flames of the torches set in the walls. Holding the sorcerer's diagram in the air, Tertön Sogyal did not dare voice what he read inscribed.

"Show it to me," the Dalai Lama commanded.

Tertön Sogyal dutifully walked toward the ruler and held the diagram in the torchlight.

SUPPRESS THUBTEN GYATSO
BORN IN THE YEAR OF THE FIRE RAT

Dizzy and nauseated, the Dalai Lama squinted in anger, now realizing the gravity of the oracle's pronouncement.

"There may be more than one person in Lhasa with the name Thubten Gyatso," the Dalai Lama said. "But only one Thubten Gyatso was born in the Year of the Fire Rat. Find out who is trying to kill me."

Tengyeling was suspected. Soon, the ex-Regent Demo was summoned to the Potala on the pretext of an important ceremony. As the former regent was ultimately responsible for the activities of his monastic estate, Demo was implicated in the assassination plot, though his direct participation was never proved. Upon Demo's arrival, the ministers ordered him shackled and threw him into Shol Prison below the Potala Palace. Demo's nephew Norbu was also tricked into coming to the Potala on the pretense that he was to be honored for his exemplary service to the Tibetan government. It did not take long before Nephew Norbu admitted being the ringleader of the plot. The black magician Nyagtrül was identified as the sorcerer assassin and rounded up from the Barkhor neighborhood and dragged to prison. More than two dozen individuals from Tengyeling were sitting in the dungeon below the Potala Palace within a week. Lhasa was abuzz with word of the assassination attempt.

The Nechung Oracle directed the Tibetan government officials to unearth additional buried spells. Another oracle was also consulted who identified a hand-size scorpion from under a willow tree in the courtyard of the temple. When attendants examined the scorpion, they found shreds of the Dalai Lama's monastic robe in its belly, which was seen as particularly harmful and inauspicious, and evidence of further black magic.

Punishment for crimes in eighteenth- and nineteenth-century Tibet was severe; corporal and capital punishment were regularly employed. After a brief trial for treason, all the accused were found guilty and sentenced to death. Even though the Council of Ministers called for the conspirators from Tengyeling to pay with their lives, the Dalai Lama intervened and forbade the death sentences, a precursor to the Tibetan leader's abolishing capital punishment in his domain.

Demo was never seen again in Lhasa. Some say he was held under house arrest in Lhasa for the rest of his life. But it is more likely that Demo was exiled to the badlands of western Tibet. Nephew Norbu and others at Tengyeling were sentenced to life in prison. The Tibetan government confiscated Tengyeling's vast estates and most of the wealth was distributed to temples across the Tibetan Plateau. The Demo incarnation line was banned, and much of the records of his previous incarnations' activities were scrubbed from the history books. One hundred statues and gold from Tengyeling were offered to Tertön Sogyal to take on his return journey to Nyarong.

As for Nyagtrül, despite the Dalai Lama's commutation of the death penalty, as well as the Nechung Oracle's strong and repeated urgings not to kill the Nyarong sorcerer, he was dead soon after imprisonment. Some say he was treated so badly by guards that he stabbed himself and died; others say he was bound in a leather bag and beaten to death. Nyagtrül's body was buried at a location named the Black Mouth at Nyen, and a black stupa was built over the top in an attempt to suppress any further negative energy. If the revenge that the spirit of Nyagtrül soon sought for his treatment in prison offers any clues, his death had certainly been horrific.

Nyagtrül's malevolent spirit did not rest in peace. Escaping from beneath the black monument, Nyagtrül began haunting Lhasa and meddling in the Dalai Lama's affairs. The black stupa above Nyagtrül's corpse cracked whenever the Dalai Lama traveled the two miles between the Potala and the gardens of his estate, and the spirit stirred up dust and windstorms at the same time. On a number of occasions, the spirit tried to enter the Medium of the Nechung Oracle and confuse the government with misguided prophecies. The Dalai Lama soon called upon the individuals whom he thought capable of suppressing Nyagtrül's spirit—Tertön Rangrik and Tertön Sogyal.

Tertön Rangrik, Tertön Sogyal's elder spiritual brother, was not keen to get involved in the esoteric clash. Such battles could last months, and he was preparing to return to his home monastery in Nyarong. Though the Dalai Lama was commanding Tertön Rangrik to carry out rituals, the elderly Nyarong lama was having none of it. His only words to Tertön Sogyal were, "You brought him here," referring to how Nyagtrül had originally arrived in Lhasa. "You put him in the ground."

Tertön Sogyal threw himself into what amounted to a spiritual war, to liberate Nyagtrül's spirit from its harmful actions. Other lamas became involved, including one of the XIII Dalai Lama's tutors, who eventually died exhausted from his own efforts. It was not until early in 1902, after Tertön Sogyal had returned to eastern Tibet, when signs appeared that the subjuga-

tion and liberation were complete. But this was only the beginning of the
XIII Dalai Lama's troubles and his esoteric battle of survival.

MARCH 2004, YEAR OF THE WOOD MONKEY

New Delhi, India

"You have interviewed so many old lamas and yogis," a friend of mine said to
me in southern France, near Sogyal Rinpoche's retreat center. Five years into
my research of the life and teachings of Tertön Sogyal, she was questioning
why I continued to return to Tibet.

"You have received the empowerments and teachings of Tertön Sogyal's treasure teachings. Why don't you just stay in one place and meditate
upon all of it?"

Her words resonated with me.

"It is as if you leave the elephant at home and go and search for his
footsteps in the forest," she said. "After all, you have Tertön Sogyal right here
in Sogyal Rinpoche!"

Perhaps I had sought out friends who told me what I wanted to hear, that
I wanted to go into retreat. My human rights work was impacting my ability to
effectively evaluate any situation in Tibet. Just being on the plane from Bangkok
to Chengdu with a cabinful of Chinese made me increasingly angry. I blamed
all Chinese for the actions of their Communist government. I deplored this vit-
riolic streak that was developing in me but could not stop it. Wangchen had told
me not to retreat but rather to use the challenging situations in daily life as my
path, to meet head-on and liberate my negative emotions when I encountered
people I find difficult. I did not want to go against my teacher's recommenda-
tions, but I yearned for the secluded caves and hermitages in the Himalayas.

By 2004, there were new international dynamics that gave me reason to question if passing information about torture and abuses in Tibet to governmental and non-government people in Washington, D.C., could be effective. The moral ground on which the U.S. government stood when pressing China to change its draconian policies in Tibet was eroding as a consequence of the Bush-Cheney doctrine of rendition, secret prisons, and use of torture. Although I supported a tough stance against China's role in Tibet, public revelations of torture at Abu Ghraib and circumstances surrounding the detention of prisoners at Guantánamo were evoking in my mind images of Lhasa's notorious Drapchi Prison. American leaders were pursuing reckless and inhumane policies that were exacerbating tensions between the United States and Muslim nations. To the ears of many in the international community, including China, American moralizing or lecturing about freedom began to sound false.

I was confused about my own investment in the U.S. government as the great champion of universal human rights. On top of that, I remained profoundly sad at the death of Khenpo more than a year before. Thoughts clicked in my mind, one after another, as I sat down in April 2004 in a New Delhi hotel for breakfast with Lodi Gyari.

Before I said anything, Lodi Gyari told me, "Now is not the time to go into retreat," while unrolling a white napkin.

"You have a fire in your belly. It is burning, so there is no use in trying to sit on a meditation cushion. Use the drive to do good in the world, accumulate a lot of positive karma. Then, when it is time to do retreat in the future, obstacles in your meditation that would have otherwise arisen will have already been purified through your positive karma.

"Besides, Matteo," he concluded, "you haven't gone to all of the pilgrimage places of Tertön Sogyal that Khenpo told you to visit. You still have to go to Nyagar in Golok." By nightfall, I had heard the same message from the Dalai Lama himself.

Over the years I was often asked by my colleagues at the International

Campaign for Tibet to brief U.S. officials on the situation in Tibet. Typically this involved sharing photos I had taken and passing along personal testimony from Tibetans. I was described as the guy with "boots on the ground" who could deliver firsthand credible reporting. In late 2004, I was asked to join an ICT-sponsored delegation of congressional staff to Tibetan refugee communities in India and Nepal. Their schedule in Dharamsala included an audience with the Dalai Lama. As the delegation was taking leave from their meeting with the Dalai Lama, Lodi Gyari motioned me to come for a private conversation with the Dalai Lama. Though I had met the spiritual leader on other religious occasions, I was never introduced to the Dalai Lama in my role as a human rights monitor in his country. The half-dozen previous times at Buddhist teachings when I met the Dalai Lama, I found that questions in my mind seemed to dissolve into the spacious expanse that you can see in his eyes. This time, however, it was different—questions remained. Was I going to endanger anyone by returning to Tibet? Had my time for such social action run its course? Would it be better if I were in solitary meditation retreat?

Lodi Gyari told the Dalai Lama the kinds of secret documents and photographs I had taken out over the previous four years, highlighting the Larung Buddhist Encampment, and my devotion to Khenpo, Sogyal Rinpoche, and Tertön Sogyal. Lodi Gyari did not, however, pose any of my questions to the Dalai Lama.

The Dalai Lama's lower lip rose in a few moments of silent thought.

"Stay the course. Follow Khenpo Jikmé Phuntsok's advice. And tell the world what is happening inside Tibet."

The Dalai Lama's words merged in my mind with Wangchen's voice, *There is no Vajrakilaya, no Buddha, no Tertön Sogyal, if there are no suffering beings to be helped.*

I asked the Dalai Lama to bless the amulet box that I always carried with me as protection throughout Tibet. A photograph of Tertön Sogyal is placed in its small window opening, and I told the Dalai Lama of the amulet's contents, including the phurba that Khenpo had given me, and the hair and other sacred relics of Tertön Sogyal.

After gazing intensely at the image of Tertön Sogyal, the Dalai Lama closed his eyes in prayer and then placed the amulet on the crown of his own head in an act of benediction. Behind the charisma and iconic smile of this holy monk lay a masterful vajrayana practitioner, who is himself an adept of the Vajrakilaya practice revealed by Tertön Sogyal.

I bowed at the waist. He placed both his hands softly on my head and said a brief prayer. I looked up into the Dalai Lama's eyes. I did not want to leave his gaze, this place of safety and truth. Just as I became aware that I was staring at the Dalai Lama, a broad smile spread across his face as he reached forward and tugged on my goatee beard.

1901, Year of the Metal Ox

Lhasa, Central Tibet

Tertön Sogyal's return to Lhasa in 1901 was not only to be his last sojourn in central Tibet, but those two and half years proved critical to his main disciple, the XIII Dalai Lama.

Upon his arrival, Tertön Sogyal took up his usual residence in Jokhang Cathedral. After some weeks, the Dalai Lama summoned him to his court in the Potala Palace.

"I was told you have a crystal tube containing a treasure teaching known as *Dispelling Flaws in Interdependence*, and that the rites specifically avert inauspicious circumstances in this day and age."

"Indeed, Kundun," Tertön Sogyal said, addressing the Dalai Lama simply as "The Presence."

"This practice is extraordinary, like a wish-fulfilling jewel, powerful and with profound implications for Tibet and the whole world."

"Why haven't you revealed the teaching?"

"The treasure casket was delivered to me in a secret cave in eastern Tibet, but the right circumstances have not coalesced for me to open the crystal casket and reveal the teaching," the tertön admitted.

It is believed that one of the unique qualities of treasure teachings is that they are revealed at precisely the time when they are most needed. Padmasambhava's treasure teachings, such as *Dispelling Flaws in Interdependence* and *The Razor,* as well as his many prophecies that appeared at the end of the nineteenth and early twentieth century, were specifically catering to Tibet's troubled time. Padmasambhava's treasure teachings and prophecies are often an antidote to threats to spiritual practice, but they are not effective until they are put into practice. Tertön Sogyal explained to the Dalai Lama that he required the assistance of a spiritual friend, a woman in a foreign land, to unlock the teaching of *Dispelling Flaws in Interdependence* contained within the crystal. However, the predestined lady lived a great distance from the Land of Snows and spoke a different language. Tertön Sogyal said she was the missing link that was needed for him to bring forth the teaching.

"I can send anyone anywhere in the world. I can provide any funds that might be needed. I can find any translators for any language that you might require," the Dalai Lama affirmed.

"She lives across a vast body of water," Tertön Sogyal said.

At this time, a robust raven landed on the windowsill of the room, cawing as it bobbed its head. Tertön Sogyal recognized the importance of the raven's arrival; it was a manifestation of the Raven-Faced Dharma Protector, who was to act as a messenger.

The Dalai Lama and Tertön Sogyal composed a letter explaining the various threats facing the Tibetan people, and that they needed this woman's assistance to decode a spiritual treasure. Affixing their seals on the letter and its translation into English, the Dalai Lama included a diamond pendant in the envelope. Tying the small package with a blessed cord, they placed it on the raven's neck. Tertön Sogyal described to the raven exactly the features of the building where the letter was to be delivered and explained that he might have to escort the woman back to Lhasa. The raven took flight westward.

Three months after the raven had been sent on his mission, on the twenty-fifth day of the lunar month, the black bird returned. The Dalai Lama and Tertön Sogyal were performing an offering ritual to Padmasambhava in the Potala when the messenger landed on the windowsill. Disheveled from the long journey, with broken feathers, the raven was exhausted.

The Dalai Lama and Tertön Sogyal continued chanting prayers to Padmasambhava and to the protector deities of the treasure teachings, while the attending monks provided the bird with blessed water and took a small locket from the raven's neck. The locket that the roaming raven had brought back was waved over smoldering juniper smoke for cleansing and then placed upon a silver tray.

The attendants placed the tray before the Dalai Lama and Tertön Sogyal. They found a small envelope inside the locket and when the tertön opened it, an exquisite perfume filled the room. Inside they found thin golden fibers tied in three delicate knots. The Dalai Lama and Tertön Sogyal had never seen such exquisite golden strands in their lives.

There was also a letter written in a language they did not understand. A group of translators were summoned by the Dalai Lama and waited in an adjacent room. In no time at all, they found a monk proficient in English.

I took a vow many lifetimes before to benefit all beings, and
to serve both of you, my teachers from past lives. Now, in this life

I have been born on land with great oceans on either side. At present, it is not possible for me to travel to the Land of the Snows. For the sake of an auspicious connection with the tertön and to assist him in revealing in writing the treasure teaching placed in his mind-stream by Guru Padmasambhava, please accept, in my stead, a lock of my hair.

She signed the letter saying that she prayed that they would meet again in the future.

Setting the crystal tube containing the treasure teaching of *Dispelling Flaws in Interdependence* on the silver tray, Tertön Sogyal gently laid the woman's golden hair across it. As he began to pray to the protector deities, the crystal rocked back and forth on the tray. A small aperture began to open in the crystal under the golden hair and an edge of textured parchment appeared. Tertön Sogyal extracted the small piece of yellow paper from the crystal. Written on the tiny scroll were mystical syllables—a mnemonic trailmarker leading the tertön back to the time when Padmasambhava hid the teaching in his own mind-stream. As soon as he saw the dakini script, the teaching flowed through Tertön Sogyal's mind.

Within two days, while making fervent prayers and consumed with joy, Tertön Sogyal decoded hundreds of folios containing spiritual practices and advice for *Dispelling Flaws in Interdependence*. Deciphering a treasure teaching of that length in only a few days without any errors was an extraordinary feat. Tertön Sogyal bestowed the empowerments and reading transmission on the Dalai Lama.

1903, YEAR OF THE WATER HARE

Lhasa, Central Tibet

The political threats to Tibet at the beginning of the twentieth century were a continuation of the geopolitical struggle between the Russian and British empires for supremacy in Central Asia. The Great Game had closed in on all fronts for the Tibetans. Russia had been expanding its territory. By the time the Trans-Siberian Railway was complete, Britain was worried that Russia might extend her reach into Tibet, and eventually India. Britain, on the other hand, had consolidated colonial control in the Indian foothills in Ladakh, Sikkim, and Bhutan. Tibet maintained its isolationist foreign policy. Britain, China, and Russia continued to negotiate trade and governing agreements about Tibet, but without Tibetan representation. In the summer of 1901, one of the assistant tutors of the Dalai Lama, a Buryatian scholar known as Dorjieff, had gone to Russia carrying a letter of greeting to the tsar from the Dalai Lama. This raised considerable suspicion that the Dalai Lama was courting Russia to oppose Britain and China. The fear of invasion by three different countries was growing more real every day.

In the fourth month of the Water Hare Year of 1903, after having received ritual and meditation instruction from Tertön Sogyal and others, the Dalai Lama entered a multiyear meditation retreat to practice *The Razor* phurba practices, among other rites. Shortly thereafter, Tertön Sogyal left on pilgrimage through central Tibet, revealing treasure teachings and practicing esoteric rituals in a continuous attempt to strengthen the Tibetan nation spiritually and to repel the British army.

British India had long been trying to communicate directly with the

Dalai Lama. Now, with the Tibetan leader in closed retreat, the letters that the British sent to Lhasa were returned unopened. Even if the Dalai Lama had not been in retreat, it is unlikely he would have responded to any communiqués from Britain. In July 1903, the British regiment led by Major Francis Younghusband crossed the Indo-Tibetan frontier without resistance. Within a month, Britain had increased her force to eight thousand men and marched northward. Younghusband finally encountered armed Tibetan resistance only a few days' ride from Lhasa. Much of the ragtag Tibetan army brandished lances, bows and arrows, and amulets believed to protect them from bullets. They were brutally massacred by Britain's troops, even as the Tibetans were retreating, much to the chagrin of many in London who still thought Younghusband was leading a trade mission.

News of the carnage quickly made its way back to the Tibetan government. The Nechung Oracle had been delivering regular pronouncements that the Dalai Lama should break his retreat and flee to Mongolia. Tibet's Cabinet of Ministers concurred with the oracle's direction and advised the Dalai Lama to leave immediately for Ulan Bator.

In the first days of August 1904, British forces marched into Lhasa. Had the Dalai Lama been in the Potala he would have had a bird's-eye view of the impressive khaki-clad legion marching through the West Gate, just below the Potala Palace. But to the dismay of Younghusband and the British, they still had no Tibetan leader with whom to negotiate. A few days prior, under the cover of night, the Dalai Lama had fled northeast to Mongolia.

Less than a month before the British entered Lhasa, Tertön Sogyal had been called to the Potala. Touching foreheads in a sign of mutual devotion and reverence, the Dalai Lama told Tertön Sogyal he must leave Lhasa. There was nothing more for the tertön to do; the battle for the life force of his country was going to take him elsewhere. Tertön Sogyal and Dalai Lama were never to meet face to face again, at least not in that incarnation.

Part IV

If we serve sentient beings by engaging in political activities with a spiritual orientation, we are actually following the bodhisattva's way of life.

THE XIV DALAI LAMA

Chapter 11

Wielding the Phurba

North and Central America

Soon after I met the Dalai Lama in Delhi, I was asked by the International Campaign for Tibet to help compile a report for the United Nations' rapporteur on torture. I revisited the anguish of the farmer who was hung from rafters, and the monk who was left in complete darkness in solitary confinement for weeks, and the man who was beaten into submission to confess a crime he had not committed. My notes from an interview with a nun in Lhasa told me, "When we were in solitary confinement, we were whipped with the policemen's leather belts. Before they dragged us into the cells, I watched my two friends shocked by electric batons in their vaginas." She had spoken with a stuttering voice, not wanting to say that she, too, had endured the same sexual abuse. I watched again the videotape of the man whose head jerked uncontrollably from beatings in Drapchi Prison; his crime was shouting, "Long Live the Dalai Lama." I found references in notebooks of inhumane treatment of political prisoners: how they were tied to trees overnight during the dead of winter; how they were made to stand erect in the searing sun for many hours and beaten if they moved; and how rubber and metal objects were used for thrashings. I remembered what Ming, the policewoman, had told me of other techniques of brutality. Writing the report did not give me, as the work once had, strength to battle against China's injustice; instead, feeling that change was slow to come, if at all, I began to sink into depression, dispirited that no one may ever act on these stories.

What I felt paled in comparison to what Tibetans in Tibet live with, which made it more difficult to admit that I was in a downward spiral psychologically. I needed a break. My friends in Washington and Colorado saw me as an adventurous human rights worker who flowed easily between the dusty world of the Tibetan highlands and the lobbies and hallways of the U.S. government, drinking butter tea with Khampa nomads with as much ease as I would drink a gin and tonic in a senator's Georgetown home.

Appearances are deceiving and I was not well. I found myself striking out with cynical comments. I ran away again—this time to a surfing village in Central America.

I accepted a long-standing invitation from a college friend, Nichole, to visit Costa Rica. Like me, Nichole had become an expatriate after university. She'd decided to homestead on the sparsely populated southwestern coast of Costa Rica, eventually developing a diving camp and eco-resort, accessible only by boat. I landed in Costa Rica with only a satchel and sandals, though Nichole could see the heavy baggage in my mind. When we arrived at our Puerto Viejo bungalow on the southeastern border with Panama, I hung my Tertön Sogyal amulet on the wall. Our time was punctuated by long stretches of silence. Nichole allowed my heart to settle, as I lay in hammocks below the palm trees and meditated in the jungle.

During our walks together in ocean spray, I began to recount my experiences. It was an emotional roller coaster, reliving my journey with saints in Tibet, and my resentment of the Chinese Communist Party. One moment I spoke of the inspiration of pilgrimage through the wild valleys of Nyarong and sacred temples of Lhasa, and the next moment I recalled the suffering of the herders and city folk who dwell there today. I told Nichole of receiving holy relics and blessed substances on the same day I was given reports from a monk's brother of his brutal beatings in prison.

Mao Zedong stressed if you repeat a lie enough times it will become thought of as truth. The Chinese government's persistence in saying that Tibet has always been part of China, and that there is social and religious freedom today in Tibet, is false. Long before Mao, one of China's venerated philosophers, Confucius, believed that before one could govern in a just and correct manner, governments "must rectify the names" and the stories of the past and present. Confucius said, "If names aren't rectified, speech doesn't follow reality. If speech doesn't follow from reality, endeavors never come to fruition. If endeavors never come to fruition, then ritual and music cannot flourish. If ritual and music cannot flourish, punishments don't fit the crime. If punishments don't fit the crime, people can't put their hands and feet anywhere without losing them." Nichole just listened.

When I see television footage of officials from Western governments, including my own, exchanging niceties with Chinese officials, I am stunned by the hypocrisy of diplomacy. Should a Chinese government agreement on environmental, economic, or security issues hold up to scrutiny by Western diplomats when its assurances on Tibetan issues are proven false? Should the U.S. government pledge to work toward a positive and cooperative U.S.-China relationship when the head of the Communist Party in Tibet says the Dalai Lama "has the face of a man and the heart of a beast," or calls him "a wolf in monk's robes" who promotes rape, murder, and child cannibalism, and who even proclaims the Tibetan leader to be the single greatest threat to the unity of the Chinese nation?

One evening Nichole asked why I needed to shed light on the stories from Tibet—why not Burma or the Middle East or even about the

Shoshone or Lakota peoples from our home state of Wyoming? "I feel a responsibility to reciprocate the generosity that my Buddhist teachers have shown me, again and again, through the wisdom they offer," I said. Though nearly all of my Tibetan Buddhist teachers live in exile, if Tibetan Buddhism survives only outside of Tibet, then eventually it will lose its very foundation.

One early morning after a week in Costa Rica, I walked to the ocean just down from our bungalow. I sat quietly on the sand, the sun's first rays stretching across the vast expanse of water. Finishing my meditation session, I waded into the morning tide to float and relax while staring into the blue above. My ears were below the water and I could hear my own breath lengthening, feeling lighter than I had in many years. The previous days in the care of Nichole had loosened the grip that was pulling me into depression. I was feeling a new beginning as I floated weightless in the sea.

My tranquil state was broken when a wave crashed over me. I began to tread water and I discovered that I had been pulled a few hundred yards away from the beach. Had I been raised swimming in the ocean rather than hiking in the mountains, I would have known that I only needed to swim perpendicular to the riptide that had pulled me out to escape its strong current. Instead, I fought against the undercurrent, precisely what one is meant not to do, which sapped my energy.

Waves arched and pushed me underwater as I was dragged farther out to sea. I yelled for help but the beach was deserted. When a large wave hit me, I swallowed water and plunged again into the churning salt water, certain I would drown. Another wave crested, I took in more water, gasping for air. Pushed under, I heard Sogyal Rinpoche's voice: "How will your mind be when you die?"

I struggled to the surface, and Sogyal Rinpoche's calm voice came again. "How will your mind be when you die?"

If there is one thing I know about the natural world from being raised in Wyoming, nature does not discriminate. I was at death's edge and I was going to drown in the Caribbean Sea.

"How will your mind be when you die?"

Again, a wave hit. When I surfaced, I heard another voice.

"Grab this."

I tried to grasp the edge of a surfboard just as another wave pounded me, but I missed the board and sank. In the dark gray bubbles, swallowing more salt water, I could see a person's legs a short distance away. But I had no physical strength. There was no sound and I felt my body begin to lighten.

My head bobbed up one last time and I took hold of the waxy board. With the last bit of life force I held on until the surfer hoisted me out of the water with one arm. He navigated us back to the beach. I heard the skidding of the board on sand. He rolled me onto the beach, where I felt warmth on my shoulders. I vomited and fell into a state of semiconscious shock, still halfway in the tunnel of death.

"How will your mind be when you die?"

When I came to and my vision cleared from the haze, the surfer was sitting next to me. I heard myself asking him where I was.

"That was a close one. Don't swim on this beach, *amico*," he said with an Italian accent. *Am I in Italy? Where is Sogyal Rinpoche?*

"You are fine now. My name is Marco. See you around."

He left before I could thank him. Time was moving in fits and starts.

My mind was clouded. Still half-afraid of breathing in salt water, my eyes bloodshot and swollen, I stumbled back to the bungalow where Nichole was just then returning with an armful of fruit from the morning market. I collapsed, mumbling something about drowning.

When I awoke an hour later my answer to Sogyal Rinpoche's question was clear: If death came at this moment, my mind would be fearful of what was next. After a decade of wandering around Tibet, Nepal, and India seeking to stabilize my mind in meditation, and attempting to realize deeply the impermanent nature of life, when the test came, I had failed.

As the day progressed, the frightful taste of death subsided and was replaced with a growing sense of joy. Everything—from the mango slices to the smiling face in the street to the warmth of the sun—was sharp, vivid, and in a constant state of appearing and dissolving. The arc of the seagull, the morning dew, Nichole holding my hand, all was fleeting. The past became a waning echo; the future behind the moon, and the present accessed through open, vivid awareness. Tasting death, I walked through the Costa Rican village transformed.

I wanted to find Marco. I had another small protection phurba in my amulet that had been blessed by the Dalai Lama and I wanted to give it to him.

At the end of a jungle path, Nichole and I found Marco playing his saxophone in a house on stilts that he had built himself almost a decade earlier.

"You look a lot better now than you did this morning," he said, giving me a hug. "We lost someone last year right where you almost drowned. It is a powerful riptide that all the locals know."

When I took the phurba out that was tied to a red blessing cord, it was as if Marco knew exactly what I was thinking. He put it around his neck and said that I need not say anything.

"I know you would do the same for me, brother, and that makes the world all right. Now, let's go have a beer to celebrate the day."

I left Costa Rica a few days later, feeling as though I had broken out of a cocoon of anxiety. Nichole kissed me good-bye, knowing I was not going to come back. I was ready to return to Tibet.

WINTER 1903, YEAR OF THE WATER HARE

Nyarong, Eastern Tibet

The Dalai Lama fled to Mongolia and Tertön Sogyal to Nyarong. Some Tibetans will say that the phurba practices ensured that Younghusband's British forces only stayed in Lhasa for a month and were unable to secure a meaningful trade deal. Some have gone so far to attribute Younghusband's late conversion to modern mysticism as a result of the ritual bombardment of phurbas directed at him; he did in fact found the World Congress of Faiths after his return to Britain. Whatever the case may be, the invasion of British forces into Lhasa prompted the Qing government to consolidate control in eastern Tibet to keep from losing ground to the British or Russians. Even before Younghusband's march into Lhasa, the Qing were positioning their troops in eastern Tibet with the intent of establishing forceful rule over the tribal chiefs and monasteries.

When Tertön Sogyal returned to Nyarong in the winter of 1903, he walked directly into the emerging battlefront between the Qing military and eastern Tibetan tribal warriors. Thousands of Qing troops were stationed in Litang, poised to begin the first-ever planned population transfer of Chinese migrants into Tibet, as well as the initial mining of the area's rich mineral deposits. It was common knowledge that if Litang was secured, the Qing army would turn north and move into Nyarong. Tibetans needed the likes of the Nyarong chieftain Amgon, whom the Lhasa government had killed more than five decades earlier, to contain the Qing as prophecies had indicated he would. Now they were left exposed.

Over the next year and a half, while Tertön Sogyal stayed in residence at Kalzang Monastery, troubled locals and tribal chiefs from Litang and Batang came to see him, telling of atrocities being committed by the Chinese troops. The Qing were looting the grain stores as well as carting off the gold and copper statues of Buddha in Dondrupling Monastery. There were imperial pronouncements restricting the number of monks who could stay in the monasteries, and orders for monks to leave monasteries to work as farmers instead. Opposition by monastic leaders led to armed conflict. Monks attempting to negotiate with the Chinese were beheaded on the spot. Within four years, during the time the Chinese troops marched from Batang to Lhasa, they had beheaded thousands of Tibetans, which earned the commanding general the infamous nickname Butcher Chao.

For Tertön Sogyal, the destruction of the state would have been fatal for Buddhism in Tibet. As part of his efforts to repel the invaders, he completed the consecration of a small temple complex, as well as a strategically placed stupa at Deer Horn Junction. While musk deer, blue sheep, and the Himalayan pheasants roamed the small forests of Kalzang Monastery, feeding on the barley cakes the monks placed outside following daily rituals, the suffering and screams of war to the south could almost be heard. Tertön Sogyal remained in retreat.

In the spring of 1905, Tibetan monks and farmers in Litang rose in armed rebellion against Butcher Chao's armies. Though they were initially successful, by the summer, additional Qing reinforcements from Chengdu arrived with German-made rifles and crushed the Tibetan resistance, razing one of the largest monasteries in Batang and killing thousands. Additional forces moved into Gyalthang farther to the south, and many defenseless monasteries met a similar fate. The brutal accounts of destruction and beheading continued to reach Tertön Sogyal from those fleeing the fighting.

NOVEMBER 2005, YEAR OF THE WOOD BIRD

Crystal Rock Hermitage, Padma, Eastern Tibet

Soon after I returned to Asia from Costa Rica, I traveled to Crystal Rock Hermitage to see Wangchen, the treasure revealer whom I had traveled with in Dzachukha and to the Jewel Cliff of Tsadra. The previous year, Wangchen had given me the directions to his hermitage; a four- or five-day bus ride from Chengdu to Padma; a couple hours of hitchhiking on old logging roads, and "where the road crosses a river by a stupa, get out and walk in the direction where the sun rises over the mountain pass."

"Come during the ninth month of the Wood Bird Year," he said, as I calculated the date on a Western calendar. That was as specific as he'd be.

Wangchen's wife welcomed me as I arrived on foot at the hermitage. With storm clouds approaching, she sent her two young children outside to collect yak dung for the fire in the cabin. She showed me to my sleeping quarters and poured me a cup of butter tea. I would not see Wangchen for a day, as he was completing a silent retreat in a nearby cave.

Just weeks before my arrival at Crystal Rock Hermitage, I had received reports from Lhasa about a monk who had committed suicide following weeks of intense Communist Party "Patriotic Education" sessions in Drepung Monastery. Half a dozen monks had been arrested after they refused to denounce the Dalai Lama in the same political indoctrination sessions. Though it was a joy to see Wangchen again, I could not contain my ill will toward the new Communist Party chief, Zhang Qingli, in Lhasa. I blamed him for the monk's suicide. Wangchen allowed me to vent about that, how the railroad to Lhasa was nothing more than China's colonialist tool, and how free trade was not liberalizing China politically, but rather emboldening and enriching the Communist regime. His thumb rolled his prayer beads as I spoke.

Wangchen shook his head; perhaps as much at the injustices as at the degree to which it disturbed the mind of one to whom he had given extensive meditation instruction on remaining in a state of equanimity. As I continued to express similar frustration at the lack of any tangible progress in recent negotiations between the Chinese government and the Dalai Lama's representatives, Wangchen encouraged me "to think more than just thirty years backward and forward. The ripening effect for positive efforts to blossom requires much patience."

Wangchen ended the evening early. As he was leaving, I remembered a phurba from Kathmandu in my pack that I had brought to offer to him, and presented it wrapped in a white scarf. Accepting it, he told me, "Now is the time for you to learn to wield the phurba. If you can't help yourself, then you can't help others," Wangchen declared. "Tomorrow morning, come to my room. And bring your anger with you."

I walked to my cabin with a storm in the distance. Sitting upright in bed with a flickering candle nearby, I concluded my evening meditation. In these formal meditation sessions, thoughts would evaporate upon arising, like mist hitting sunlight. I could remain simply aware in that pregnant vastness between the end of one thought and before the next one began. That awareness would seem to expand beyond time, into a space of vivid awareness of awareness itself.

When I was not sitting on my meditation cushion, when I was confronted with episodes of torture and unjust political situations, that spaciousness vanished. I lay awake with angry thoughts darting through my mind.

One of the hermitage's acolytes pushed my door open after I'd spent a few hours of sleeplessness. The young monk carried a shovel with hot coals and poured the embers into a large urn next to my bed. Stepping outside, he grabbed a blackened kettle, placed it on the coals, and, without a word, departed. My watch showed three thirty A.M. I took the monk's action as a wake-up call and concluded Wangchen wanted me at his cabin well before dawn.

Overnight the rain had turned to snow and the hillside was laced with moonlight as I walked to my teacher's cabin. Wrapped in a thick cloak, Wangchen did not move when I entered. I bowed three times and took a seat in the small space between his meditation box and the wooden shrine. Practitioners such as Wangchen often sit in a box no bigger than four feet square all day and night meditating. Remaining in an upright posture throughout the hours of darkness, they make a vow not to lie prone for a week, a month, six months, even a lifetime for some yogis who view sleep merely as a distraction from meditation and prayer.

Wangchen had the phurba I had offered him hitched in his belt. As a committed Vajrakilaya practitioner, he always had one. I hoped Wangchen would show me how to use the phurba practice to subjugate another person— maybe the Communist Party chief himself. I wanted to go at him the way Uncle Apu had stabbed the effigy so many years before.

As ideas about the multiple uses of the phurba ritual bounced inside my mind, Wangchen was resting in meditation, eyes wide open and, as usual, never blinking. The enveloping silence pulled me into meditation as well. The engine of my thinking began to slow, leaving an increasingly lucid space, enhanced by the expanse of Wangchen's own undistracted mind.

"Should you wish to look into the essential nature of mind, do not fabricate or transform anything, and do not 'meditate,' but rather, allow whatever arises to be liberated by itself, without inviting or following after thoughts," Wangchen said in a monotone voice.

"By settling into the natural state, one's thoughts are liberated spontaneously. At all times and in every type of behavior, this alone is sufficient as the universal method of liberation. Sustaining this natural condition, there is not the slightest thing to be done. Just rest evenly in awareness."

Wangchen's words sliced away the animosity in my mind. Thoughts arose, but like waves, they returned to the vast and spacious ocean from where they came. And then there was just awareness.

"This thought-free awareness is where your phurba practice begins, and ends," Wangchen said, pulling me into his gaze.

"Now, when a pleasant thought begins to emerge in your mind, you try to claim it and grasp hold of it as 'mine,' don't you? Or, when an unpleasant thought forms, you try to push it away, no? This is where so much of your suffering begins—in the *thinking* about thoughts."

I had heard this kind of teaching before from Wangchen on how we are a slave to thinking, grasping and reifying thoughts, and being led away in distraction like an ox by a nose ring. That thoughts arise in the mind is to be expected, he explained, "but as a spiritual practitioner, it is what you do, or in this case, *don't do,* with the thoughts. This is a crucial point."

He told me to sit in meditation. I adjusted my crossed legs, straightened my spine, and exhaled.

"Zhang Qingli!" Wangchen said, catching me off guard.

My mind exploded into an angry haze on hearing the name of the Communist Party leader in Lhasa.

"Instead of acting from that swirling rage that is within you at this moment, recognize it just for what it is—a powerful force of energy—and let that force blaze your awareness, not your anger," Wangchen counseled.

"Don't concentrate on the object—that person in Lhasa—of your anger, but rather, rest in *that which knows*. Rest in the awareness itself, without any particular focus."

Wangchen repeatedly stoked my powerful emotions as we sat together. This was not a peaceful process. After some time, I found the resentful thoughts would arise just as they had before but they had no power to stick in my mind. When I did not think about the thoughts, the thought itself simply evaporated, leaving only thought-free awareness.

"Now, Matteo, you are liberating your anger," Wangchen said. "This is the real meaning and ultimate instruction for wielding the phurba. This is how you will speed toward enlightenment and, as a bodhisattva, bring benefit to others!"

WINTER 1906, YEAR OF THE FIRE HORSE

Nyarong, Eastern Tibet

Despite a blisteringly fierce winter, Butcher Chao's armies continued their advance westward toward Lhasa, and north through Nyarong. Young monks had recently returned to Kalzang Monastery from a scouting mission to witness the movement of Chao's troops. Though the mountainous terrain and deep valleys challenged the army and their mules, they were still moving quickly and were within a day's ride of Kalzang Monastery.

Late one afternoon, Tertön Sogyal's wife and son entered his retreat cabin. They had prepared the horses to leave Nyarong. Kalzang Monastery was in Butcher Chao's sights. They must flee immediately.

"Surely the troops would have wanted to bring the head of the Dalai Lama's teacher back to their general, Butcher Chao," Lodi Gyari told me at his office in Washington, D.C. "Not only was he of Nyarong blood, but as the Dalai Lama's teacher, Tertön Sogyal would have also been identified as part of the Tibetan government in Lhasa. This is the reason for the bounty on his head."

To disguise Tertön Sogyal as a wandering pilgrim, Pumo offered her husband a knitted hat to cover his trademark nest of dreadlocks and suggested that he wear a tattered cloak. This would get them through Upper Nyarong, where most villagers would recognize the tertön. She did not want even the locals to know that their spiritual father was departing the region—they would make a big processional of it and word would reach Butcher Chao.

Riding through the dark forests of Upper Nyarong, they continued northeast, where Tertön Sogyal had been a bandit as a young boy. They stopped briefly for tea and to let the horses rest until they were well beyond Butcher Chao's armies. At each stop, they would burn juniper incense and roast barley flour as an offering to the local protectors, requesting safe passage through their domain.

Tertön Sogyal's visions and his conversations with protective deities told of tumultuous times ahead for the Tibetan people, and indeed for the Dalai Lama. Now, with Butcher Chao's armies moving from Chengdu across southeastern Kham en route to Lhasa, the fifty-two-year-old tertön was awaiting signs from Padmasambhava to direct him. Should he return to Nyarong to contest Butcher Chao's military with mantra as he had done with the British? Should he return to Lhasa to conduct rituals on the Tibetan government's behalf even though the Dalai Lama was still in exile? Or were there treasures to be revealed in parts of Tibet where Tertön Sogyal had not yet ventured in this life?

In June 1908, the Dalai Lama left Mongolia and, after passing through northeastern Tibet and a holy mountain in China, arrived in Peking. He wanted to negotiate directly with the Qing emperor to stop Butcher Chao's armies from attacking monasteries in Litang, Nyarong, and Derge and to halt their advance on Lhasa. Although the Tibetan leader was received ceremonially by the Qing Imperial Court, and performed Buddhist rituals at their request, the emperor and empress were dismissive of the Dalai Lama's concerns. While the Dalai Lama was in residence at the Yellow Palace in Peking, both the emperor and empress unexpectedly died. Though he was called upon to conduct the funeral rites for both, he realized that the Qing could never be trusted and so decided to return to Tibet's capital even while Butcher Chao's armies were rampaging across southeastern Tibet.

While the Dalai Lama made the arduous overland trip to Lhasa, Tertön Sogyal was at Dzogchen Monastery in eastern Tibet. On the twenty-ninth day of the tenth month of the Earth Bird Year in 1909, Tertön Sogyal had a visionary conversation with the dakini known as the Awesome Protectress of eastern Tibet, in which he asked how to protect the Dalai Lama. She replied:

> *When efforts were made in accord with the Guru's [Padmasambhava's] prophecies,*
> *Some perverse individuals [Tibetans] turned favorable signs into the opposite*
> *And thus a firm foundation for the destruction of Tibet's well-being was laid.*
> *Even now, reliance on the deceptive allure of temporarily apparent endowments*
> *Like a dream, a shooting star, a flash of lightning, is misplaced.*
> *The strength of demonic forces of the dark side being ever greater,*
> *I see no chance for the well-being of the teachings and living beings in Tibet.*
> *The earlier affirmation of your own longevity,*
> *Through association with the "life-giving" dakini revelation*
> *And the Dispelling Flaws in Interdependence treasure revelation,*
> *Was the grace of Orgyen Padmasambhava.*
> *Now, given the conjunction of karma, immediate circumstances, and unfortunate*
> *   times,*
> *If you cannot succeed through the religious polity, there are no other means.*
> *Once the medicinal tree of physical health is spoiled at the root,*
> *The foliage of beneficial activity will automatically dry up.*
> *Even if you meet success through the religious polity,*
> *The signs should still be closely examined.*
> *If it is the final and unalterable conclusion, remain in equanimity,*
> *If not absolutely final, the means of improvement are those that I have prophesied.*
> *There is nothing more than those, and obstacles will still hinder success.*

Then, the dakini protectress spoke in a foreboding tone:

If you do not succeed, but fall between the jaws of two quarreling demons,
The prevalence of the teachings in Tibet will be snuffed out,
All the masters of the teachings will fade away like rainbows in the sky,
Nominal representatives will remain, but they will not serve the teachings,
With the extinguishing of the teachings, living beings will not know happiness,
The life span of masters who serve the teachings will dwindle in equal measure,
And some prominent individuals will attack the teachings.
The milk lake of the monastic assembly will be laced with black poison,
Some malign ones within your own ranks will go the way of the demons,
And as a result, even your worldly estate will be lost to demonic forces.

"Tertön Sogyal had told the government officials in Lhasa time and again that they needed to change their self-serving ways," Lodi Gyari once explained.

"Many of these officials were more concerned with their own welfare than for the Tibetan people they were meant to serve. Indeed, the demonic force of the dark side was pulling many Tibetan officials and monks away from genuinely serving Padmasambhava, the Dalai Lama, and Tibet.

"While not excusing the brutality of armies, Tertön Sogyal would not have felt that the British and Qing should be blamed completely for Tibet's weakened political standing," Lodi Gyari explained. "Younghusband and Butcher Chao were only taking advantage of a situation we ourselves had created. We cannot escape the consequence of our actions—this is karma at work."

After five years in exile the Dalai Lama returned to Lhasa in the Earth Bird Year in late 1909. His stay at the Potala would be brief. Butcher Chao was slicing west from Chamdo through pockets of the Tibetan army, while in Lhasa the Qing representative's troops were engaged in sporadic gun battles

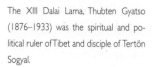

The XIII Dalai Lama, Thubten Gyatso (1876–1933) was the spiritual and political ruler of Tibet and disciple of Tertön Sogyal.

with Tibetans. Butcher Chao remained at his command post about a six days' ride from Lhasa.

The Nechung Oracle began insisting that the Dalai Lama flee Lhasa again. This time, as allegiances had changed, the oracle advised the Dalai Lama to seek political refuge to the south in British India. By early February 1910, Lhasa was surrounded by Butcher Chao's troops, with orders to bring the general the Dalai Lama's head. The night before the planned siege of Lhasa, the Tibetan leader and a small entourage left the Potala undetected and escaped into the night. The Qing army realized only the next day that the Dalai Lama had fled and were late in pursuit. While a small battalion of Tibetan militiamen stalled the Qing army, the Dalai Lama was able to cross the border into Darjeeling and was given protection by the British. The Dalai Lama began petitioning the British and Russians to support Tibet in the international geopolitical arena, though both governments refused in the face of possible backlash from the Qing court.

Butcher Chao's control of Lhasa marked the first time in Tibet's long history that a foreign force directly controlled the Tibetan capital. Yet their stay in Lhasa would be short-lived. Soon after the Dalai Lama arrived in India, revolution broke out across China. By November 1911, with the Republican Revolution in full force, Sun Yat-sen rose to lead the Nationalist Party as the Qing Dynasty quickly dissolved. Butcher Chao was recalled from his post and received the same treatment he had inflicted upon so many across the Tibetan Plateau—execution by beheading in Chengdu. With the Qing military command in disarray, central Tibet became free of foreign troops and the Dalai Lama returned to Lhasa in the Water Rat Year of 1912. Before the Dalai Lama entered Tibet, he issued a proclamation that cut all official ties with the Qing and declared Tibet an independent country, stating that even the ceremonial lama-patron relationship that had existed for centuries between Tibet and the dynasties in China had "faded like a rainbow in the sky."

I stood with Wangchen and his family under the brilliant sky in a crisp morning breeze. I had my backpack on and was saying farewell after ten days at the hermitage. I did not attempt to articulate my appreciation for the teachings; Wangchen had said many times the best way to thank him was to apply the instructions, not merely voice gratifying words. After Wangchen touched his forehead to mine he sent me away, saying, "The phurba that you gave me was a most auspicious gift. But know that the physical phurba is only a reminder for the sublime practice of liberating anger upon arising—this is now your practice, so persevere."

Chapter 12

Continuing the Pilgrimage

1910, Year of the Metal Dog

Golok, Eastern Tibet

Traveling east on horseback from Dzogchen Monastery, Tertön Sogyal, his wife, son, and attendants crossed into the Machu River watershed of southern Golok. They steered past the southern turnoff toward Kandze, where Butcher Chao's troops occupied Darge Monastery. The Nyarong clan continued northeast between highland spruce forests and rolling golden grasslands that extended as far as the eye could see. In the mountain meadows and along the river basins they passed herds of yaks numbering in the thousands, tended by teenage nomads. In the lowland watersheds, where barley terraces were planted, they passed no more than a dozen houses in any village. When the children and women of the villages saw Tertön Sogyal, they left their farming duties and ran after him, seeking his blessing.

This was the first time Tertön Sogyal had ventured to Golok, which rivaled Nyarong in its reputation for rough characters and dangerous bandits. Outsiders, including the few English and Russian explorers or Christian missionaries who tried to survey Golok in the late 1800s, were either forced to retreat by tribal scouts, or fell to the sword of one of the Golok tribes or roaming bandits. Even the monasteries needed protection. A common description of this area ran, "Golok is full of wolves, bandits, and monks, and most of the time you can't tell the difference between them." Tertön Sogyal secured the patronage of one of the four Golok chieftains; without such protection and support, he and his entourage would have been unable to stay in the region.

For the next fifteen years, Tertön Sogyal traveled widely among the Golok tribes. He made regular attempts to resolve regional water and territorial disputes between Tibetan tribal leaders and the Hui Muslim population of the northeastern frontier—sometimes through discussion but more often through ritually removing obstacles. He also intervened during various armed clashes between the Hui and Han Chinese, which resulted in his becoming a spiritual mentor for many non-Tibetans in the fertile valleys around Rebkong and northward toward Xining. In particular, Tertön Sogyal was hosted by Ma Qi, the reigning Muslim warlord east of Lake Kokonor, to perform blessings and give Buddhist discourses to the warlord's family. Eventually, Ma Qi's daughter studied at Tertön Sogyal's encampment, assisting the tertön in revealing treasure teachings.

It was through the patronage of such supporters that Tertön Sogyal was able to oversee the woodblock carving and printing of his collected treasure revelations, a time-consuming and costly venture, as paper and ink were not readily available. Tertön Sogyal's corpus of revealed spiritual practices and vajrayana rituals filled over seventeen volumes. His renown was such that not only were traditional scroll paintings commissioned of him, but he sat for a formal photograph portrait in Mandigar, and was recorded chanting in Xining. His response to this new technology was, "Indeed, that is a likeness of my face and of my voice, but for the true blessings to enter your heart, it is more important to have devotion."

The most enduring relationship Tertön Sogyal forged during this period was with Jamyang Khyentsé, an incarnation of the great Khyentsé Wangpo, who died in 1892. When Jamyang Khyentsé Chökyi Lodrö was twenty-eight years old, he sought out Tertön Sogyal because, "by the mere mention of the tertön's name an unfabricated devotion arose in his heart." Their meeting was but another chapter in their long reincarnation history; one that continues to this day. Tertön Sogyal empowered Jamyang Khyentsé as a lineage holder of all his treasure teachings, in particular that of *The Razor* and *Dispelling Flaws in Interdependence*. Jamyang Khyentsé would go on to become one of the most influential lamas from eastern Tibet. On the eve of the Communist invasion of eastern Tibet in 1947, Jamyang Khyentsé recognized a young boy from Lakar town as the reincarnation of Tertön Sogyal. Seven years later, before fleeing into exile, Jamyang Khyentsé took the boy to Lhasa, where they met the nineteen-year-old XIV Dalai Lama in the Potala Palace. That boy was Sogyal Rinpoche.

Sogyal Rinpoche and the XIV Dalai Lama's future relationship would play out not in the Himalayan region but rather in the West. Sogyal Rinpoche arrived in England to study comparative religion at Cambridge in 1971. He was one of the first lamas in the West, who, as the Dalai Lama has noted, saw working for the Tibetan cause as spiritual practice. Sogyal Rinpoche took the Dalai Lama's example as his guide—a reversal, in a sense, of their teacher-disciple relationship from their previous lives in the nineteenth century. Wherever he has been in the world, Sogyal Rinpoche has passed on the Dalai Lama's message of universal responsibility, compassion, and human values. So it was no coincidence that over the decades following the Dalai Lama's first visit to the West in 1973, which Sogyal Rinpoche helped organize, the Dalai Lama became the patron to Sogyal Rinpoche's organization, Rigpa, and guided its development. In August 2008, more than half a century after their first meeting in the Dalai Lama's temple in Lhasa, it was the Dalai Lama himself who consecrated Sogyal Rinpoche's Buddhist temple in southern France. With statues and images of Padmasambhava,

Tertön Sogyal, the XIII Dalai Lama, and other Buddhist saints and deities, I joined over a thousand others in the temple to listen to Sogyal Rinpoche address the Dalai Lama following the ceremonial opening of the temple. Sogyal Rinpoche said, "We think of this temple as a tribute to the Tibetan people, who have undergone so much in order to hand the Buddhist teachings down to the present day, and who are unable to practice them freely in their homeland. We know that by maintaining Tibet's Buddhist tradition here authentically in the West, we can play a part in preserving Tibetan culture and keeping its unique traditions alive."

In 1920, the Year of the Metal Monkey, one of Tertön Sogyal's students invited the tertön and his family to take up residence in a remote valley about a day and a half on horseback from Dodrupchen Monastery. The valley was a pristine environment for meditation. Financial support and protection was secured from a local Washul Kaduk tribal chief. Tertön Sogyal's wife encouraged him to become more sedentary because he was approaching his mid-sixties. After checking with various divinations, they decided to relocate to what would become known as the Nyagar Encampment, named after the Lama from Nyarong.

When they were packing their few belongings and loading the yaks for the move, a monk by the name of Namgyal, from Khamgon Monastery, arrived. Bowing before Tertön Sogyal, he offered a quill pen and paper and requested the tertön write a prayer for causing the Buddha's teachings to flourish.

Tertön Sogyal was just beginning to write when a vision of a red dakini appeared, and said, "Wait! When the time comes, I'll speak the prayer to you!" Tertön Sogyal placed the pen on the table and told the young Namgyal that he would have to wait for the prayer, and then invited the young monk to come to live with his family at Nyagar.

Black yak-hair tents were strapped to the sides of yaks, tent poles forming a V silhouette against the skyline, as the caravan moved out. Four mastiffs, used to protect the camp from bandits and wolves, barked and ran alongside the caravan. A dozen yogis and other meditators in the party walked with the caravan. Proceeding slowly on a white horse, after half a century of travel and pilgrimage, Tertön Sogyal knew he was riding to his last encampment. When they arrived at Nyagar, they lived in the tents until rock houses were constructed.

OCTOBER 2007, YEAR OF THE FIRE PIG

Golok, Eastern Tibet

Conditions had ripened in my life enabling me to make the pilgrimage to the last of the four places Khenpo had instructed me to go—the Nyagar Encampment in the region of Golok. After eight years, I was finally going to finish the task that Khenpo had mapped out. One of the bodyguards of the Dalai Lama in India once asked me how it was that I continued to go in and out of Tibet without arousing the suspicion of the Chinese; I pulled my collar down to show him that small meteorite phurba Khenpo had give me. The incredulous look on the security guard's face indicated that he relied on more conventional means to carry out his duties.

As I was stuffing my backpack with provisions for the journey to Golok, I realized the four places Khenpo had told me to go to paralleled the sacred sites the historical Buddha told his disciples to visit. Just before Shakyamuni Buddha passed into nirvana, he told his disciples they should be concerned most with applying his spiritual instructions, but, if they were to commemorate the Buddha's life and teachings, they should make pilgrimages to four places: Lumbini, in current-day Nepal, where the Buddha was born; the bodhi tree in Bodhgaya, where he attained enlightenment; the park where the Buddha first taught in Saranath; and Kushinagara, where the Buddha passed into nirvana. These four places correlated with the locations Khenpo had told me to visit; Kalzang Monastery was where Tertön Sogyal's spiritual birth occurred; the Cave That Delights the Senses is the location where Tertön Sogyal revealed the phurba teachings that removed obstacles to his own awakening; Lhasa was where Tertön Sogyal first taught the phurba practice to the Dalai Lama; and the Nyagar Encampment is the site where Tertön Sogyal passed into nirvana.

Southern Golok is as large as Texas and California combined, and I did not know the exact location of the Nyagar Encampment. Tertön Sogyal's biography offers few geographical hints; and in previous years, nobody in Nyarong or Lhasa had been able to tell me anything about the site of Nyagar. Leaving Chengdu, I traveled west along the same Sichuan road that I had come to know as well as any highway in Wyoming. Two noodle shop owners near the petrol stations before Dartsedo now even remembered my usual order of "fried garlic-broccoli noodles, no MSG."

Through the Erlan Shan jungle and mountain pass, which historically divided China and Tibet, we drove through the steep shaded valley of Dartsedo and then up two thousand feet of switchback highway, cresting onto the wide horizons of the Tibetan Plateau, and continued northwest into Golok. There are fewer roads in Golok than in other parts of eastern Tibet, which means fewer economic migrants from China's interior have settled here. But the wildness in the eyes of the Golok horseman must also contribute to Chinese newcomers' reticence in relocating to this harsh environment of high-altitude, windblown grassland.

In the county town, I inquired at different temples about the location of Nyagar. A few monks had heard of the place but did not know the site, and others had never heard the name. At one monastery, however, I was told that an elderly hermit named Dorje would likely know the location. The abbot, pleased that I was on pilgrimage and asking about Tertön Sogyal, dispatched a monk and the monastery's jeep to drive me to Dorje's hermitage. The steel-framed vehicle smelled of gas and oil and looked as though it had been rolled a time or two. We bounced along single-track dirt roads before heading directly up a river for two miles, water nearly as high as the top of the bald tires. Turning north, we continued across rolling arid grassland well above thirteen thousand feet. The driver, who was a monk, had his outer shawl tied around his waist like an oversize belt, and muscular arms exposed to the late morning chill. He knew his way around, as for generations his family had led mule and yak trains here loaded with brick tea protected from water by leather panniers. Nomads today still use this same route for quicker travel from Dartsedo into the interior of eastern Tibet's highlands that bend and rise into Golok's endless rolling hills, most of the time on motorcycles rather than horseback.

It turned out that Dorje was the reincarnation of the lama who had performed the cremation rites over Tertön Sogyal's body in 1926. From Dorje's southern-facing hermitage, he passes most of his days either reciting scriptures or resting his gaze in the cloudless sky. Like so many of the meditators whom I had met on my pilgrimage, his eyes are a gateway to a provocative immensity and reflect outwardly the spacious skylike quality within his being. And similarly to how other hermits reacted when I appeared unannounced, after months or years of silence, Dorje seemed to have almost expected my arrival, having told his attendant that morning to collect some sacred relics from behind lock and key so that he could place them inside a brocaded amulet, which he gave me when we met.

We made offerings of cabbages, apples, and a five-pound chunk of butter just purchased from a nomad camp we had driven past. Tea was poured and we began speaking about Tertön Sogyal. Two monks with windburned cheeks crouched by the woodstove, listening to Dorje's stories while feeding kindling to the fire.

The elderly lama told us that a few years before Tertön Sogyal passed away, the tertön revealed a number of precious stones with various protection mantras and symbols appearing in relief from the rocks' surface. These protection stones had been hidden by Padmasambhava and were meant for the Dalai Lama, though only one of them ever made it to the Tibetan leader, and that was after Tertön Sogyal had died.

"Tertön Sogyal never stopped working to care for the Dalai Lama and the Tibetan people," Dorje said matter-of-factly. "He was like the moon's reflection in the ocean, never staying in one place, rising and falling throughout his entire life—so much journeying to benefit others! And Tertön Sogyal's care continued through his reincarnations Khenpo Jikmé Phuntsok and Sogyal Rinpoche."

Dorje was too frail to travel to Nyagar, but he sent two monks with me to show me the route. After one last cup of butter tea, we jumped back into the jeep, poured three plastic 7UP bottles of gasoline into the tank, and headed toward Nyagar. We stopped the jeep where a landslide blocked the way; local nomads lent us horses so we could ride the last ten miles. Cool late-afternoon winds were blowing in a storm from the east and the sky was darkening. After two hours of riding and walking, we came over the last mountain pass before Nyagar. In the distance, on a grassy hillside, I saw the stone outlines of what was once Tertön Sogyal's encampment—a small temple, a stupa, and a dozen rock huts. Nothing remained except rubble, and I could not help but wonder why Khenpo had told me to come here. We prostrated in the direction of the distant encampment, and started a fire to make a smoke offering of juniper branches, paying respect to the land spirits and mountain deities before continuing to Nyagar.

Nyagar lay in ruins. Some of the rock houses had fallen down after Tertön Sogyal's death, but the temple and stupa had been torn down by hand, rock by rock, in the mid-1960s after the Communist takeover of Tibet. We meandered silently through the stones as if they were grave markers. Drizzle made the jade-green moss and orange lichen that covered most of what was once a temple shine. I walked alone higher on the south-facing slope and sat next to Tertön Sogyal's stone hut. After nearly a decade of pilgrimage in Tertön Sogyal's footsteps, I found myself sitting next to the rock remains of his home. The only life inside the broken walls was clumps of grass now being struck by droplets of rain.

The sting of impermanence pierced me again, but this time it did not morph into a joyful awareness as it had in Costa Rica. When I was so close to death in Costa Rica, Sogyal Rinpoche's voice questioned how my mind would be when I die. Here, on this barren mountainside, I realized the answer to that question. How I will be at the moment of my death is completely dependent upon my actions right now, in this present moment. And the avenue through which we can access the present moment is our own clear, pristine awareness, neither ensnared in the past nor worrying about the future. The spiritual path of the bodhisattva is about integrating whatever circumstances arise right now, whatever presents itself, not only the inspiring moments but the painful situations as well. The path of living in the world is about working to bring about the conditions for others to find security and contentment—and this can only occur when we are fully cognizant of reality as it presents itself, situation by situation. Both the spiritual and political paths are accomplished by maintaining clear awareness of what is clearly before us. And when death arrives, the only thing remaining to do is simply to merge one's present awareness with the clarity of mind itself, for the past is complete and the future unknowable. As I have heard Sogyal Rinpoche say many times, "the next life or the next breath, which will come first is uncertain." Even our teachers' bodies pass away—the Buddha, Tertön Sogyal, the XIII Dalai Lama, and Khenpo.

But the fact that everyone must die, and that we cannot say when death will occur, only reinforces why we must strive to maintain the state of awareness, and act compassionately from that space of pure knowing.

My balloon of expectations was completely punctured on that mountainside. There was no more sadness, no more spiritual yearning or political agenda. Sitting in the rain among the rock and rubble, there was no anticipation. I was not trying to accomplish anything. I was not encumbered by hope or immersed in fear. I released trying to accomplish, to win, or to overcome. And, the worry of losing, or being defeated, or getting caught by the Chinese, evaporated. In the absence of hope and fear, I felt the blessing of all my teachers descend with the falling rain.

The edge of the day's sunlight was fading over a distant mountain. My companions were walking toward me and I knew they were cold and wanted to go home. In the last moments amid the ruins, I had the overwhelming feeling that I needed to mark this sacred location, just as the Buddha's disciples marked the place where their teacher had passed into nirvana. Before we departed drenched down the valley, I vowed to build at Nyagar a new reliquary-stupa—a symbol of enlightenment—in honor of Tertön Sogyal and his life and teachings.

I spoke to the leaders of the local community and nearby monastery about the construction. We agreed upon the division of responsibility; mine to secure patronage and collect relics from different Tibetan lamas, and theirs to coordinate the local nomads and monks to build the structure. My first opportunity to secure sacred relics came in Washington in October 2007, just a few weeks after my return from Tibet; the Dalai Lama was in the U.S. capital to receive the Congressional Gold Medal. The day before the award ceremony, at a hotel in Georgetown, I spoke to the Tibetan leader about Tertön Sogyal and the stupa.

"I'm here to report back to you on my pilgrimage in Tertön Sogyal's footsteps," I said to his approving nod. I presented him with a photo album of all the sky-eyed yogis, meditating hermits, and scholarly abbots I had met in his homeland, as well as images of sacred peaks, holy grottoes, and consecrated lakes associated with Tertön Sogyal. There were photos of Tertön Sogyal's relics and treasures, including phurbas and statues. And I told him I intended to write a book about Tertön Sogyal.

"Tertön Sogyal was the great protector of the Tibetan nation," the Dalai Lama said, turning the pages slowly. "He was a most powerful master. A very rare master."

The last photographs of the book showed the remnants of the Nyagar Encampment. I pointed out the structures that had once been Tertön Sogyal's house and temple, and showed him where the new stupa would be constructed. I asked the Dalai Lama if it was possible to receive any relics from his collection in India to place inside the structure in Golok.

"Come to Dharamsala. I will give you a very blessed relic pill. You must place it inside for consecration. This pill was made from holy substances, and with power of meditation."

The timing worked well. I was already planning to be in Nepal the next February for a retreat with Abbot Namdrol, and after that I was to meet the Speaker of the U.S. House of Representatives, Nancy Pelosi, as well as a U.S. congressional delegation, in Dharamsala.

MARCH 2008, YEAR OF THE EARTH RAT

Dharamsala, North India

"These are not just protests," I stressed to Speaker Pelosi in Dharamsala when she asked me about the reports I was receiving from Tibet in the third week of March 2008. We were preparing to leave in the motorcade to the Dalai Lama's residence. "This is a full-scale uprising against Chinese rule on a scale we have not seen since the 1950s."

Just weeks before we traveled to India, the Tibetan Plateau had erupted in unrestrained demonstrations against the Chinese government. It began on March 10 on the forty-ninth anniversary of the Tibetan Uprising that preceded the Dalai Lama fleeing into exile. At a time when China was trying to project an image of harmony, with the Olympics in Beijing just five months away, the Chinese authorities were caught off guard. Thousands of Tibetans—from Lhasa to Kandze, from Xining to Chengdu, in Kirti, Labrang, Machu, Nyarong, and elsewhere—monks, nuns, nomads, poets, teachers, businessmen, and farmers spontaneously rose up to say that it is the Dalai Lama who represents their interests, not the Chinese state. This was an explosion of pent-up resentment fifty years in the making.

Throughout the spring of 2008, Tibetan protests spread like wildfire to every corner of the plateau. Nearly all of the some two hundred protests were peaceful, but a handful turned violent, most notably in Lhasa on March 14, when some Tibetans attacked Chinese migrants and burned their shops. Some Chinese died. The Chinese government quickly tried to represent all of the protests as a part of a violent riot, releasing video of looting and police cars on fire in Lhasa.

The authorities sealed off Tibet and enforced a news blackout except for state-run media, kicking out foreign journalists and cutting off Internet and cell phone service across the region. It was only a matter of time, despite the blackout, before we began receiving reports of the thousands of Tibetan detained, and cell phone images of unarmed monks and farmers shot dead while peacefully demonstrating, and cell phone videos of detained protestors being stomped on and beaten with batons by Chinese police in Lhasa. The overwhelming and brutal force with which China responded to the Tibetans' peaceful protests confirmed that the Chinese state retains no other means than force and intimidation with which to govern.

The sheer number of demonstrations and its unorganized yet unifying voice of protest clearly evidenced the failure of Beijing's decades-old policies in Tibet. Certainly two principal flashpoints for Tibetans' discontent has been their economic marginalization and the suppression of their Buddhist faith. But above all, what these protestors demonstrated was their unwavering devotion that they have in the Dalai Lama and their yearning for his return to their homeland. If the Chinese leadership believes that their profound crises in Tibet will pass after the Tibetan leader dies, then they are denying themselves the *only* opportunity to secure a durable resolution with their Tibet problem. Precisely because the Dalai Lama will pass away, time is now against the Chinese. If it is harmony the Chinese leadership is seeking in Tibet, then they will find it *only* in direct, face-to-face discussions with the Dalai Lama.

As the Dalai Lama greeted Speaker Pelosi along with her Republican and Democratic colleagues from the U.S. Congress, Lhasa was under curfew. I knew in eastern Tibet, Tibetan horsemen continued to ride across the grasslands in jubilant euphoria, publicly singing the Dalai Lama's long-life prayer, even while the Chinese paramilitary fanned across the wide plateau. The Dalai Lama called upon his Tibetan compatriots and the Chinese security forces to act nonviolently.

The Dalai Lama led the congressional delegation, surrounded by a bubble of armed American, Tibetan, and Indian security agents, into his residence through a throng of reporters and crowds of refugees waving Tibetan and American flags. I followed the delegation, having been brought to Dharamsala by the International Campaign for Tibet to help provide cultural and religious context to the visit of the Americans. Arriving in a small meeting room, the delegation took their seats as the Dalai Lama removed his flip-flops and sat cross-legged in an overstuffed chair. For an hour they discussed the situation in Tibet and his efforts to find a solution through dialogue with the Chinese government. The solidarity was heartening for me to see, even though it did not translate directly into alleviating the anguish inside Tibet. China's Ministry of Foreign Affairs was trying to convince the world that the Dalai Lama had instigated the riots and demonstrations in Tibet. When asked by one of the congressmen what he thought of China's charges against him, the Dalai Lama responded, "The Chinese government is demonizing me. On a personal level, as a Buddhist, this is good for my practice of increasing tolerance to others' views. But as the leader of the Tibetan people, I have the responsibility to say the Chinese are making baseless accusations."

As tea was served, I heard the drone of monks chanting in a chapel nearby. The Dalai Lama occasionally thumbed his prayer beads, seeming to join the monks for a moment of silent recitation. During a break in the meeting, I walked to the chapel. An old monk invited me in, where, before the group of twenty monks, with the elderly Khamtrul Rinpoche and the Medium of the Nechung Oracle presiding, a dozen phurbas were standing up-

The author and the XIV Dalai Lama, Tenzin Gyatso, at his residence in Dharamsala, India, in March 2008.

right on the shrine. Tertön Sogyal's phurba practice—*The Razor*—was being conducted on the instruction of the Dalai Lama in an attempt to quell the violence in Tibet. *Om Benza Kili Kilaya Hung Phet, Om Benza Kili Kilaya Hung Phet.*

Soon after Speaker Pelosi's motorcade departed, and the BBC, CNN, and other media crews dispersed, the Dalai Lama joined the twenty monks in the private chapel and presided over the phurba ritual. The Dalai Lama never loses sight of the ultimate goal—the cessation of suffering for all, including those in Beijing demonizing him, calling him "a devil in monk's robes."

I was given an aspirin-size sphere of condensed-powder relics from the Dalai Lama without ceremony that same day.

A month after I returned to America from Dharamsala, I received a message that the stupa in Golok was nearly complete. I could barely believe the news. It was miraculous, given that its construction must have taken place during the most serious part of the riots and ensuing crackdown. The message indicated that I should return to eastern Tibet as soon as possible and bring the final installment of relics to place inside the stupa. I telephoned Sogyal Rinpoche to tell him the news, as he had given his blessing, support, and a host of sacred relics to enshrine in the heart of the stupa.

China's security forces continued at their all-time high, as protests in different parts of Tibet continued. I doubted I should travel to the region. Golok, like the rest of the Tibetan Plateau, was under martial law. When I phoned two Chinese friends who had recently driven from Litang to Xining through Golok, they spoke of paramilitary presence in riot gear wherever they went, riot police checkpoints at intersections of cities and villages, and restricted travel. If I attempted to go to the stupa in Nyagar, my presence could endanger my Tibetan friends. While my motto over the last decade had been to "ask for forgiveness rather than permission" when traveling to restricted places in Tibet, this time I decided to check with a more informed source than my own bravado. I contacted Khamtrul Rinpoche—known for his mastery of divination—to ask him for insight.

"If I travel to Nyagar, is it safe for the Tibetans with whom I will have contact?"

A reply was quickly sent back, with an obstacle-removing prayer composed by Khamtrul Rinpoche for the venture.

"Go to Nyagar. Do no politics. Protect yourself by supplicating the Raven-Faced Dharma Protector."

WINTER 1926, FIRST MONTH OF THE YEAR OF THE FIRE TIGER

Nyagar Encampment, Golok, Eastern Tibet

Tertön Sogyal called his daughter-in-law to help him walk above the dozen stone huts at Nyagar. Sonam Drolma held the hand of the seventy-one-year-old tertön as they circumambulated mantra-carved stones on the north end of the encampment and then continued up the grassy knoll to take in the expansive view. Looking south and west on the hillside, the Ja Valley was deep and thick with pine and juniper forests. To the northwest, a single yak trail disappeared into the windswept pass that leads to Larung Valley. To the east, glacial water flowed from the peaks above the eight holy lakes of Dzongdün on the border of Aba. Tertön Sogyal's breath was labored but his eyes were clear and soft. They had recently returned from Nubzor Monastery, a day's ride away, where he had bestowed what would be his final tantric empowerments, *The Most Secret Wrathful Vajrakilaya* and *Dispelling Flaws in Interdependence*.

Among the wild animals that roamed around Nyagar, Tertön Sogyal sat quietly looking into the distance with his daughter-in-law by his side. After some time, he told her that he was going to die within a week, but that she should not despair.

"All that is born must die. I have done all that I could for the people of the Land of Snows.

"As for the twelve treasure teachings that remain unfinished, I will summon the protectors and they will return the treasure objects among the lakes and grottoes of all the places I have traveled throughout the Land of Snows. My future incarnations will return to find them."

A few days before Tertön Sogyal passed away, he called his wife into his room after morning rituals were complete. He handed her a piece of paper with a prayer and said, "I dreamed I was in the Crystal Cave of Padmasambhava last night when a dakini appeared and spoke this to me. Please be sure that young monk Namgyal receives a copy." Pumo looked down at the last prayer Tertön Sogyal wrote, touching it to her crown after reading.

Buddha, Dharma and Sangha, and the Lord of Shakyas, Shakyamuni Buddha
Avalokiteshvara, Manjushri, and Vajrapani, and Maitreya,
The sixteen Great Elder Teachers,
And Padmasambhava—
Through your power and through your truth,
May the lives of the teachers be secure!
May the spiritual community increase and dwell in harmony!
May all circumstances hostile to the Dharma be pacified!
May the activities of study and practice grow and spread!

"These words are the mother's last advice," Tertön Sogyal said, referring to the Protectress of Mantras, who had guided and assisted him throughout his life with prediction and prophecy. "There is still much more to this, and it will be explained, when the time is right."

On the tenth day of the first month of the Fire Tiger Year of 1926, Tertön Sogyal was helped by his attendant to sit upright in his bed and cross his legs in meditation posture, while his wife placed a wool blanket over his shoulders. A profound peace settled as he rested his hands on his knees and entered a deep stillness.

Khandro Pumo sat at his bedside. The great yogi was unmoving, in a profound state of meditation. His piercing eyes were at once gazing outwardly to the world with compassion, while inwardly abiding in the pristine clarity, resting in his own pure nature. As the mist rose and dissolved in the vast expanse of the morning sunlight, Tertön Sogyal exhaled his last breath.

Cumulus clouds were circling as we walked toward the mountain pass before the Nyagar Encampment. The motorbikes local nomads had loaned us coughed to a halt on the steep incline. For each three slow steps at seventeen thousand feet, I recited the prayer that Khamtrul Rinpoche had composed, asking the Raven-Faced Dharma Protector to assist, which concluded with the phrases, "May all obstacles be dispelled. May all positive circumstances increase. Swiftly perform the activities of protection I request of you." Despite the warnings in Chengdu that no foreigners would be allowed onto the plateau, and the many paramilitary check-posts and patrols of riot police in Dartsedo, Kandze, and elsewhere, we arrived at Nyagar without incident. This was the first time I had traveled without mishap: no flat tires, no multi-day engine delays, no check-post fiasco on the road.

Ascending the ridge, I looked down to what was no longer a barren hillside full of rubble, but rather what appeared to be a blossom on the mountainside. Just as a lotus flower blooms in the muck of a dirty pond, so, too, did this stupa rise in the swirling dark clouds of anger and aggression. Just weeks before, while the Chinese paramilitary was deploying and setting up their own camouflaged encampments with mounted automated weapons, the stones at Nyagar were being stacked into a shrine.

I paused on the crest above. The stupa was a sign of hope, and a reminder that we all have the promise to rise above our own anger and aggression and ignorance so that we may benefit others. Before walking down the mountainside to Nyagar, I prostrated to the stupa that represents for me enlightened action in all its forms—from phurba-wielding tantric deities to saints and yogis of the past; from my kind teachers today to all the swift and selfless compassionate activity that goes unnoticed each day in the world. Approaching the stupa, I was completing a nearly decadelong pilgrimage. The outer journey had been sketched by the life and travels of Tertön Sogyal. And through that sacred topography where I ricocheted between inspiration and sadness, meditative stillness and anger, an inner pilgrimage was born, a pathway that continually brought me back to where the vast potential for enlightened action abides, and is always present.

I do not claim to have benefited anyone along my pilgrimage or from my human rights work. All I can say is that I have tried to apply what my teachers have taught me, and that I have given voice to what I have witnessed. In politics, ultimately, there are no winners, for every politician will die and every government will fall—the wise, durable question is not if a political system will survive, but when will it fail? Because everything is impermanent, including politicians and their governments, we have a responsibility to effect change that will bring about the conditions right now for others to find contentment and happiness.

Accomplishing the spiritual path means doing what each of us needs to do for ourselves to bring about true and lasting contentment, beyond suffering. And accomplishing the path of social engagement means creating the conditions for others to find the same lasting satisfaction. These remain my commitments as I continue along the journey, the path of doing what is right and just, story by story, stone by stone. Following in the footsteps of the master, we return to the place before the journey begins—to that space of infinite possibility where the bodhisattva makes the commitment:

For as long as space exists
And sentient beings endure,
May I, too, remain,
To dispel the misery of the world.

I stood below the thirty-foot-tall stupa: square base, dome-shaped body from which a spire rose, crowned with a lunar and solar disk and finally a parasol. Buried directly underneath the structure was a pile of swords, knives, bullets, and two rifles. The entire stupa was made of rocks that had once been Nyagar's temple and stone houses. Monks were chanting auspicious hymns while placing wet juniper branches on a fire, offering incense to all the enlightened beings of the past, present, and future. Two nomad boys arrived bareback on palominos. They watched as I climbed up to the dome on a makeshift pole ladder tied together with hemp. A monk helped me open the heart-center of the stupa by removing a few stones. We set a golden-silk-wrapped container of relics inside, adding to the contents within—hundreds of volumes of sacred scriptures draped in brocade, statues of Buddha, Padmasambhava, and Vajrakilaya, mantra-infused medicines, and fragrant juniper powder. Replacing the stones to close the small portal to the relics, we sealed the substances within so that blessings may emanate outward for generations to come. Before climbing down the ladder, I placed a small wooden engraved sign by the portal with the name that Sogyal Rinpoche had bestowed upon the site—THE ENLIGHTENMENT STUPA OF TERTÖN SOGYAL, VICTORIOUS IN ALL DIRECTIONS.

Epilogue

During the construction of the Enlightenment Stupa of Tertön Sogyal, and while visiting hundreds of holy sites throughout Tibet, the Himalayas, and Southeast Asia over the last decade, I realized the importance of revitalizing sacred pilgrimage sites. In response to this need, in 2009 I founded Nekorpa, a nonprofit organization dedicated to the protection and conservation of pilgrimage sites throughout the world. Through restoration and maintenance, environmental stewardship, and the documentation of spiritual knowledge associated with the sites, along with publication of pilgrimage guides, I believe sacred sites are needed more than ever as places where individuals can cultivate compassion and deepen their spiritual practice to generate peace within themselves and their communities. I now serve on the Executive Council of the International Network of Engaged Buddhists, and on the board of directors of Rigpa Fellowship and the Conservancy for Tibetan Art and Culture. I continue to study under Sogyal Rinpoche and Abbot Namdrol Rinpoche, and remain dedicated to helping Lodi Gyari with his efforts to protect Tibet's unique Buddhist heritage.

I follow daily news from Tibet, including the aftermath of Tibetan protests against Chinese rule and the resounding call for the Dalai Lama's return that spread across Tibet in the spring of 2008. The protests of 2008 shook the Chinese Communist Party and its assumptions about Tibetans. Like most observers, I had hoped that Beijing would listen to the Tibetans' voices. Sadly this was not the case. The repressive and often violent response by Beijing to the peaceful protests was another missed opportunity to steer a different course after decades of failed policies. Despite intimidations, detentions and arrests, beatings, and even deaths, Tibetans have not abandoned their resolve to live according to their distinct Tibetan identity and are demonstrating a resurgence of faith in the Dalai Lama's leadership and Middle Way approach. Solidarity between Tibetans in and out of Tibet has been strengthened in this dark period. In an effort to find space to express their views, Tibetan intellectuals, writers, bloggers, poets, and environmentalists in Tibet and China have taken unprecedented risks to share their informed perspective. Reprisals by the authorities against these courageous individuals are taking place as you read this book.

China's Communist Party leaders continually underestimate the resilience of the Tibetans, which the prominent author Shogdung, who was detained in April 2010 for his writings, encapsulated when he wrote in *The Line Between Sky and Earth*, "Freedom is a hundred times, nay, a thousand times more valuable than my life." With such determined Tibetan spirit, now is the time for the Chinese government to resolve its Tibet problem with honest face-to-face discussions with the Dalai Lama. Time is against Beijing; the Dalai Lama is seventy-five years old. The Dalai Lama's vision of a harmonious society based upon mutual respect is not only good for Tibetans but ultimately for China and the Chinese people. May the Tibetans and Chinese find a way forward toward freedom and peaceful coexistence.

In Gratitude

I drew profound inspiration and counsel for my pilgrimage and for the writing of *In the Shadow of the Buddha* from a number of teachers to whom I pay homage with 1,008 prostrations—to His Holiness the Dalai Lama for exemplifying how a realized bodhisattva acts in the world; to Khenpo Jikmé Phuntsok for his protection and the phurba; to Sogyal Rinpoche for his continued blessing, love, and wisdom; to Lodi Gyari Rinpoche for his trust, encouragement, and exceptional support; to Abbot Namdrol Rinpoche for his sublime instructions; to Khamtrul Rinpoche for his advice and divinations; and to Wangchen for being a guide along the path in Tibet. All of these masters have brought the timeless wisdom of the Dharma, the person of Tertön Sogyal, and the spiritual lineage of Padmasambhava alive for me in different ways. I pray that *In the Shadow of the Buddha* may contribute, in some small way, to accomplishing the vision of all these masters, like a drop of virtue added to the vast ocean of their compassionate activity.

I deeply appreciate the many lamas, yogis, monks, and nuns who recounted the oral history of Tertön Sogyal and other mystics of the time, and am grateful for the protective rituals they performed on my behalf. These include Kyabjé Trulshik Rinpoche, the late Chagdud Rinpoche, the late Sherab Ozer Rinpoche and the late One-Eye Wangde of Kalzang, the late Amchi Chime of Lumorab, Tulku Thondup Rinpoche, Neten Chokling Rinpoche, the late Adeu Rinpoche, Tsikey Chokling Rinpoche, Dzigar Kongtrul Rinpoche, Orgyen Tobgyal Rinpoche, Chökyi Nyima Rinpoche, Rabjam Rinpoche, Tsoknyi Rinpoche, Arjia Rinpoche, Lama Zopa Rinpoche, Gelek Rinpoche, the Medium of the Nechung Oracle Thubten Ngodrup, Venerable Matthieu Ricard, Khenpo Gyurme Tsultrim of Shechen, the late Uncle Apu, Choyok Tashi of Namgyal, Mayumla Tsering Wangmo of Lakar, Ama Damchö of Bhutan, Lama Yonten of Lerab Ling, Ama Adhe, Ani Karin of Kopan, and the late Amdo Jampa. A handful of other lamas in Tibet have not been mentioned here, but to them, too, I offer my profound gratitude and prayers. May I soon repay the karmic debt I have amassed.

The auspicious prayers, presence, and boundless love of my wife, Monica Garry-Pistono, are a constant source of inspiration and ultimately brought this book to fruition, for which I am eternally grateful.

My mother, Francey Pistono, and James Hopkins read many drafts of this book and spent painstaking hours offering me insights—thank you for your dedication to this project. I am grateful to my father, Chico, and his wife, Sandy, and my brother, Mike, and sister-in-law Dominique, and the rest of my family who supported me even when it meant that I spent less time in Wyoming, Montana, and Colorado. Josh Elmore, Joseph Wagner, and Mark Rovner influenced my path in distinctive ways for which I am extremely appreciative. And to Marco Orlandelli, *grazie tante* for saving my life in Costa Rica.

A number of scholars have provided a consistent stream of astute insights and translations for me over the years. I am especially grateful to Patrick Gaffney, who offered extremely prudent guidance at various stages of the writing, and to Adam Pearcey, whose wise counsel and erudition I appreciate and admire. My travels with Antonio Terrone greatly enhanced my appreciation of contemporary tertöns. Sangye Khandro, Lama Chonam, Venerable Tenzin Jamchen (Sean Price) and Gyurme Avertin translated for me at important junctures when I was carrying out research and retreat practices at Yangleshö, and Venerable Lozang Zopa's assistance was crucial. And I learned a great deal from Matthew Akester in Kathmandu and Gen Pema Wangyal in Washington, D.C., the late E. Gene Smith, Daniel Goleman, and Erik Pema Kunsang all kindly advised me on how to present esoteric material and Tibetan history to a wide readership.

The spiritual kinship I have with everyone within Rigpa is a treasure without which I would not have entered the mandala of Tertön Sogyal's practices. I want to thank especially Joanne Baltad, Ane Damchö, Volker Dencks, Seth Dye, Pete Fry, Mauro De March, the late Ian Maxwell, Philip Philippou, Kimberly Poppe, Dominique Side, and Dhanphat Singh for their insights and support. I am a beneficiary of Lotsawa House's translations and Rigpa's extensive library of teachings on Tertön Sogyal terma practices, as well as the oral history of Tertön Sogyal's life as recounted by Dilgo Khyentsé Rinpoche and Nyoshul Khen Rinpoche. May Rigpa's beneficial activity flourish and increase further and further!

Readers who offered encouragement and constructive critiques of *In the Shadow of the Buddha*'s nascent narrative include Hubert Decleer, Judy Feldmann, Marni Kravitz, Ligaya Mishan, Michael Tweed, and the poet Gary Snyder, whose sagacious counsel came at precisely the right moment. Appreciation goes to Brian Tart, Amy Hertz, Jessica Horvath, Amanda Walker and the team at Dutton, Penguin Group, and Hay House in London; it has been a pleasure working with you. I am grateful to my literary agents in Washington, D.C., Gail Ross and Howard Yoon, who saw my story as a book the very moment they heard it. And I thank Jocelyn Slack for rendering the map of Tibet, and Robert Beer for the line drawing of the phurba.

To all the nuns and monks who offered hospitality, to the villagers and nomads who pointed me in the right direction, to the Khampa business-men and Hui Muslim truck drivers who picked me up when I was hitch-hiking; to the hermit scholars and dusty pilgrims who welcomed me on the path; and to the *nagma chang* maidens in Lhasa and fellow travelers, I remain indebted to your kindness.

Kathmandu is the city where I feel most at home and this has much to do with the friendship and hospitality of Frances Howland and the Maharajgang crew. Many others in Nepal contributed to *In the Shadow of the Buddha* with their insights over the last decade, including the Dalai Lama's former representatives in Nepal, Samdup Lhatse and Wangchuk Tsering, and their staff; and those with whom I spent time at the Tibetan Refugee Reception Center, including Konchok Chodak, Dorje Damdul, Dawa Drolma, Katrina Edwards, Gendun Rinchen, Thubten Shash-tri, Ganden Tashi, and Lumboom Tashi. Appreciation goes to Nedon, Norbu Zangpo, and the late Ang Phinjo Sherpa from the Khumbu, and to Amchi Dekyi Yangzom, who kept me healthy. Thanks for the insights of Judith Amtzis, Tamdin Dorje, Carroll Dunham, Mikiko Okuma, Marcia Schmidt, Chris Tomlinson, Lopon Sonam Tsewang, Roberto and Cicci Vitali, and to Ngakpa Rangbar for the phurbas. And for those with whom I communicated on human rights and refugee issues at the embassies of the United States and India, and the United Nation's High Commission for Refugees in Nepal, thanks for your action.

I thank Tenzin Geyche Tethong, Tenzin Taklha, Chhime Rigzing Chhoeky-apa, and Jamphel Lhundup of the Private Office of His Holiness the Dalai Lama in Dharamsala. I have gained key insights into *satyagraha* from Professor Samdhong Rinpoche, former chairman of the Kashag of the Central Tibetan Administration, and thanks also to Jigmey Namgyal. Tashi Tsering of Amnye Machen Institute provided suggestions for my research that were very helpful. Venerable Gyaltsen, Venerable Tenzin Choephel, and Phelgye Kelden from Nechung Monastery all helped me understand the connections Tertön Sogyal had with Tibet's State Oracle.

The board of directors and past and current staff of the International Campaign for Tibet (ICT) have been extremely helpful. In particular, I worked closely with John Ackerly, Mary Beth Markey, Bhuchung Tser-ing, Lesley Rich, Kelley Currie, Tsering Jampa, Kate Saunders, Van Ly, Tenzin Dhongthog, and Royce Priem—I admire their dedication to social justice and human rights, and thank them for their unflinching support. I am especially grateful to ICT's chairman, Richard Gere, for the confidence he has placed in me, and for writing the foreword to *In the Shadow of the Buddha*. I thank the former staff of the Tibet Informa-tion Network, and those with whom I communicated at the China and Nepal desks at Amnesty International in London. I am grateful to the Conservancy for Tibetan Art and Culture and the Smithsonian Center for Folklife and Cultural Heritage for the opportunity to work on the Smithsonian Institution's *Tibetan Culture Beyond the Land of Snows* program from 1998 to 2000.

I wish to respectfully acknowledge the Speaker of the U.S. House of Representatives, Nancy Pelosi, for her leadership on human rights in

China and Tibet and her senior policy advisor, Jonathan Stivers, for his steadfast attention to Tibetan issues. And I am proud to have known Wyoming's late senator Craig Thomas, whose support for the Dalai Lama and the Tibetans was demonstrated time and again in key legislation. I appreciate greatly the efforts of those U.S. congressional offices that made use of reports and photographs of human right abuses, as well as those individuals at the National Security Council in the administrations of President Bill Clinton and President George W. Bush, and the U.S. Department of State's Bureau for Democracy, Human Rights and Labor; Bureau for Population, Refugees and Migration; and Office of Chinese and Mongolian Affairs. The late Julia Taft, and Paula Dobriansky, former Special Coordinators for Tibetan Issues, and their staff, deserve special mention for their work.

I have benefited greatly from my communications with a number of writers, professors, and authorities on Tibet, China, India, the Himalayas, and Buddhism, including Robbie Barnett, Katia Buffetrille, Kathy Butler, Victor Chan, Sam Chapin, Brot Coburn, Michael Cohn, Suzette Cooke, Philip Denwood, David Germano, Jonathan Green, Steven Goodman, Pico Iyer, Sarah Jacoby, Greg Kruglack, Jonathan Lipman, Steve Marshall, Gaetano Maida, Gary McCue, Hemanta Mishra, Rebecca Novick, Chokyi Nyima (Richard Barron), the late Alexander Piatigorsky, Xiao Qiang, Ngawang Sangdrol, Jeremy Schmidt, Ron Schwartz, Tadeusz Skorupski, Heather Stoddard, Warren Smith, Robert Thurman, Gray Tuttle, Jeff Watts, Harry Wu, Sonam Zoksang, and Lhasa University alumni who will remain unnamed. I am also grateful to the University of Wyoming's Anthropology Department for my ethnographic training and the School for Oriental and African Studies at the University of London.

For support, advice, and inspiration while completing the manuscript, gratitude goes to Dawa-la and the Gyari family in the United States, India, and Japan, Nichole DuPont, Darren Fischer, Peter Gabriel, Daymond Hoffman and the crew in Haines, Gary Holthaus, Harsha Navaratne, Amanda Kiessel and everyone at the Islander Centre in Sri Lanka, Middle Path Travels in Delhi, Maura Moynihan, Karpo Pondi, Mollie Rodriquez, Rick Rogers, Lisa Schermerhorn, Josh Silver, Ajan Sulak Sivaraksa, John Wasson, Eric Weiner, Liz Welch, Kelly Welch, and Kate Yonkers. And for use of photographs, thanks to Heinz Nowotny, The Jacques Marchais Museum of Tibetan Art, and Venerable Matthieu Ricard.

Please note that respectful titles for teachers and lamas have sometimes been shortened for the benefit of a general audience—no lack of respect is intended. *In the Shadow of the Buddha* is above all an oral history. For all omissions and errors in my recounting of these inspiring and tragic stories that were offered by devoted and brave individuals, I take full responsibility.

Finally, but certainly not least, I want to honor the host of enlightened deities, the Protectress of Mantras and the Raven-Faced Dharma Protector, and all the local mountain and land guardians. With folded hands, I beg you to forgive my transgressions or any offense I may have caused! May your sphere of protection extend to all! And for accepting my offerings of *serkyem* and juniper smoke in exchange for a mudslide and accident-free pilgrimage, I thank you! *Lha gyal lo!*

Yangleshö, Nepal

May 27, 2010

In the fourth month of the Metal Tiger Year

Dramatis Personae

Amgon (d. 1865) Chieftain from Tertön Sogyal's home region of Nyarong who forcibly overtook much of eastern Tibet. Perpetuated a culture of violence in Nyarong. Also known as Gönpo Namgyal.

Chao Erfeng (1845–1911) Infamous general of the late Qing era who led military campaigns throughout eastern Tibet. His troops eventually reached Lhasa in 1910. His brutal character and methods of execution earned him the nickname Butcher Chao.

Dakini (Tib: Khandro) Female embodiment of enlightened energy, sometimes manifesting in a human form while other times as ethereal beings who protect Buddhist teachings, including treasure teachings.

Dalai Lama, XIII, Thubten Gyatso (1876–1933) Spiritual and political ruler of Tibet and disciple of Tertön Sogyal.

Dalai Lama, XIV, Tenzin Gyatso (b. 1935) Reincarnation of the XIII Dalai Lama, ruled Tibet until 1959 and currently resides in exile in northern India.

Dargye Father of Tertön Sogyal.

Demo (1855–1899) Regent of Tibet before the XIII Dalai Lama's accession to power in 1895; implicated by association in an assassination plot of the XIII Dalai Lama; full name is Ngawang Lobsang Trinley Rabgye.

Dodrup, Hermit (1865–1926) Scholar-meditator with whom Tertön Sogyal collaborated on composing philosophical treatises; full name is Dodrupchen Jikmé Tenpé Nyima.

Dorje Dudjom (eighth century) Minister of religion in Tibet, close disciple of Padmasambhava, accomplished Vajrakilaya practitioner, and previous incarnation of Tertön Sogyal.

Jamyang Khyentsé, or **Jamyang Khyentsé Chökyi Lodrö** (1893–1959) Reincarnation of Jamyang Khyentsé Wangpo, and student of Tertön Sogyal. Recognized Sogyal Rinpoche as the reincarnation of Tertön Sogyal.

Khamtrul Rinpoche (b. 1927) Close associate of the XIV Dalai Lama in Dharamsala, lineage holder of Tertön Sogyal and Nyala Pema Duddul treasure teachings, ritual master at Namgyal Monastery, and historian.

Khenpo, or **Khenpo Jikmé Phuntsok** (1933–2004) One of the two simultaneous reincarnations of Tertön Sogyal, and the author's charismatic teacher, who remained in Tibet throughout the Cultural Revolution, and later in the 1980s established the Larung Buddhist Encampment. Teacher of the current XIV Dalai Lama and Abbot Namdrol.

Khyentsé, or **Jamyang Khyentsé Wangpo** (1820–1892) Eminent master and tertön of the nineteenth century and teacher of Tertön Sogyal.

Lerab Lingpa Another name for Tertön Sogyal.

Lodi Gyari (b. 1949) Special Envoy of His Holiness the Dalai Lama and chief interlocutor with the Chinese government, mentor to the author, who resides outside of Washington, D.C. Reincarnation of Khenpo Aten Jampal Dewé Nyima. Also known as Gyari Gyaltsen.

Lungtok, Master (1829–1902) Meditation master whom Tertön Sogyal studied with and served for nearly a decade; full name was Nyoshul Lungtok Tenpai Nyima.

Ma Qi (1869–1931) Prominent Hui Muslim warlord in northeast Tibet who maintained cordial relationship with some Tibetan lamas; Tertön Sogyal had strong connection with his daughter in 1913; father of Ma Bufang.

Ming Half-Han and half-Tibetan policewoman with whom the author was intimately involved for a short period.

Namdrol, Abbot (b. 1953) Present-day scholar, principal disciple of Khenpo Jikmé Phuntsok, lives near Yangleshö Cave outside Kathmandu, and the author's teacher.

Nechung Oracle State Oracle of Tibet whose medium is a monk from Nechung Monastery; responsible for protecting the Dalai Lama and strengthening the Tibetan government. Current medium lives in Dharamsala, India.

Nyagtrül (d. 1899) Taken over by dark forces and attempted to assassinate the XIII Dalai Lama with sorcery; also known as Nyarong Tulku or Shiwa Tulku.

Norbu Tsering, or **Nephew Norbu** (d. 1899) Mastermind behind the failed 1899 assassination plot of the XIII Dalai Lama; nephew of Regent Demo.

Padmasambhava (eighth century) "Father of Tibetan Buddhism," vajrayana master from the land of Oddiyana, which some scholars identify with the modern-day Swat Valley region of Pakistan; established Buddhism in Tibet and concealed treasure teachings throughout Tibet to be revealed at the most opportune time. Also known as Guru Rinpoche.

Pema Duddul (1816–1872) Visionary and meditation master, first teacher of Tertön Sogyal, founded Kalzang Monastery in 1860, attained rainbow body. Also known as Nyala Pema Duddul.

Pumo, or **Khandro Pumo** (d. 1949) Spiritual wife of Tertön Sogyal.

Protector Incorporeal, nonhuman beings who vow to protect and guard the teachings of the Buddha and his followers; "worldly" protectors are akin to local spirits, while "wisdom" protectors are emanations of enlightened beings.

Protectress of Mantras A female incorporeal protector whose principal duty is to safeguard the teachings of the Great Perfection.

Raven-Faced Dharma Protector An incorporeal protector with whom Tertön Sogyal had a special connection.

Rigdzin Namgyal (d. early 1950s) Son of Tertön Sogyal and Khandro Pumo, accomplished meditator.

Rudra Embodiment of self-cherishing ego, depicted as a mythical cannibalistic ogre.

Sogyal The contraction of Sonam Gyalpo, which means "King of Merit."

Sogyal Rinpoche One of the two simultaneous reincarnations of Tertön Sogyal, author of the *Tibetan Book of Living and Dying*, who resides in France, and is the author's teacher.

Sonam Drolma Mother of Tertön Sogyal.

Sonam Gyalpo Tertön Sogyal's birth name, which means "King of Merit."

Yogi Sonam, or **Sonam Thayé** Accomplished meditator to whom Tertön Sogyal was sent by Nyala Pema Duddul, and who oversaw Tertön Sogyal's first meditation retreats and training.

Tertön Literally, "treasure revealer," indicating someone who is a revealer of spiritual teachings and ritual objects buried in Tibet by Padmasambhava in the eighth century; emissaries of Padmasambhava.

Tertön Rangrik (1847–1903) Principal student of Nyala Pema Duddul, senior spiritual brother to Tertön Sogyal, and founder of Lumorab Monastery in Nyarong; full name is Tertön Rangrik Dorje Kusum Lingpa.

Tertön Sogyal (1856–1926) One of Tibet's great mystics of the late nineteenth and early twentieth centuries, teacher and advisor to the XIII Dalai Lama.

Trisong Detsen, King (742–797) Thirty-seventh king of Tibet, responsible for inviting Padmasambhava to Tibet to firmly establish Buddhism.

Vajrakilaya Tertön Sogyal's principal meditational deity, whose vajrayana implement, a three-sided phurba, is used to vanquish the self-cherishing ego.

Wangchen (b. 1952) Contemporary treasure revealer from eastern Tibet with whom the author studied and traveled.

Yeshe Tsogyal, Lady Accomplished vajrayana practitioner; spiritual wife of Padmasambhava who assisted in the concealment of treasure teachings.

Younghusband, Francis (1863–1942) British army officer and explorer who led the first invasion of Lhasa in 1904 and, after a mystical experience in Tibet, went on to found the World Congress of Faiths.

Zhang Qingli (b. 1951) Communist hardliner; party secretary of Tibetan Autonomous Region.

Notes

Pages xii–xiii, Tibet map. The map was designed by the author and hand-illustrated by Jocelyn Slack. Tibetan font is courtesy Sogyal Rinpoche. Lodi Gyari, Pema Wangyal, Adam Pearcey, Monica Garry-Pistono, Jeremy Schmidt, John Ackerly, and John Wasson gave critical topographical comments. The drawings in the four corners of the map are of Jokhang Cathedral in Lhasa, the Enlightenment Stupa of Tertön Sogyal at Nyagar, Kalzang Monastery in Nyarong, and the Cave That Delights the Senses at Tsadra Rinchen Drak near Palpung.

Part I
Page 1 *"A pilgrimage through wild, open lands . . ."*: Dalai Lama 1990b.

Chapter 1

The Mission Begins
Page 8 *"Less than a year earlier in June 2001 . . ."*: International Campaign for Tibet (hereafter ICT) 2004a, pages 63–74; Tibetan Center for Human Rights and Democracy (hereafter TCHRD) 2001; for video of the destruction that was smuggled out by monks who wrapped the mini-DV tape around a pencil and walked it across the Himalayas, through Nepal, and to India, see TCHRD 2002. See also the ICT 2004b video *Devotion and Defiance: Communist Party Crackdown on Buddhism in Tibet,* www.tibetpolicy.eu/resource-center/

multi-media/186-devotion-and-defiance-communist-party-crackdown-on-buddhism-in-tibet.

Page 8 *"Other dramatic images and firsthand reports . . .":* Liu 2001; Eckholm 2001.

Page 9 *"Biko was an antiapartheid leader in South Africa . . .":* Gabriel 1980. See also Attenborough 1987 and Woods 1978.

Page 14 *"During Uncle Apu's years as a hermit-yogi . . .":* For an overview of the Varjakilaya phurba practice, see Khenpo Namdrol Rinpoche 1999.

Page 16 *"For more than forty years, beatnik poets . . .":* Snyder 1983; Ginsberg 1970; Merton 1973.

Page 16 *"When the Dalai Lama escaped . . .":* Dalai Lama 1977, 1990a; also for comprehensive account of events leading up to Dalai Lama's escape, see Tsering Shakya 1999.

Page 18 *"For as long as space exists . . .":* See also Shantideva 1997, 10:55.

Chapter 2

Following in the Footsteps of the Master

Page 20 *"I found the challenge of academia . . .":* My professor of Indian philosophy at the School of Oriental and African Studies was the eccentric Russian intellectual Alexander Piatigorsky (see Iosseliani 2008, *Philosopher Escaped*). We had extensive conversations about the challenges of merging spirituality and political action; he believed the closest the world has seen to perfecting the two was Mahatma Gandhi's *satyagraha*. Under Professor Piatigorsky and Professor Skorupski, I completed my M.A. thesis, entitled "Reflections on Dependent Origination in the Light of Nāgārjuna's Interpretation of Truth." University of London, School of Oriental and African Studies. Master's Thesis.

Page 20 *"One afternoon at university, over tea . . .":* Over two million copies have been printed of *The Tibetan Book of Living and Dying,* in fifty-seven countries in thirty-two languages.

Page 24 *"Before Tertön Sogyal died in 1926 . . .":* Tertön Sogyal predicted that there would be two principal reincarnations, and he also indicated he would emanate beneficial activity through hundreds of future practitioners. Also, when the meditation master Sonam Zangpo journeyed to the Dugsta Temple in Bhutan in the 1960s, he came across a philosophical discourse by the monk Gendun Rinchen from the famed Tiger's Lair. Sonam Zangpo was struck by the similarities in tone and content to writings by Tertön Sogyal, whom Sonam Zangpo had met some decades before in eastern Tibet. Sonam Zangpo asked that Gendun Rinchen be brought to him and it is said that at this time he recognized him as one of three incarnations of Tertön Sogyal. According to this version, it is said of these three reincarnations of Tertön Sogyal, one would be a strict monk (Khenpo Jikmé Phuntsok), one would be a learned hermit (Gendun Rinchen), and one a yogi with unconventional "crazy wisdom" (Sogyal Rinpoche).

Page 24 *"A prophecy regarding Tertön Sogyal's reincarnation..."*: Part of the prophecy of
Tertön Dzongter Kunzang Nyima, the second son of Dudjom Lingpa, reads:

Nanam Dorje Dudjom [previous incarnation of Tertön Sogyal]
Will certainly ripen into two fruits:
One, a turquoise dragon holding up a jewel for all to see,
The other, his voice resounding everywhere like a lion's roar.

Also, in October 1993, Khenpo Jikmé Phuntsok stated in Lerab Ling, Sogyal
Rinpoche's retreat center in southern France, "In one of the treasures of Lerab
Lingpa [Tertön Sogyal] which is called *The Complete Gathering of Teachings*—the
Ka Yongdzok Düpa—there are two appendices: the *Dojang Chima* and the *Dojang
Chimé Chima*. In the latter, the "Later Discourses," it is clearly predicted that
Lerab Lingpa would have two reincarnations, and that both of them would be
of enormous benefit to the teaching and to sentient beings."

Page 26 *"By late 2000 the enormous encampment..."*: See also Germano 1998, pages
53–94.

Page 27 *"Thousands of students arrived..."*: For biographies of Khenpo Jikmé Phuntsok, see Khenpo Sodarjey 2001; Pistono 2008. Thanks to David Germano
for sharing with me his unpublished research on the life of Khenpo Jikmé
Phuntsok.

Chapter 3

A Different Kind of Pilgrimage

Page 32 *"Its library houses the hand-carved woodblocks..."*: See also www.lotsawahouse
.org/tsullo.html.

Page 32 *"Tsullo's biography is based on Tertön Sogyal's journals..."*: Tsullo 1974, 2002.

Page 40 *"In order to achieve his aim to split the country..."*: The scholar-monk Geshe
Sonam Phuntsok died a short while after being released from prison. See also
ICT 2004, 2007.

Part II

Page 45 *"Beings are by nature buddhas..."*: Hevajra Tantra. Translation courtesy Rigpa.

Chapter 4

From Bandit to Saint

Page 47 *"This is the home of the protective deity..."*: The full name is Heights of Eternal Snow (pronounced "Kawalungri"). It is the principal sacred mountain in
Nyarong. A photograph of the mountain from the southern side was one of
the examples used by the United States Mint in designing the Congressional
Gold Medal awarded to the Dalai Lama on October 17, 2007. The other two
mountains on the gold medal are Amnye Machen and Chomolungma (Mount
Everest).

Page 49 *"Tertön Sogyal's birth in Upper Nyarong had been prophesied . . .":* David Germano provided me the following quote found in *The Magical Mirror of Exceeding Clarity: An emanation of the Tantric Yogi Dorje Dudjom:*

Will come in upper Nya in Kham,

Karmically fit to be a yogi with disciplined balance

In front of a three peaked snow mountain to the west of a great water,

In the dragon year and named Lerab Lingpa [Tertön Sogyal].

Page 50 *"The whole of Tibet was thought to be . . .":* Dudjom Rinpoche 1991, page 938.

Page 50 *"Padmasambhava accepted their request . . .":* Dudjom Rinpoche 1991, page 513; Yeshe Tsogyal 1993, page 60.

Page 51 *". . . the father of Tibetan Buddhism . . .":* For biographies of Padmasambhava, see Rigpa 2004; Tulku Thondup 1996; Jamgön Kongtrul 1980; Dudjom Rinpoche 1991; Nyoshul Khenpo 2004; Sogyal Rinpoche 1989; Yeshe Tsogyal 1993; Yeshe Tsogyal 1978; Ngawang Zangpo 2002.

Page 51 *"It was because of his overarching power . . .":* Mantrayana is often equated with vajrayana Buddhism; from a teaching the Dalai Lama gave in Dharamsala, India, on March 21, 2004. See also Rigpa 2004, page 14.

Page 52 *"It is said that he was able to slice solid stone . . .":* Tulku Thondup 1996, page 105; Tarthang Tulku 1995, page 45.

Page 52 *"With his concern for the development of future practitioners . . .":* Tulku Thondup 1986, 1996; Terrone 2010.

Page 54 *"Gönpo Namgyal, known simply as Amgon . . .":* My textual and oral history research into the life of Gönpo Namgyal and Nyarong was enhanced by my conversations and interviews with Lodi Gyari, the late Sherab Ozer Rinpoche, and the late One-Eye Wangde of Kalzang Monastery, and Tashi Tsering of Amnye Machen Institute. See also Tashi Tsering 1986; Jamyang Norbu 1986. Aten Dogyaltshang 1993; *China Tibetology* 1991; Yeshe Dorje 1997, 1998; Yudru Tsomu 2006; Sherab Ozer 1981; Teichman 1922.

Page 55 *"The word around Upper Nyarong's pine-filled valleys . . .":* Oral history of Sonam Gyalpo's father and "Sure Shots" is from interviews with the late One-Eye Wangde and Khamtrul Rinpoche. See also Tsullo 1974, pages 17–21; Khamtrul Rinpoche's unpublished biography of Tertön Sogyal; Khamtrul Rinpoche 1992.

Page 57 *"When there is a war between devils . . .":* Yeshe Dorje 1998.

Chapter 5

Taking What Is Given

Page 58 *"Richard Gere had just flown in . . .":* United States House of Representatives 2002.

Page 61 *"It stayed there for the next week of eastward travel . . .":* ICT 2004, pages 64–74; Tibet Information Network (hereafter TIN), April 18, 2002.

Page 62 *"By the time Dargye ascended the staircase . . .":* Yeshe Dorje 1998.

Page 63 *"We are what we think..."*: Byrom 1993, verses 1–2.

Page 65 *"May bodhichitta, precious and sublime..."*: See Dalai Lama III 1982, page 136.

Page 69 *"By morning, Dargye knew he no longer..."*: Oral history of Sogyal's youth from interviews with Khamtrul Rinpoche, the late One-Eye Wangde, Lodi Gyari, and the late Sherab Ozer Rinpoche. See also Khamtrul Rinpoche's unpublished biography of Tertön Sogyal.

Page 71 *"In the narrow prison courtyard..."*: For prison photos, see ICT 2004a, page 77.

Page 72 *"I learned later in the week the two prisoners..."*: The main aim of the Patriotic Education campaign in Tibetan areas, which reaches even the most remote monasteries and nunneries, is to tighten Communist Party control over religion and undermine the influence of the Dalai Lama in society and religious institutions.

Chapter 6

Disappearing Bodies

Page 74 *"As Sogyal rode westward to Yogi Thayé's encampment..."*: Yogi Thayé, or Lama Sonam Thayé (aka Chomden Dorje), was one of the two main "heart-sons" of Nyala Pema Duddul, the other being Tertön Rangrik Dorje. He passed the lineage of Nyala Pema Duddul on to Tertön Sogyal. He was renowned as an emanation of Gyalwa Chokyang, one of the twenty-five disciples of Padmasambhava. Born into the family of Akalbu, he became a yogi who dressed in white and wore his hair in a topknot. He assisted in the construction of the main temple at Kalzang Monastery and took responsibility for all Pema Duddul's disciples after their master attained the rainbow body.

On August 12, 1998, Sherab Ozer Rinpoche, abbot of Kalzang Monastery in Tibet, performed a ceremony in Lerab Ling in southern France, during which he offered the throne of Kalzang Monastery to Sogyal Rinpoche as the heir to Tertön Sogyal.

Page 74 *"First, contemplate the preciousness of being free and well favored..."*: This is a series of contemplations meant to turn the mind's interest away from the mundane world and toward spiritual practice. Translation courtesy of Nalanda Translation Committee.

Page 75 *"Soon, Sogyal received instructions from the deepest source of wisdom..."*: See also Dalai Lama 2000.

Page 77 *"I walked to Lumorab Monastery..."*: Tertön Rangrik Dorje, Kusum Lingpa (1847–1903), established Lumorab Monastery in 1896 with the XIII Dalai Lama's patronage.

Page 78 *"When they opened the door to the room after four days..."*: Uncle Achung, also known as Khenpo Achung (1918–1998), lived and taught at Lumorab Monastery in Upper Nyarong, which is closely associated with the great Nyingma Monastery of Mindroling in central Tibet. He studied for many years at Sera Monastery in Lhasa, and had many disciples in the area around Nyarong, Tre-

hor, and Kandze. Apart from reports in the local press, Achung is discussed in
Kapstein 2004 and *Noetic Sciences Review* 2002. The current Dalai Lama also said
(see Dalai Lama 2004, page 169), "Two years ago a Tibetan yogi who practiced
the Great Completeness [Dzogchen] style of meditation in the Nyingma tradition achieved a state of the complete disappearance of his gross physical body,
which we call 'achieving a rainbow body.' His name was Achok [Achung], and
he was from Nyarong. He studied philosophy from time to time at a Geluk
monastic university near Lhasa called Sera, and he also received teachings from
my junior tutor Trijang Rinpoche, but his main teacher was the Nyingma lama,
Dudjom Rinpoche. Although he practiced Tantra according to both the old
and new schools of Tibetan Buddhism, his main practice was the recitation of
'Om Mani Padme Hum' and its accompanying meditation. Until about three
years ago, he frequently said he hoped to have the opportunity of meeting the
Dalai Lama in this lifetime. Then, one day he called on his followers to perform offerings for the sake of the Dalai Lama's life. After they made offerings,
he surprised them by announcing that he would leave. He put on his saffron
monastic robe and told them to seal him inside his room for a week. His disciples followed his request and after a week opened the room to find that he had
completely disappeared except for his robe. One of his disciples and a fellow
practitioner came to Dharamsala, where they related the story to me and gave
me a piece of his robe." See also Rigpa International 2000.

Page 79 *"What remained are hair and nails..."*: Also quoted in Kapstein 2004.

Page 79 *"During my stay at Lumorab Monastery..."*: Chöpel Gyatso was a monk who
taught widely in the Nyarong and Kandze area. In 1957, the Chinese Communists jailed him in Dartsedo. He was held at Dorje Drak Monastery, which
was being used as a prison. Ama Adhe was in prison with Chöpel Gyatso—
see Ama Adhe 1997, pages 108–113. Ama Adhe told me that seven reincarnate lamas, including Chöpel Gyatso, died one evening in prison but that it
was not at the direct hand of the prison guards—rather, the lamas decided
to eject their consciousness. The late One-Eye Wangde and the late Lama
Chime concurred, saying that the seven lamas chose to leave their body and
die so as not to allow the Chinese Communists to incur negative karma by
beating them.

Page 83 *"With Ol' Penam's motionless eyelids open..."*: Ol' Penam is the moniker for
Lama Pema Namgyal. The reincarnation of Ol' Penam was born to Dawa and
Lodi Gyari in Virginia, U.S., and after being recognized, began his studies at
the exiled Mindroling Monastery in India.

Page 87 *"I knew the city had many laogai prisons..."*: See also, Wu 1993.

Chapter 7

In the World but Not of It

Page 91 *"These were the very kinds of instructions that Tertön Sogyal..."*: For mural images and brief commentary, see Baker 2000.

Page 94 *"Although Yahoo! admitted their moral error..."*: For technical reports on the Chinese government's malware attacks on the Dalai Lama's Private Office, the Tibetan government-in-exile in India, and Tibetan support groups in the West, see Nagaraja and Ross Anderson 2009; *Information Warfare Monitor* 2009.

Page 95 *"As one commentator put it..."*: Kurlantzick 2010.

Page 100 *"Khyentsé and another eminent lama, Jamgön Kongtrul..."*: See Ferrari 1958; Jamgön Kongtrul 2003; Ngawang Zangpo 2001. Ringu Tulku 2006; Ricard 1996; Tulku Thondup 1996; Smith 1970, 2001; Gardner 2006; and www.lot sawahouse.org/khyentsewangpo/index.html.

Page 100 *"But for now, Sogyal had..."*: For every treasure teaching, Padmasambhava specified a custodian whose duty was to propagate the teaching. Usually this involved the responsibility of publishing the treasure teaching, an expensive endeavor involving woodblock carving, and paper and ink production. The most important role of the treasure custodian, however, was to either teach the text himself or arrange for the textual transmission from a qualified master. The two principal custodians of Tertön Sogyal's treasures were Khyentsé Wangpo and Thubten Gyatso, the XIII Dalai Lama.

Page 101 *"From that moment on, Sogyal took..."*: When Tertön Sogyal affixed his tertön seal to treasure texts or some prayers he authored, he sometimes signed with his treasure revealer name of Lerab Lingpa, or his secret name of Trinlé Thayé Tsal, meaning "Potential of Boundless Enlightened Activity."

Page 101 *"It is through the auspicious link with a consort..."*: See also Jacoby 2007.

Page 107 *"Whatever arises, in pure awareness..."*: Khenpo Jikmé Phuntsok 1987. Translation courtesy Lotsawa House.

Page 110 *"The* Washington Post *reporter..."*: Pan 2004.

Part III

Page 113 *"Though my view is higher than the sky..."*: Courtesy Lotsawa House.

Chapter 8

In Service to the Dalai Lama

Page 116 *"In particular, just as the abbot..."*: Thupten Jampa Tsultrim Tenzin 1998, pages 582–583; translation in Akester (forthcoming), where it states, "Padma gling pa', the other gTer ston lauded as a [teacher] of the young XIII Ta la'i bla ma in the official biography, was evidently an alias (gTer ming) for one of the highest dignitaries in the dGe lugs pa order, the ninth 'Phags pa lha incarnation mKhas grub ngag dbang blo bzang 'jigs med bstan pa'i rgyal mtshan (1849–1900)." Note: for readability for the general reader in the main text of this book, I do not use Wylie transliteration and have made the spelling of Tibetan names consistent. In the footnotes, however, I have retained other authors' transliteration styles. Tertön Sogyal was not the only vajrayana master employing mantras and wrathful ritual against the British army's cannons and bullets; there were other yogis called upon to control the weather and avert the foreign devils. But Tertön Sogyal was the only who became the Dalai Lama's personal teacher and advisor. And one of the Vajrakilaya practices that Tertön Sogyal deciphered in 1895 would become the principal practice in the Tibetan government's liturgical arsenal, used side by side with the XIII Dalai Lama's attempts to modernize Tibet's army. See Stoddard 2006.

Page 117 *"Regent Demo, who was in charge of the country's political affairs . . ."*: A regent, chosen by Tibetan government ministers, ruled Tibet during the years in which the Dalai Lama had not yet ascended to the throne. In the middle of the seventeenth century, the institution of the Dalai Lama had risen to religious and political rule, coinciding with the Gelug school rise to power. In the previous four centuries, the Sakya and Karma Kagyü schools competed for rule in Tibet through the patronage from three dynasties; Mongol Yuan (1271–1368), Chinese Ming (1368–1644), and Manchu Qing (1644–1911). These patrons of Tibetan Buddhism, to varying degree, provided monetary support and military backing. The Tibetan Buddhist lamas in turn provided spiritual legitimacy to their rule. This symbiotic relationship, known as *cho-yon* bond, or "lama-patron," where the lay community supports the ordained monks and nuns, as found in many countries in Asia, was adopted in Tibet as a national policy. The roots of this "lama-patron" relationship reach back to the thirteenth century, when the Mongol descendants of Genghis Khan, namely his grandson Prince Goden and later Kublai Khan, ruled over the largest land-based empire in the history of the world, extending from southern China to Korea, throughout Central Asia, into modern-day Russia, Iran, and eastern Europe. It was in 1240 when the Mongols invited a leading Tibetan religious hierarch to Yuan court and adopted Tibetan Buddhism as the empire's state religion, and thus began the "lama-patron" relationship. Contacts between Tibet and Ming China rulers were limited throughout the fourteenth through the sixteenth century, but the "lama-patron" relationship did endure. In 1644, the foreign Manchus, who established the Qing Dynasty, overthrew the Chinese Ming emperors. It was this Qing Dynasty, in their last years of their imperial rule of China, that would not only be a threat to the XIII Dalai Lama's life, but to the existence of Tibet as an independent nation. Whether with the Mongols, Chinese, Manchus, or even into the early Republican period in the twentieth century, Tibetan Buddhist leaders bestowed teachings, tantric empowerments, and blessing upon their benefactors, who in turn gave economic and martial support as well as conferring imperial titles upon the religious hierarchy. Tibetan Buddhism has never treated politics and religion separately. Tibetan nationalism commenced in the eighth century when King Trisong Detsen gained rule over the Tibetan Plateau through the esoteric achievements of Padmasambhava. From the Tibetan nation's inception, politics and religion have been inseparable and remain so today. Any notion that rule of the country should not flow from Buddhist principles would be foolish. Buddha's teachings on impermanence, causality or karma, and compassion are the very foundation on which Tibet's leaders should govern, whether ordained monks or lay officials. It is from these fundamental Buddhist principles that leaders are meant to glean the needed wisdom to rule effectively and fairly. And the embodiment of the merging of politics and spirituality is found in the institution of the Dalai Lama. Also, see Tuttle 2005.

Page 118 *"Painting cement apartment blocks with a Tibetan façade . . .":* See Barnett 2006.

Page 119 *"Most of the political prisoners in Lhasa in 2004 . . .":* See Schwartz 1994; Marshall 1999, 2000. For current lists of political prisoners in Tibet, which utilize data from the Tibet Information Network and the Dui Hua Foundation, see www.cecc.gov/pages/victims, as well as ICT's www.savetibet.org/action-center and www.missingvoices.net.

Page 119 *"Some of the nuns had been released . . .":* For photos and description of Drapchi Prison, see ICT 2004, pages 83–87.

Page 124 *"Science and technology are powerful tools . . .":* Dalai Lama 2005b, pages 9–11.

Page 124 *"See these two solitary confinement cells . . .":* A Chinese court sentenced Tenzin Delek Rinpoche, a prominent and well-respected Tibetan lama, and Lobsang Dhondup to death on December 2, 2002, for their alleged involvement in a string of explosions that injured several people in Kandze Tibetan Autonomous Prefecture and Chengdu (the capital of Sichuan Province). Lobsang Dhondup was executed on January 26, 2003. Tenzin Delek remains in Chinese custody. For photo of the prison where Tenzin Delek Rinpoche and Lobsang Dhondup were held the day before the latter was executed, see ICT 2004, page 76. The U.S. Congressional-Executive Commission on China reported on February 10, 2003, that the execution of Lobsang Dhondup was "particularly disturbing" because it was "carried out in haste," "in a manner which may have violated the laws of the People's Republic of China," and that PRC officials had defaulted on their commitment to Lorne Craner, Assistant Secretary of State for Democracy, Human Rights and Labor, to undertake a lengthy judicial review of the case. Also, see Human Rights Watch 2004.

Page 126 *"Today the lack of interest in human rights . . .":* Kurlantzick 2010.

Page 126 *"The message was clear . . .":* Although the Dalai Lama does not advocate independence for Tibet, a CNN poll in February 2010 showed that nearly three-quarters of Americans believe Tibet should be an independent country. See: www.cnn.com/2010/WORLD/asiapcf/02/18/tibet.poll/index.html.

Page 130 *"The People's Government . . . forbids any person . . .":* See also TIN 2001 and Pistono 2002.

Chapter 9

The Merging of Politics and Spirituality

Page 136 *"The significance of the Dalai Lama reconnecting..."*: Tsullo 1974, pages 131–136.

Page 136 *"Furthermore, the British had already..."*: Das 1988.

Page 136 *"The Dalai Lama and his regent conscripted..."*: Stoddard 2006.

Page 138 *"Any influence on the Dalai Lama..."*: See also Goldstein 1973, where he writes, "One of the most salient features of traditional political life in Tibet was the intense and pervasive competition for power and prestige that took place within the ranks of the politically relevant, particularly within the aristocratic lay-official segment of the government. Plots, disputes, and confiscations were key elements in the dynamics of the system."

Page 140 *"They assist the government-in-exile and the Dalai Lama..."*: See also Khamtrul Rinpoche 2009.

Page 144 *"The Tibetan government sent an urgent message..."*: Tsullo 1974, page 165; Thupten Jampa Tsultrim Tenzin 1998, page 155; and Nechung 2004, pages 53–54. The oral history that I collected in interviews with Khamtrul Rinpoche, Nechung elder monks, and the present Medium of Nechung Oracle offer a similar conclusion to the narrative. Khamtrul Rinpoche told me, "At the same time, the Tibetan government prepared to send the abbot of Nechung Monastery, Trinley Chöpel, to eastern Tibet to meet Tertön Sogyal and the statue and escort them both back to Lhasa. By the time the abbot of Nechung had arrived in eastern Tibet, Tertön Sogyal had entrusted the statue to his own teacher, Jamyang Khyentsé Wangpo. Before leaving Lhasa, the oracle had told the abbot, 'Initially there may be some obstacles to obtaining the statue. However, if you were to open the jeweled rice-container of Khyentsé Wangpo, you will find a sealed scroll. This scroll is a Guru Yoga text, also a treasure object discovered by the great Tertön Sogyal.' When the Nechung abbot met Khyentsé Wangpo, the great lama said that the statue was needed to protect eastern Tibet, and that he did not intend to let it be taken. The abbot remembered the instruction from the oracle and he asked Khyentsé Wangpo if he might open the jewel rice-container on his prayer table. Upon its being opened, the Guru Yoga text indeed was found atop the rice. Khyentsé Wangpo recognized the writing to be in Tertön Sogyal's hand. Reading aloud the conclusion of the scripture, Khyentsé Wangpo then said, 'This text instructs the disciple how to merge their mind with the wisdom mind of the Guru, and that is the ultimate protection. You can take the Wish-Fulfilling Jewel Guru Statue—I will keep this sacred text in its stead.' Nechung Rinpoche soon found Tertön Sogyal in a nearby hermitage and, with a large entourage, escorted the Guru statue and the tertön back to Lhasa."

The text entitled *The Guru Yoga of the Profound Path* was incorporated in the daily scriptural recitations by Nechung Monastery, and is still practiced today at their exiled monastery in Dharamsala, India. Thanks to Adam Pearcey for translating the Guru Yoga sadhana for the author.

Page 145 *"The Wish-Fulfilling Jewel Guru was taken . . .":* One week after the enthronement of the Guru statue in the Jokhang, the Dalai Lama ordered that the statue should join him in the Chamber of Joyful Clear Sound in the Potala Palace. Once again, the statue was placed on a palanquin and ceremonially escorted to the Potala, where it sat before a statue of the Great Fifth. The Dalai Lama's biography states that these two statues provided an auspicious condition necessary for the Tibetan leader to receive empowerments into esoteric practices that the Great Fifth had received in vision. With the blessed presence of the statues, it was as if the XIII Dalai Lama was carrying out a ceremony with Padmasambhava and the Great Fifth by his side. After the Dalai Lama had received the needed empowerment, the Guru statue returned to the Jokhang.

Page 146 *"Lodi Gyari is also a quiet phurba practitioner.":* Lodi Gyari was recognized at a young age as the reincarnation of Khenchen Jampal Dewé Nyima, also known as Gyurme Pendé Özer (Khenpo Aten), who was one of the main teachers of Dudjom Rinpoche Jikdrel Yeshe Dorje. Jampal Dewé Nyima's principal teacher was Mipham Rinpoche, and he also studied with Nyoshul Lungtok, Tertön Rangrik Dorje, Jamgön Kongtrul, and Jamyang Khyentsé Wangpo. Jampal Dewé Nyima was primarily connected with Lumorab Monastery in Nyarong. See Nyoshul Khenpo 2005, pages 425–426; Gyari 2006; www.rigpawiki.org/index.php?title=Lumorap_Monastery.

Page 150 *"Nearly two volumes of Padmasambhava instruction . . .":* Tertön Sogyal 1985, volume "pha." Padmasambhava prophesized two custodians for *The Razor* treasure: Khyentsé Wangpo and Thubten Gyatso, the XIII Dalai Lama. By the time Tertön Sogyal discovered the treasure, Khyentsé Wangpo had already passed away. Thus the Dalai Lama was the individual who bore custodial responsibility for disseminating the Vajrakilaya treasure.

Page 154 *"Descend to what is known as Raven Valley . . .":* Part of this signpost's instruction can be found in Ngawang Zangpo 2001, page 211.

Page 156 *"Of this there is not the slightest doubt!":* Tsullo 1974, pages 188–215; Thupten Jampa Tsultrim Tenzin 1998, page 691. Quoted in Akester (forthcoming).

Page 158 *"Whatever joy there is in this world . . .":* Shantideva 1997, VIII, 129. Courtesy Lotsawa House.

Chapter 10

Trouble on the Path

Page 161 *"If, on the other hand, the temples were built . . .":* Tsullo 1974, page 233; Thupten Jampa Tsultrim Tenzin 1998, pages 225–226. Quoted in Akester (forthcoming).

Page 162 *"The celestial beings told the Dalai Lama . . .":* Thupten Jampa Tsultrim Tenzin 1998, pages 220–222.

Page 162 *"Demo had held the influential regency..."*: For history and photographs of Tengyeling Monastery, see Alexander 2005; Petech 1973.

Page 163 *"On the occasion of hosting a ritual..."*: The narrative of this episode is based primarily on Nyarong oral history, and sources include the late Sherab Ozer Rinpoche, Khamtrul Rinpoche, Tashi Tsering, Lodi Gyari, and the late One-Eye Wangde. Gelek Rinpoche was enormously helpful to me about the episode. Also, see Tsullo 1974, pages 243–245; Thupten Jampa Tsultrim Tenzin 1998, pages 239–242. English sources that deal with parts of the episode are found in Goldstein 1991, pages 42–43; Kawaguchi 1979, pages 374–382; Tsipon Shakapa 1976, pages 75–76. Matthew Akester provided me Tibetan sources, which include Hor khang bSod nams dal 'bar, Ram pa rNam rgyal dbang phyug, and bShad sgrva dGa' ldan dpal 'byor in Bod kyi lo rgyus rig gnas dpyad gzhi'i rgyu cha bdams bsgrigs volume 8, and Blo bzang rgya mtsho in volume 19. Mullin 1988, pages 37, 40–45 erroneously writes that Tertön Sogyal and Lerab Lingpa are two different people associated with the XIII Dalai Lama; Lerab Lingpa was another name used by Tertön Sogyal.

Page 174 *"Tertön Sogyal recognized the importance..."*: The narrative of this story follows the oral history of Khamtrul Rinpoche, and differs from the Tsullo 1974 pages 250–269. Khamtrul Rinpoche received the oral history from Lama Norkho (died c. 1956), who was his teacher for astrology and medicine. Lama Norkho heard it from his uncle, Karma Lhaksam, who was a monk-attendant of Tertön Sogyal, and who couriered messages on horseback between the XIII Dalai Lama and Tertön Sogyal, and apparently read the missives along the way. The XIII Dalai Lama was the treasure custodian.

Page 177 *"Britain, China, and Russia continued to negotiate..."*: The Sino-Anglo Convention of 1906 recognized Chinese sovereignty over the region and the Anglo-Russian Convention of 1907, though the Qing were unaware, recognized the suzerainty of China over Tibet. See Smith 1996, page 162; Goldstein 1989, page 830.

Page 177 *"In the fourth month of the Water Hare year..."*: Tsullo 1974, pages 220–222; Thupten Jampa Tsultrim Tenzin 1998, pages 194–198, 283.

Part IV

Page 179 *"If we serve sentient beings by engaging in political activities..."*: Dalai Lama 2005a, page 24. The full quote is, "The political struggle for the restoration of Tibetan freedom should not be seen in the same light as we view ordinary politics. The Tibetan political struggle is aimed at preserving Tibetan identity and culture, a culture that is closely related to Buddhism and its fundamental principle of compassion. This culture has the potential to benefit not only Buddhists, but also nonbelievers. This being the case, I do my best to serve the cause of Tibet. As a Buddhist monk, I see this as a spiritual practice, which will not only make my life meaningful, but also lead me to the path of enlightenment. If we serve sentient beings by engaging in political activities with a spiritual orientation, we are actually following the Bodhisattva's way of life. Therefore, I call upon Tibetan spiritual figures, as they have influence in the community, to work for the cause of Tibet."

Page 183 *"Confucius said, 'If names aren't rectified...'"*: Confucius 1998, pages 139–140.

Page 183 *"Should the U.S. government pledge..."*: See Lin 2008 and Reuters, June 1, 2000, "Dalai Lama Responsible for Rape, Cannibalism, Murder Says Beijing."

Chapter 11

Wielding the Phurba

Page 187 *"Even before Younghusband's march into Lhasa, the Qing..."*: From the Manchu perspective, Tibet had long been a protectorate of their empire, ever since they overran the Han's Ming Dynasty in 1644. Though a foreign power ruling China, the ethnic Manchu's Qing Dynasty claimed that same patron role that the Mongols had established in the thirteenth century with the Tibetan lamas. See also Tuttle 2005.

Page 187 *"Thousands of Qing troops were stationed in Litang..."*: Coleman 2000; Epstein 2002.

Page 193 *"Late one afternoon, Tertön Sogyal's wife..."*: Tertön Sogyal and Khandro Pumo had two sons, one who died at the age of five, and the other, Rigdzin Namgyal, who became an accomplished lay tantric practitioner. The late One-Eye Wangde and the late Lama Chime both recounted to me how Rigdzin Namgyal would spend extended periods in seclusion, usually meditating completely naked in his one-room cabin on the mountainside. Attendants would bring tea in the morning and, upon returning in the afternoon, often find that he had not taken his tea or, indeed, moved. Later in his life, it was said that dust would collect on Rigdzin Namgyal's shoulders and thighs while sitting in thought-free awareness for days on end. Rigdzin Namgyal later married Sonam Drolma of the Horshul Choyu tribe of Golok, and they had a son, the monk Chöpel Gyatso.

Page 195 *"When efforts were made in accord with..."*: Tsullo 1974, pages 392–393. Translation from Akester (forthcoming).

Page 198 *"Soon after the Dalai Lama arrived in India..."*: Bell 1987, page 429.

Page 198 *"Before the Dalai Lama entered Tibet..."*: Tsipon Shakapa 1967, pages 246–247.

Chapter 12

Continuing the Pilgrimage

Page 200 *"Tertön Sogyal secured the patronage of one of the four Golok chieftains..."*: Thanks to Tulku Thondup Rinpoche for sharing with me his oral history of Dodrup Tenpai Nyima and Tertön Sogyal's life in Golok. During this period, Tertön Sogyal started to build a monastery at the Khemar Encampment but because of warring tribes, he had to abandon it unfinished.

Page 200 *"Eventually, Ma Qi's daughter studied..."*: Tsullo 1974, pages 509–518, 567–580.

Page 200 *"Tertön Sogyal's corpus of revealed spiritual practices ..."*: Tertön Sogyal 1985.

Page 200 *"Indeed, that is a likeness of my face and of my voice ..."*: For the photograph story, I collected oral histories from Gurong Gyalse via Humchen Chenaktsang in Xining, Alak Serthar in Rebkong, and Khamtrul Rinpoche in Dharamsala. According to Gurong Gyalse (d. 2002) the photographer was his father, the influential entrepreneur and forward-thinker Alak Gurong. Alak Gurong provided Tertön Sogyal and entourage his Mandigar compound just to the west of the Machu (Yellow) River to use as a base while he taught in Rebkong and Achung Namdzong. It was in this house that Alak Gurong decided to celebrate a treasure revelation of Tertön Sogyal, where he dove into the frozen lake at Nyenbo Dzari and retrieved an ancient Buddha statue. Gurong prepared a simple throne and, having arranged a low table with tantric accoutrements, requested Tertön Sogyal to take a seat. Gurong then retrieved his sturdy tripod stand, black cape, and square box in which he inserted the dry-plate negative using the gelatin silver process. Tertön Sogyal had never seen such equipment, much less his own photograph, which Gurong soon produced of the fifty-six-year-old tertön. Also, see Dongkawa, Orgyen 2000. Thanks to Gen Pema Wangyal in Washington, D.C., for his assistance on researching Alak Gurong. According to Khamtrul Rinpoche, soon after the photo was taken, when Tertön Sogyal was in Xining with the Muslim warlord Ma Qi, the tertön was recorded chanting a *chö* ritual on what was likely a 78 rpm copper gramophone etcher. Both the photograph and voice recording are said to have been spread into China, as Tertön Sogyal had Chinese disciples, as well as relations with the family of Ma Qi. The voice recording has not been found. For more information and photographs of Alak Gurong and family, see *Da lta ba* 2005; Gurong Gyalse 1994; Humchen Chenaktsang 2005. It is also during this time that Tertön Sogyal met Gendun Chöpel, who described Tertön Sogyal: "He was not very tall. He had a bluish complexion, long dreads, and a tuft of hair wrapped in some red material." See Stoddard 1985, pages 137–138.

Page 201 *"That boy was Sogyal Rinpoche ..."*: Before leaving Tibet in the spring of the Wood Sheep Year 1955, Jamyang Khyentsé Chökyi Lodrö and his protégé Sogyal Rinpoche met the young XIV Dalai Lama in the Potala Palace. During this meeting, Jamyang Khyentsé continued, like his predecessors and Tertön Sogyal, to offer to the Dalai Lama Padmasambhava's prophecies, which he had received in visions, for practices, geomantic placement of temples and stupa, and the construction of statues that would provide some measure of protection for the Dalai Lama and Tibetans.

Page 202 *"We know that by maintaining Tibet's Buddhist tradition ..."*: I felt we had come full circle. The temple in Lerab Ling had been built on ground consecrated by the Dalai Lama himself in the year 2000, when he presided over the conclusion of two weeks' group practice of *The Razor* by thirty Namgyal monks, and conferred its initiation, as a prelude to the Buddhist teaching he gave to twelve thousand people. This was the first time this powerful phurba practice, following the arrangement written by the XIII Dalai Lama, and with all of its associations for the Dalai Lamas and for Tibet, had taken place in the Western world. Also, see Dalai Lama 2007, page 253.

Page 202 *"After checking with various divinations..."*: Kunzang Nyima, the brother of Dodrup Tenpai Nyima, was responsible for inviting Tertön Sogyal to Nyagar, and securing support. Before Tertön Sogyal died, the tertön gave Kunzang Nyima his black yak-hair tent. Tulku Thondup told me that Kunzang Nyima never slept in a house again, saying, "Why should I sleep in home when I can sleep in the house of the XIII Dalai Lama's teacher every night!"

Page 206 *"These protection stones had been hidden..."*: See Tsullo 1974, pages 469–472, 567–569; Thupten Jampa Tsultrim Tenzin 1998, pages 647–649; Keutsang Trulku Jamphe Yeshe 2001, page 256. One of the three precious *lha-do* stones revealed by Tertön Sogyal was offered to the XIII Dalai Lama after the tertön passed away. The stone had an image of red Tamdrin and green Dorje Pakmo on either side. The Dalai Lama told the author that he carried this lha-do stone on his person for protection when he fled Lhasa in March 1959. The Dalai Lama said, "There were quite a number of sacred things that remained in Potala, but I left from Norbulingka. So when I left, those things that were available in Norbulingka, I took those things. I carried with me that lha-do, [which] the XIII Dalai Lama kept in the Norbulingka, and one vajra and one phurba."

Page 210 *"Throughout the spring of 2008, Tibetan protests spread...."*: For the authoritative analysis of the March 2008 Tibet uprising, see Barnett 2008; ICT August 6, 2008; Woeser March 2008, April 2010; Smith 2009; Wang Lixiong 2009; ICT March 2009; ICT May 2010.

Page 212 *"Tertön Sogyal's phurba practice—The Razor..."*: *The Razor* was indeed the phurba practice that Tertön Sogyal and the XIII Dalai Lama used to combat aggression from the British in 1903–04, the Qing Dynasty in 1910, and later the Muslim warlords in northeastern Tibet. *The Razor* was also practiced by Nechung Monastery leading up to and during the XIV Dalai Lama's escape from Tibet in March 1959. The ultimate purpose of *The Razor* remains the same—to bring about conducive circumstances for spiritual practice.

Glossary

(Tib) Tibetan

(Skt) Sanskrit

(Ch) Chinese

Amdo (Tib) Northeastern region of Tibet; one of the three regions traditionally considered to constitute Tibet. The area is now largely within the Chinese provinces of Qinghai and parts of Gansu and Sichuan.

Avalokiteshvara (Skt) [Tib: Chenrezik] The Buddha of Compassion; the embodiment of the compassion of all the Buddhas, regarded by the Tibetan people as the progenitor of the race and patron saint of the country. The Dalai Lamas are believed to be manifestations of Avalokiteshvara.

Bardo (Tib) Commonly used to denote the intermediate state between death and rebirth, but in reality bardos are occurring continuously, throughout both life and death, and are junctures at which the possibility of enlightenment is heightened.

Barkhor (Tib) Literally the "middle circuit," which specifically in central Tibet means the walkway used for circumambulating Jokhang Cathedral in Lhasa.

Bodhichitta (Skt) The compassionate wish to attain enlightenment for the benefit of all beings.

Bodhisattva (Skt) Someone who has aroused bodhichitta, the compassionate wish to attain enlightenment for the benefit of all beings and who engages in actions that bring them to that state. The bodhisattva vows not to remain in nirvana until all beings have attained enlightenment.

Buddha nature The potential for enlightenment inherently present in every sentient being.

Chenrezik (Tib) See *Avalokiteshvara.*

Dakini (Skt) Female embodiment of enlightened energy, sometimes manifesting in a human form while other times as ethereal beings who protect Buddhist teachings, including treasure teachings. Female lamas and the spiritual wives of male lamas are often given the Tibetan epithet *khandro,* meaning "dakini."

Dharamsala A former British hill station in Himachal Pradesh, northern India, currently the seat of the Dalai Lama and of the Tibetan government-in-exile.

Dharma (Skt) The Buddha's teachings. It has many shades of meaning, including "the spiritual path," or "spirituality" in general.

Dorje (Tib) A ritual scepter symbolizing compassion and skillful means. In vajrayana rituals, the dorje represents the masculine principle and is the counterpart of the bell, which represents the feminine principle and the wisdom of emptiness. The union of skillful means and wisdom is the enlightened mind.

Dri (Tib) A female yak.

Dzogchen (Tib) See *Great Perfection.*

Gelug (Tib) One of the four main traditions of Tibetan Buddhism, and the latest school of the Sarma schools; founded by Tsongkhapa in the fifteenth century on the basis of the Kadampa tradition.

Geshe (Tib) An academic title given to a monk who has finished a corresponding Ph.D.-level spiritual and philosophical education at one of three monasteries, Drepung, Sera, or Ganden. The Dalai Lama passed his Geshe examinations in 1959 just before he fled into exile.

Great Game The struggle for control of Central Asia between the British and Russian empires between 1830 and 1900, which included Tibet. Soldiers, spies, explorers, cartographers, and even monks participated and died. The term "Great Game" was coined by Rudyard Kipling, and the historian Peter Hopkirk has written extensively on the period.

Great Perfection (Tib: Dzògchen) The most ancient and direct stream of wisdom within the Buddhist tradition of Tibet.

Golok (Tib) A region in eastern Tibet. Until the 1950s, Golok was divided into three main districts: Akyong Boom, Wangchen Boom, and Padma Boom.

Guru Yoga (Skt) A meditation practice that focuses on the teacher, who is often visualized in an enlightened form.

Jokhang (Tib) Considered the most sacred temple in Tibet; home to the Jowo Rinpoche statue.

Kalzang Monastery Founded by Nyala Pema Duddul in 1860, and later became the seat of Tertön Sogyal.

Kham (Tib) Eastern region of Tibet; one of the three regions traditionally considered to constitute Tibet. Currently divided between Sichuan and Yunnan provinces and the Tibet Autonomous Region. Tibetans from Kham have their own dialects and customs and are known as khampas.

Khenpo (Tib) A title for one who has completed the major course of studies of about ten years' duration of the traditional branches of Buddhist philosophy, logic, monastic discipline, and ritual; can also refer to the abbot of a monastery.

Lama (Tib) [Skt: Guru] A spiritual teacher.

Lama-Patron Relationship The mutually supportive relationship in which the lay community or government supports the monastics, and the lamas in turn give the lay community spiritual counsel and blessings. In Tibet, this relationship was adopted as part of their international relations, whereby Tibetan lamas gave spiritual legitimacy to successive foreign patrons who offered martial and monetary support to the lamas. This was initiated during the Mongolia Yuan Dynasty (1271–1368), to a limited degree maintained with the Chinese Ming (1368–1644), and then continued into the Manchu Qing (1644–1912) and Republican period (1912–1949).

Lhasa (Tib) Literally "the abode of the gods"; the former capital and largest city in Tibet, and home of the Dalai Lamas. Population prior to 1959 was approximately 30,000. Today the population of the Lhasa is approximately 350,000, of which 60–80 percent is Chinese.

Mantra (Skt) Sacred syllables used in vajrayana practice to protect the mind from negativity and ordinary impure perceptions; also used to invoke meditational deities.

Nirvana (Skt) Literally "extinguished" in Sanskrit and "beyond suffering" in Tibetan; enlightenment itself. It is the state of peace that results from cessation and total pacification of all suffering and its causes.

Nyarong (Tib) Region in eastern Tibet; current-day Sichuan Province; Tertön Sogyal birth region.

Old Translation School [Tib: Nyingma] The oldest school of Tibetan Buddhism, which follows the original translations of the teachings of the Buddha into Tibetan. These translations were carried out up until the late tenth century.

Sometimes known as the "Earlier Translation School"; distinguished from the Sarma or "New Schools" (Kadam, Kagyü, Sakya, and eventually Gelug), which followed the later translations made from the mid-eleventh century onward.

Pharping A town south of Kathmandu, Nepal, near the sacred caves of Yangleshö and Asura, blessed by Padmasambhava.

Potala (Tib) The principal palace and residence of the Dalai Lamas, constructed in Lhasa by the V Dalai Lama in the mid-seventeenth century upon the ruins of an old palace and hermitage erected more than a thousand years before by the kings of Tibet. Up until the Chinese invasion, it housed much of Tibet's central government. Namgyal Monastery is located within the massive thousand-room compound.

Samyé (Tib) The first Buddhist monastery in Tibet, built during the time of King Trisong Detsen; name means "inconceivable."

Phurba A three-bladed, single-pointed dagger representing skillful means of compassion and the destruction of the self-cherishing ego; principal ritual implement of Vajrakilaya.

Rimé (Tib) The ecumenical, nonpartisan, and nonsectarian movement fueled by Jamyang Khyentsé Wangpo and Jamgön Kongtrul and their disciples in eastern Tibet in the nineteenth century.

Rinpoche (Tib) Literally means "Precious Jewel," or "Great Precious One." Honorific title used for spiritual teachers, often denoting having been recognized as an incarnate lama. "Rinpoche" is a not an academic title like "Geshe" or "Khenpo."

Samsara (Skt) The cycle of conditioned existence, birth, and death, which is characterized by suffering in which one is continually reborn; the cause of samsara is ignorance.

Shiwa (Tib) Tertön Sogyal's birth village in Upper Nyarong, eastern Tibet.

Splittist Communist Party criminal term for a Tibetan advocating for independence from China; a general label for anyone advancing secession in China; also known as "separatist."

Stupa (Skt) [Tib: Chorten] A reliquary monument symbolizing the enlightened mind of the Buddhas; can vary in size and shape, but often has a wide, square base, a rounded middle, and a tall conical section at the top.

Tantra (Skt) A text of the vajrayana. Tantra begins with the view that the final attainment or result has been within the mind from the very beginning, but has been obscured by ignorance.

Terma (Tib) Spiritual treasures hidden by Padmasambhava and Lady Yeshe Tsogyal in the earth, sky, and water, as well as in the minds of disciples, to be revealed at the appropriate time by tertöns, or treasure revealers.

Tertön (Tib) Literally "treasure revealer," indicating tertöns discover or reveal spiritual teachings and ritual objects that were hidden in Tibet and throughout the Himalayas during the eighth century by Padmasambhava and Lady Yeshe Tsogyal. See *Terma*.

Tibet Traditionally composed of three main areas: Amdo (northeastern Tibet), Kham (eastern Tibet), and U-Tsang (central and western Tibet); a term that is used today by China to denote only the Tibet Autonomous Region (Ch: Xizang zizhiqu), which was established by the People's Republic of China in 1965 and covers the area of Tibet west of the Drichu River (Ch: Yangtze), and includes part of Kham; the rest of Kham and Amdo have been incorporated into Chinese provinces, and where Tibetan communities were said to have "compact inhabitancy," those areas were designated as Tibetan Autonomous Prefectures (TAP) and Tibetan Autonomous Counties (TAC).

Tibet Autonomous Region Tibetan area west of the Drichu River (Ch: Yangtze) and south of the Kunlun Mountains. This is the only area recognized by modern-day China as "Tibet" and is referred to as Xizang. The area was formally constituted as an "autonomous region" in 1965.

Tsampa (Tib) Flour made of ground roasted barley grains, which traditionally constitute, together with butter, yak meat, and tea, the staple of Tibetan people.

Tulku (Tib) Literally "emanation body"; the reincarnation of a previous spiritual master who, at the time of death, was able to direct his next rebirth. Used in common speech to refer to any incarnate lama, who is also often called "Rinpoche." Chinese publications often incorrectly translate Tulku as "Living Buddha."

United Front The wing of the Chinese Communist Party responsible for external and internal propaganda concerning "minorities" in China, including Tibetans; devoted to forming broad alliances with non-Party and often with non-Chinese sectors, particularly by co-opting "patriotic upper strata" to facilitate acknowledgment of the Party's supremacy.

Vajrayana (Skt) The Diamond *(vajra)* Vehicle *(yana)*. The tantric branch of Mahayana Buddhism utilizing a wide variety of methods, including mantra and visualization of deities, giving great emphasis to the role of the teacher. Vajrayana Buddhism relies upon the tantras and is the main form of Buddhism in Tibet and Mongolia. Vajrayana also spread in China, which in turn transmitted it to Vietnam, Korea, and Japan.

Vajrakilaya (Skt) Wrathful deity who embodies the enlightened activity of all the

Buddhas and whose practice is renowned for removing obstacles, destroying forces hostile to compassion, and purifying the spiritual pollution that is
prevalent in this age; commonly depicted with six arms, three faces, standing
in a raging inferno and wielding a phurba.

Yogi (Skt) A practitioner of yoga. The Tibetan word for yoga means "union with the
natural state"; yogis seek to unite their mind with the actual nature of things.
Often the word *yogi* holds the connotation of someone who has some degree
of spiritual realizations.

Bibliography

Akester, Matthew (forthcoming). *The rJe 'bum sgang lha khang and other follies: rNying ma pa ritual architecture in the resurgence of the modern Tibetan state. Journal of the International Association of Tibetan Studies.*

Alexander, André. 2005. *The Temples of Lhasa: Tibetan Buddhist Architecture from the 7th to the 21st Centuries.* Serindia.

Ama Adhe. 1997. *The Voice That Remembers: A Tibetan Woman's Inspiring Story of Survival.* Wisdom Publications.

Aten Dogyaltshang. 1993. *A Historical Oration from Khams: The Ancient Recitation of Nyag Rong.* Edited by Tashi Tsering. Amnye Machen Institute.

Attenborough, Richard. 1987. *Cry Freedom.* Universal Pictures.

Baker, Ian. 2000. *The Dalai Lama's Secret Temple: Tantric Wall Paintings from Tibet.* Thames and Hudson.

Barnett, Robert. 2006. *Lhasa: Streets with Memories.* Columbia University Press.

Barnett, Robert. May 29, 2008. "Thunder from Tibet." *The New York Review of Books.* Volume 55, Number 9.

Bell, Charles. 1987 (reprint). *Portrait of a Dalai Lama: The Life and Times of the Great Thirteenth.* Wisdom Publications.

Byrom, Thomas. 1993. *Dhammapada: The Sayings of the Buddha.* Shambhala.

China Tibetology. 1991. *History of Monasteries in Kandze, Kham: A Clear Mirror of Buddhism,* Volume 1. China Tibetology Publishing House.

Coleman, Bill. 2002. *The Uprising at Batang: Kham and Its Significance in Chinese and Tibetan History,* in Epstein 2002.

Confucius. 1998. *The Analects.* David Hinton. Counterpoint.

Congressional-Executive Commission on China. February 10, 2003. *The Execution of Lobsang Dondrub and the Case against Tenzin Delek: The Law, the Courts, and the Debate on Legality.* See www.cecc.gov/pages/news/lobsang.php.

Da lta ba (journal). 2005. Volume 2. *dGu rong tshang gi zhabs* rjes. Xining.

Dalai Lama. 1977. *My Land and My People: The Original Autobiography of His Holiness the Dalai Lama of Tibet.* Potala Corp.

Dalai Lama. 1990a. *Freedom in Exile: The Autobiography of the Dalai Lama.* HarperCollins.

Dalai Lama. 1990b. *My Tibet.* University of California Press.

Dalai Lama. 2000. *Dzogchen: The Heart Essence of the Great Perfection: Dzogchen Teachings Given in the West.* Snow Lion Publications.

Dalai Lama. 2004. *Mind of Clear Light: Advice on Living Well and Dying Consciously.* Atria Books.

Dalai Lama. 2005a. *Gems of the Heart.* Tibetan Women's Association Publication.

Dalai Lama. 2005b. *Universe in a Single Atom: The Convergence of Science and Spirituality.* Morgan Road Books.

Dalai Lama. 2007. *Mind in Comfort and Ease: The Vision of Enlightenment in the Great Perfection.* Wisdom Publications.

Dalai Lama III, Sonam Gyatso. 1982. *Selected Works of the Dalai Lama III: Essence of Refined Gold,* with commentary by Tenzin Gyatso, the Fourteenth Dalai Lama. Translated and edited by: Glenn H. Mullin. Snow Lion Publications.

Das, Sarat Chandra. 1988 (reprint). *Journey to Lhasa and Central Tibet.* Cosmo Publications.

Do Khyentsé. 1997. *Autobiography of Do Khyentsé Yeshe Dorje.* Sichuan Nationalities Publishing House of Chengdu.

Dudjom Rinpoche. 1991. *The Nyingma School of Tibetan Buddhism: Its Fundamentals and History.* Translated by: Gyurme Dorje and Matthew Kapstein. Wisdom Publications.

Eckholm, Erik. June 22, 2001. "Monitors Say China Pushes Tibet Monks from Study Site." *The New York Times.*

Epstein, Lawrence (editor). 2002. *Khams pa Histories: Visions of People, Place and Au-*

thority. PIATS 2000: Tibetan Studies: Proceedings of the Ninth Seminar of the International Association for Tibetan Studies, Leiden, 2000. Brill.

Ferrari, Alfonsa. 1958. *Mk'yen Brtse's Guide to the Holy Places of Central Tibet.* Edited by: Luciano Petech. Istituto Italiano per il Medio ed Estremo Oriente.

Gabriel, Peter. 1980. *Melt.* Geffen.

Gardner, Alexander. 2006. *The Twenty-five Great Sites of Khams: Religious Geography, Revelation, and Nonsectarianism in Nineteenth-Century Eastern Tibet.* Ph.D. dissertation, University of Michigan.

Germano, David. 1998. "Re-membering the Dismembered Body of Tibet: Contemporary Tibetan Visionary Movements in People's Republic of China," in Goldstein and Kapstein (editors), *Buddhism in Contemporary Tibet: Religious Revival and Cultural Identity.* University of California Press.

Ginsberg, Allen. 1970. *Indian Journals.* Dave Haselwood Books.

Goldstein, Melvyn C. May 1973. *The Circulation of Estates in Tibet: Reincarnation, Land and Politics. Journal of Asia Studies,* Volume XXXII, No. 3.

Goldstein, Melvyn C. 1991. *A History of Modern Tibet, 1913–1951: The Demise of the Lamaist State.* University of California Press.

Gurong Gyalse. 1994. *Biography of Gurong Gyalse.* Nationalities Publishing House of Gansu.

Human Rights Watch. 2004. *Trials of a Tibetan Monk: The Case of Tenzin Delek.* www .hrw.org/reports/2004/china0204.

Humchen Chenaktsang, and Yeshe Ozer Drolma. 2005. *The Ngak Mang Book Series and Journal: A Collection of Histories Concerning the Ngak Mang Rebkong Monastery.* Nationalities Press in Beijing.

Information Warfare Monitor. March 29, 2009. *Tracking Ghostnet: Investigating a Cyber Espionage Network,* in JR02-2009.

International Campaign for Tibet. 2004a. *When the Sky Fell to Earth: The New Crackdown on Buddhism in Tibet.*

International Campaign for Tibet. 2004b. *Devotion and Defiance: Communist Party Crackdown on Buddhism in Tibet.* (DVD). www.tibetpolicy.eu/resource-center/ multi-media/186-devotion-and-defiance-communist-party-crackdown-on-buddhism-in-tibet.

International Campaign for Tibet. 2007. *The Communist Party as Living Buddha: The Crisis Facing Tibetan Religion Under Chinese Control.*

International Campaign for Tibet. August 6, 2008. *Tibet at a Turning Point: The Spring Uprising and China's New Crackdown.*

International Campaign for Tibet. March 2009. *A Great Mountain Burned by Fire: China's Crackdown in Tibet.*

International Campaign for Tibet. May 2010. *A "Raging Storm": The Crackdown on Tibetan Writers and Artists after Tibet's 2008 Protests.*

Iosseliani, Otar. 2008. *Philosopher Escaped.* Lokomotive Film Studio. (DVD)

Jacoby, Sarah H. 2007. *Consorts and Revelation in Eastern Tibet: The Auto/Biographical Writings of the Treasure Revealer Sera Khandro (1892–1940).* Ph.D. dissertation, University of Virginia.

Jamgön Kongtrul. 1980. *Precious Garland of Lapis Lazuli* in *Dakini Teachings.* Translated by: Erik Pema Kunsang. Shambhala.

Jamgön Kongtrul. 2003. *The Autobiography of Jamgön Kongtrul: A Gem of Many Colors.* Translated by: Richard Barron. Snow Lion Publications.

Jamyang Norbu. 1986. *Warriors of Tibet: The Story of Aten and the Khampa's Fight for the Freedom of their Country.* Wisdom Publications.

Kapstein, Matthew T. 2004. "The Strange Death of Pema the Demon Tamer," in *The Presence of Light: Divine Radiance and Religious Experience.* University of Chicago Press.

Kawaguchi, Ekai. 1979 (reprint). *Three Years in Tibet.* Ratna Pustak Bhandar.

Keutsang Trulku Jamphe Yeshe. 2001. *Memoirs of Keutsang Lama: Life in Tibet after the Chinese "Liberation."* Paljor Publication.

Khamtrul Rinpoche (unpublished). *A Brief Biography of the Great Treasure Revealer [Tertön Sogyal] Lerab Lingpa Known as the Drop Thread of Purity, He Who Is Freed from the Cloud Covering of the Two Obscurations, Who Has Thoroughly Completed All Clear Light Appearances of Wisdom and Compassion, Who Showers the Beneficial and Blissful Rays of the Profound and Highest Secret Tantra.* Translated by: Acharya Nyima Tsering. Edited by Mike Gilmore. Dharamsala.

Khamtrul Rinpoche. August 12, 1992. *Teaching.* Lerab Ling, 18.00 Tape 117.

Khamtrul Rinpoche. 2009. *Memories of Lost and Hidden Lands: The Life Story of Garje Khamtrul Rinpoche.* Translated by: Lozang Zopa. Chime Gatsal Ling.

Khenpo Jikmé Phuntsok. 1987. *Drops of Advice from My Heart.* Serthar Buddhist Academy.

Khenpo Namdrol Rinpoche. 1999. *The Practice of Vajrakilaya.* Snow Lion Publications.

Khenpo Sodarjey. 2001. *Biography of His Holiness Jigmey Phuntshok Dharmaraja.* Translated by: Arnaud Versluys. Hua Xia Cultural Publishing House.

Kurlantzick, Joshua. March 1, 2010. "The Downfall of Human Rights." *Newsweek.*

Lin, Paul. April 25, 2008. "Nationalism Is Beijing's Brainchild." *Taipei Times.*

Liu, Melinda. September 9, 2001. "Trouble in Shangri-La; A Religious Crackdown Targets Tibetans in Remote Sichuan." *Newsweek.*

Lodi Gyaltsen Gyari. 2006. "Himalayan Crossings," in *Himalaya: Personal Stories of Grandeur, Challenge, and Hope.* National Geographic.

Lotsawa House. www.lotsawahouse.org

Marshall, Steven D. 1999. *Hostile Elements: A Study of Political Imprisonment in Tibet, 1987–1998.* Tibetan Information Network.

Marshall, Steven D. 2000. *Rukhang 3: The Nuns of Drapchi Prison.* Tibet Information Network.

McGranahan, Carole. 2001. *Arrested Histories: Between Empire and Exile in 20th-century Tibet.* Ph.D. dissertation, University of Michigan.

Merton, Thomas. 1973. *Asian Journals.* New Directions Publishing.

Mullin, Glenn. 1988. *Path of the Bodhisattva Warrior: The Life and Teachings of the Thirteenth Dalai Lama.* Snow Lion Publications.

Nagaraja, Shishir, and Ross Anderson. March 2009. *The Snooping Dragon: Social-Malware Surveillance of the Tibetan Movement.* University of Cambridge Technical Report 746 (ISSN 1476-2986).

Nechung Monastery. 2004. *History of Nechung.* Dharamsala.

Ngawang Zangpo. 2001. *Sacred Ground: Jamgön Kongtrul on Pilgrimage and Sacred Geography.* Snow Lion Publications.

Ngawang Zangpo. 2002. *Guru Rinpoche: His Life and Times.* Snow Lion Publications.

Noetic Sciences Review. May 2002. *The Rainbow Body. Institute of Noetic Sciences Review,* No. 59.

Nyoshul Khenpo. 2005. *A Marvelous Garland of Rare Gems: Biographies of Masters of Awareness in the Dzogchen Lineage.* Translated by Richard Barron. Padma Publications.

Orgyen Dongkawa. 2000. *The Life Story of Gurong Gyalse, Reincarnation of Mipham: A Cloud of Offerings to Delight Manjushri.* Gansu Nationalities Publishing House.

Petech, Luciano. 1973. *Aristocracy and Government in Tibet, 1728–1959.* Istituto Italiano per il Medio ed Estremo Oriente.

Philip, Pan. March 14, 2004. "Buddhist Monks Keep Refuge in China Alive; Settlement has Survived Government Crackdown." *The Washington Post.*

Pistono, Matteo. September 2002. "Tolerance and Totalization; Religion in Contemporary Tibet." Himal Southasia.

Pistono, Matthew. 1997. "Reflections on Dependent Origination in the Light of Nāgārjuna's Interpretation of Truth." University of London, School of Oriental and African Studies. Master's Thesis.

Pistono, Matthew. 2008. "Master Scholar of Fearless Sublimity—A Biography of the Lord of the Dharma, Choje Jikme Phuntsok Rinpoche," in the journal entitled *The Fifth Anniversary of Choje Jigme Phuntsok Junge.* New Delhi.

Ricard, Matthieu. 1996. *Journey to Enlightenment: The Life and World of Khyentsé Rinpoche, Spiritual Teacher from Tibet.* Aperture.

Rigpa. 2004. *A Great Treasury of Blessing: Book of Prayers to Guru Rinpoche to Celebrate the Wood Monkey Year 2004–2005.* Dharmakosha for Rigpa.

Rigpa International. January 2000. "On an Island of Wish Fulfilling Jewels," in *The Rigpa Journal.* The Tertön Sogyal Trust.

Rigpa Shedra Wiki. www.rigpawiki.org

Ringu Tulku. 2006. *The Ri-Me Philosophy of Jamgön Kongtrul the Great: A Study of the Buddhist Lineages of Tibet.* Shambhala.

Schwartz, Ronald D. 1994. *Circle of Protest: Political Ritual in the Tibetan Uprising.* Columbia University Press.

Shantideva. 1997. *The Way of the Bodhisattva.* Padmakara Group/Shambhala.

Sherab Ozer. 1981. "A History of Nyarong Gönpo Namgyal," in *The Collected Historical and Cultural Materials of Kardze Tibetan Autonomous Prefecture,* Volume 1.

Smith, E. Gene. 1970. "Jam mgon Kong sprul and the Nonsectarian Movement," in Kongtrul's *Encyclopedia of Indo-Tibetan Culture,* Parts 1–3. International Academy of Indian Culture. New Delhi.

Smith, E. Gene. 2001. *Among Tibetan Texts: History & Literature of the Himalayan Plateau.* Wisdom Publications.

Smith, Warren. 1997. *Tibetan Nation: A History of Tibetan Nationalism and Sino-Tibetan Relations.* HarperCollins.

Smith, Warren. 2009. *Tibet's Last Stand? The Tibetan Uprising of 2008 and China's Response.* Rowman & Littlefield.

Snyder, Gary. 1983. *Passageway through India.* Grey Fox/City Lights Press.

Sogyal Rinpoche. 1989. *Dzogchen and Padmasambhava.* Rigpa.

Sogyal Rinpoche. 1992. *Tibetan Book of Living and Dying.* HarperCollins.

Stoddard, Heather. 1985. *Le Mendicant de l'Amdo.* Société d'Ethnographie.

Stoddard, Heather. 2006. *The Great Phi gling dmag zlog of 1888: The first hands-on confrontation between Tibet and the British Raj with the participation of leading lineage hold-*

ers of the '1 900 Sngag mang Phur thog gos dkar lcang lo can', lay mantrins of Reb kong, Amdo, in the Dga' ldan Pho brang state military ritual to 'Turn Back the Philing' Foreigners. International Association for Tibetan Studies. Bonn.

Tarthang Tulku. 1995. *Masters of the Nyingma Lineage.* Volume 11, Crystal Mirror Series.

Tashi Tsering. 1986. "Nyag rong Mgon po rnam rgyal: a nineteeth-century Khams pa Warrior," in *Soundings in Tibetan Civilization.* South Asia Books.

Teichman, Eric. 1922. *Travel of a Consular Officer in Eastern Tibet: Together with a History of the Relations between China, Tibet and India.* Cambridge University Press.

Terrone, Antonio. 2010. *Bya rog prog zhu: The Raven Crest—The Life and Teachings of Bde chen 'od gsal rdo rje, Treasure Revealer of Contemporary Tibet.* Ph.D. dissertation, Leiden University.

Tertön Sogyal 1985. *The Collected Visionary Revelations and Textual Discoveries of Lerab Lingpa [Tertön Sogyal].* Published in Byllakuppe by Pema Norbu Rinpoche, reproduced from a set of the Nyarong block prints from the library of Dilgo Khyentsé Rinpoche. Library of Congress MARC/MODS Record: 85904374.

Thupten Jampa Tsultrim Tendzin. 1998. *The Wondrous Garland of Precious Gems: A Brief Summary of the Ocean-Like Life and Liberation of the Thirteenth Incarnation of the Incomparably Gracious Lord of the Victorious Ones, the Crowning Ornament of All Samsara and Nirvana Including the Heavens [Biography His Holiness the XIII Dalai Lama].* Sherig Parkhang.

Tibetan Center for Human Rights and Democracy. 2001. *Destruction of Serthar Institute: A Special Report.* Washington, D.C.

Tibetan Center for Human Rights and Democracy. 2002. *Destruction of Serthar Institute,* www.tchrd.org/videos/.

Tibet Information Network. April 18, 2002. "Religious Work for the New Century; the Implementation of Party Policy in Sichuan Province." Special Report.

Tibet Information Network. July 16, 2001. "Propaganda and the West: China's Struggle to Sway International Opinion on the Tibet Issue." Special Report.

Tibet Information Network. August 10, 2001. "Lhasa Authorities Reinforce Dalai Lama Birthday Celebration Ban." News in Brief.

Tsering Shakya. 1999. *The Dragon in the Land of Snows.* Columbia University Press.

Tsipon Shakabpa. 1967. *Tibet: A Political History.* Yale University Press.

Tulku Thondup. 1986. *Hidden Teachings of Tibet: An Explanation of the Terma Tradition of Tibetan Buddhism.* Wisdom Publications.

Tulku Thondup. 1996. *Masters of Meditation and Miracles: The Longchen Nyingthig Lineage of Tibetan Buddhism.* Shambhala.

Tsullo (Tshul khrims bzang po). 1974. *The Esoteric Biography of Tertön Sogyal* [the shortened title being *The Marvelous Garland of White Lotuses*]. Sanje Dorje. New Delhi.

Tsullo. 2002. *The Biography of Tertön Sogyal* [*gTer chen Las rab gling pa'i rnam thar*]. Serthar Buddhist College [*gSer ljongs bla ma rung rig nang bstan slob grwa chen mo*]. Serthar.

Tuttle, Gray. 2005. *Tibetan Buddhists in the Making of Modern China*. Columbia University Press.

United States House of Representatives March 7, 2002. Committee on International Relations Hearing on *U.S. Policy Considerations in Tibet* (78–084PDF 2002/Serial No. 107–67).

Wang Lixiong and Tsering Shakya. 2009. *The Struggle for Tibet*. Verso.

Woeser. July 4, 2008. "The Fear in Lhasa, as Felt in Bejing" at www.highpeaks pureearth.com/2008/09/fear-in-lhasa-as-felt-in-beijing-by.html.

Woeser. April 7, 2010. "Happiness Under Gunpoint" at www.highpeakspureearth .com/2010/04/happiness-under-gunpoint-by-woeser.html.

Woods, Donald. 1978. *Biko*. Paddington Press.

Wu, Harry. 1993. *Bitter Winds: A Memoir of My Years in China's Gulag*. John Wiley & Sons.

Yeshe Dorje and Ozer Thaye. 1998. *The Biography and Spiritual Songs of Nyala Pema Duddul*. Sichuan Nationalities Publishing House of Chengdu.

Yeshe Tsogyal. 1978. *The Life and Liberation of Padmasambhava*. Dharma Publishing.

Yeshe Tsogyal. 1993. *The Lotus Born: The Life Story of Padmasambhava*. Translated by Erik Pema Kunsang. Shambhala.

Yudru Tsomu. 2006. *Local Aspirations and National Constraints: A Case Study of Nyarong Gönpo Namgyal and His Rise to Power in Kham (1836–1865)*. Ph.D. dissertation, Harvard University.

Resources

In the Shadow of the Buddha *www.matteopistono.com*

Visit video and photo galleries from *In the Shadow of the Buddha*, read interviews with Matteo Pistono and follow his blog.

The International Campaign for Tibet *www.savetibet.org*

The International Campaign for Tibet works to promote human rights and democratic freedoms for the people of Tibet.

Nekorpa *www.nekorpa.org*

Nekorpa is nonprofit organization dedicated to the protection and conservation of pilgrimage sites throughout the world.

The Bridge Fund *www.bridgefund.org*

The Bridge Fund is a nonprofit, nonpolitical organization working to improve the lives of Tibetan communities across the Tibetan Plateau through education, health care, cultural heritage preservation, environmental conservation, and business development.

Sogyal Rinpoche and Rigpa Fellowship *www.rigpa.org*

Rigpa aims to present the Buddhist tradition of Tibet in a way that is both completely authentic, and as relevant as possible to the lives and needs of modern men and women.

Khenpo (Abbot) Namdrol Rinpoche *www.knamdrol.org*

Find out more about the projects that Khenpo Namdrol Rinpoche supports, and access select teachings and practices.

The Conservancy for Tibetan Art and Culture *www.tibetanculture.org*

The Conservancy for Tibetan Art and Culture is dedicated to the preservation of Tibet's living cultural heritage in Tibetan cultural areas and communities around the world.

Index

ABOUT THE AUTHOR

Matteo Pistono is a writer, photographer and practitioner of Tibetan Buddhism. He lived and traveled throughout the Himalayas for a decade, bringing to the West firsthand accounts and photos of China's human rights abuses in Tibet. He is the founder of Nekorpa, a foundation working to protect sacred pilgrimage sites around the world. Pistono and his wife, Monica, divide their time between Wyoming, Washington, D.C. and Asia.

www.matteopistono.com